Do's and Don'ts Around
A Country Guide to Cultural and Social Taboos and Etiquette

By Gladson I. Nwanna, Ph.D

EUROPE

World Travel Institute
Baltimore, Maryland

Library of Congress Cataloging-in-Publication Data

Nwanna, Gladson I.
Do's and don'ts around the world : a country guide to cultural and social taboos and etiquette: Europe / Gladson I. Nwanna.
p. cm. -- (International traveler's resource guide)
ISBN 1-890605-00-X
1. Travel etiquette--Europe--Handbooks, manuals, etc. 2. Europe-Social life and customs--Handbooks, manuals, etc. I. Title.
II. Series.
BJ2137.N8333 1998
395'.094--dc21 97-19643
CIP

Cover Design by Adrienne Waite

Printed in Canada

Acknowledgement

A lot of people have helped me with this project, giving me everything from encouragement and typesetting to editorial advice and help. I would especially, like to thank, Mrs. Phyllis Desbordes, Dr. Sydney E. Onyeberechi and Mr. Thomas J. Wilcox for their relentless assistance in editing parts of the chapters, and for other valuable suggestions, Ms. Bernadette R. Rose for her wonderful typing and editing skills, and Ms. Miatta Dabo and Adrenne Waite for their assistance in numerous ways.

A special thanks goes to the various personnel of foreign embassies and foreign government tourist bureaus in the U.S. and to government ministries abroad whose efforts in completing the exceedingly lengthy questionnaire made it all possible.

Preface

Several countries are at the crossroads of economic, social and cultural change and are undergoing profound changes. The trend towards globalization and integration of world economies are all a part of the forces transforming and changing social and cultural practices through out the world. One obvious outcome of this evolving and dynamic process is the change in social and cultural norms and practices; changes that have in some countries resulted in relaxation and/or accommodation of, and in other countries led to re-affirmation and tightening of the status quo with respect to social and cultural practices and other rules of etiquette.

Every year people travel out of their countries to one or more foreign countries. For the majority of these travelers their utmost wish is for an exciting and incident-free stay in the host country. Unfortunately, many of these travelers do not have an incident-free stay abroad. Even among those for whom safety is not a major issue, there is almost always the one spoiler, an embarrassing moment or encounter. Seasoned travelers have not escaped this spoiler, nor have they come up with a permanent solution to this seemingly unimportant, but unconformable nuisance. One can only think of a partial cure that, at best, guarantees the chance of minimizing part of such episodes. That cure is this book; a book that catalogues important and often forgotten **do's and don'ts** around the world.

In this book, I provide a country-by-country **DO's and DON'TS.** The aim of this book is to highlight areas and topics that, as a traveler to a foreign country, you may want to watch out for and take appropriate precautions against. I suggest that before traveling or upon arrival at your destination, you re-verify those topics and practices you hold so dearly. An important source of such a verification process will be the embassies, consulates and tourism bureaus representing those countries or regions.

This book is unique in many ways, not the least being the format. Some topics in the book may even appear to be repeated. This was deliberate on the part of the author. It was also deliberate to leave the various topical items as presented instead of arranging and/or grouping them by topics. This arrangement underlies the importance and emphasis the author chose to attach to every topical item and the conviction that all of the items warrant a glance or two by every foreign-bound traveler.

Other unique features of the book include the broad headings used to address the various topical items such as "Is customary, Is allowed...Is disallowed, Is a crime etc". Again this was deliberate. But importantly, it was done so as to reflect the difficulty in addressing the issue of **DO's and DON'TS** among countries. This arrangement is intended to also serve as a cautionary note to potential users of this book. This is more so, considering that even within countries a wide range of different and sometimes conflicting cultures and practices exist and in many cases there is only a fine line between what is acceptable or not acceptable. In essence, disagreements abound.

In effect, while the information conveyed in this book is useful and should help relieve some anxiety among foreign travelers, extreme caution should also be taken in interpreting any particular response for any given country. Ideally, this book should be taken only as a reference guide aimed at alerting you and increasing your awareness to issues, practices and behavior in other countries.

Not withstanding readers who may disagree with my choice of headings or with the responses to the topical items despite my earlier cautions, this book also carries the benefit of drawing information from sources I considered reliable and official. Virtually all of the information contained in this book in response to the various topical issues or questions came via a questionnaire and was provided by the embassies and/or representatives of the respective countries.

Another unique feature of this book is its wide appeal. Most of the information should be useful to every international traveler, irrespective of the country of origin or country of destination. This goal was of particular interest to me and provided the driving force in the search for questions and issues to include in the questionnaire.

Every effort was made to include important questions, issues and areas of potential concern to international travelers and to seek answers and guidance for you, the traveler. As I compiled and concluded my questionnaire and put the final touches to this book, it became very obvious that some issues of equal or greater importance are bound to be left out. It also became clear that certain items in this book may become contentious, controversial and may even generate heated arguments and debate. This, of course is not the intended purpose of the book.

Neither the issues nor the questions raised, nor items and topics treated in this book was expected to be exhaustive. I appeal to those of you who may have other concerns and comments about this book to kindly send them to me. Similarly, I ask the same for those who may detect errors that may have slipped my attention. Such feedback will help me immensely in improving future editions. It is virtually impossible to embark on a project, and a subject matter as this without anticipating concerns, particularly given the differences in customs, contents and social practices and norm even within the same national boundaries.

It is my expectation that the information contained in this book will make a big difference, particularly in ensuring a safe, enjoyable, rewarding and hitch-free trip for millions of overseas-bound travelers. It certainly should save you numerous embarrassing moments and hopefully provide you with more fun-filled times and happy memories. Suggestions and letters should be mailed to Public Relations Department, WTI, P.O. Box 32674 Baltimore, Maryland 21282-2674, USA.

POSTSCRIPT

Some Important Assumptions & Observations to keep in mind as you read this book, and as you travel abroad.

As I traveled through various foreign countries, I made some personal observations that should help you understand and better appreciate the contents, style and coverage of this book. They include:

The response to the various topical items in this book was intended to address the social and cultural norms and etiquette expected to prevail in largely urban centers of the countries profiled. While they should apply equally well in rural and suburban centers, I have observed that

(a) urban residents are generally more tolerant and understanding of foreigners than rural, particularly on issues dealing with social and cultural norms and decorum. This may be due to the degree and frequency of exposure and contact between foreigners and urban residents than with the rural residents. This, however, may not be the case with law enforcement issues. (see section c)

(b) you stand a greater chance of being stared, looked at with curiosity in rural areas or by rural residents than in urban areas or those exposed to urban living. In some areas, expect some rural residents, particularly children, to walk along with you or even want to touch you. It is all part of the curious feeling you should expect. This is likely the case when you have some "foreignness" in you, often due to your color or some other outstanding and distinguishing features. While this may seem awkward and discomforting at times to the foreigner, similar feelings, are often shared by the other parties. My suggestion is to feel relaxed now that you've been alerted. Most of the times it usually doesn't signify danger as you may be apt to think or feel. A good friendly smile from you may just do the magic. You may also notice that rural residents tend to be reserved and often shy.

Having made these observations, I caution that because of the more culture-minded nature of rural residents and their less tolerant attitude towards any form of contravention or violation of strongly held cultural norms and decorum, you can expect in some cases, strong negative feelings and even hostility from some quarters. Interestingly, the signs of such contravention are often clear to an alert international traveler. Either a Good Samaritan citizen will quickly alert you or you will find both children and some adults making threatening signals or physically attempting to harass you. Under such a circumstance, you may be better of stopping and asking for anyone around who understands your language to seek some understanding or clarification. Alternatively, cease and desist from doing whatever you are doing or may have been doing. For the most part, misunderstandings often stem from doing something as opposed to saying something, unless you are attempting to communicate in the local dialect or language.

(c) I have also observed that law enforcement authorities in rural areas tend to be more sympathetic and tend to forgive easily. In other words, despite the higher tolerance level and higher degree of understanding of foreigners, you stand a greater chance of getting into trouble with the law and getting arrested when you contravene the law in urban areas than in the rural areas. This should not be a reason or an excuse to want to deliberately test or flaunt the system during your visit to rural areas.

(d) Expect to be stopped and questioned by law enforcement when you stray into areas that are either prohibited to foreigners or appear segregated e.g. by color, or class or other distinct characteristics of which you do not appear to fit. Stating your case or claiming your ignorance calmly, and politely may be your best move.

(e) If you need assistance (outside law enforcement), expect mixed reactions from both urban and rural sector residents. How much real help you get will depend on the country, as much as where in the country you may be located. Deliberate attempts to misdirect a foreigner is not unusual. It is not unusual to find acts of hospitality and effort to assist a foreigner either. I have experienced both. Generally, rural residents tend to do better. You should rely more on law enforcement officers.

(f) Surprising as it may sound to many readers, life and activities in several countries of the world are still male-dominated and this permeates the prevailing culture. As a female international traveler, expect this state of affairs to manifest itself in the manner that may not only run contrary to your upbringing and expectations, but may be a source of unwarranted attention and embarrassment to your person. Although you may not be able to change things, at least you can learn to be aware of them and to place them to your own comfort level. The idea and trend towards equal rights of the sexes is hardly taken seriously in several developing countries, and you are better of not pushing it and not expecting much of it during your brief stay abroad. Similarly, keep in mind that once in a foreign country, you are subject to the, rules, regulations and laws of that country, including their constitution and not those of your country. To think or act otherwise is to expose yourself to potential risks of all types.

(g) If you love taking photographs as many international travelers do, particularly, first-timers, you need to be cautious of where you go to photograph and who or what you photograph. One of the most common incidents encountered by international travelers stems from taking photographs. In almost every country, taking photographsof military installations, barracks, posts, hardware (in fact, anything military) is prohibited. If you are caught, you are most likely to be detained, questioned, jailed or tortured. You can also bet your camera or video camera that the film or tape will be confiscated or destroyed. Similarly, while the taking of personal photographs inside the airport is allowed in several countries, there is equally a large number of countries where it is prohibited. It is safer to inquire first at the airport information desk if it is ok to take photographs. I will also suggest the same precautions if you must take a photograph of a sacred site, object or of someone. While some people in some countries may not object, photographing a person without asking permission may be an invitation for trouble. When such permission is sought and granted, do not be surprised if the person demands money (before or after) in return as compensation.

(h) Finally, always remember that you are a foreigner and not a citizen of the country or local. This means taking extra precautions in what you say and do, how you say and do things, as well as when and where you say and do them. Things that a local may get away with, you may not be so fortunate as to get away with. Hence, avoid feeling like a resident and be alert to locals who try to con or trick you into committing a crime or an offense. Furthermore, remember that several countries are still ruled by the military who are usually less tolerant of so many things, including their perception of foreigners and their interpretation of rules of laws.

(More of these observations can be found in the book (**Practical Tips for American Traveling Abroad: Ignore them at Your own Risk.** ISBN #: 1-890605-09-3; 263 pages, $19.99; Also available on-line for purchase and downloading at www.worldtravelinstitute.com)

DISCLAIMER:

Neither the publisher nor the author can accept responsibility for errors or omissions that may occur, nor will they be held responsible for the experiences of readers while they are traveling. The information contained in this book is meant to serve only as a guide and to assist you in your travel plans. This information is neither all inclusive, exhaustive nor cast in bronze. You are advised to verify and reconfirm all information mentioned in this book with your travel agent, travel advisor, travel bureaus and with embassies and consulates of the country (ies) you plan to visit before embarking on your trip.

OTHER RESOURCES

As a web or internet-accessible international traveler, you may find the following web sites useful, particularly, their links to several other instructive travel and country-related sites: **http://travel.state.gov/travel_pubs.html;**
http://travel.state.gov/travel_warnings.html. I encourage you to explore other country, travel and culture-related sites.

TABLE OF CONTENTS

AUSTRIA

AUSTRIA	Is customary Is allowed Is permissible Is used. Is OK	Is not customary Is frowned upon	Is disallowed Is forbidden Is a crime	(See last page for comments on items referenced here)
Smoking in public	✓			1
Eating in public	✓			
Not flushing public toilet			✓	
Spitting in public			✓	
Feeding animals & birds in public	✓			2
Whistling in public		✓		
Drinking alcohol in public		✓		
Kissing in public	✓			
Breast feeding in public		✓		
Drunkenness (in public)			✓	
Cursing in public		✓		
Religious preaching in public		✓		
Begging (panhandling) in public		✓		
Giving money to beggars/panhandlers	✓			
Giving food/drink to beggars/panhandlers	✓			
Brushing teeth in public (other than in restrooms)			✓	
Strolling with pets in major public roads/streets		✓		
Chewing gum in public	✓			
Chewing gum in government offices	✓			
Combing hair in public (other than in toilets/restrooms)		✓		
Undressing/dressing in public			✓	
Wearing of dark glasses indoors in public places		✓		
Public display of wealth	✓			
Praying openly in public in non-designated areas		✓		
Walking bare feet in public		✓		
Chewing tobacco in public		✓		
Trimming one's finger or toe nails in public			✓	
Laughing aloud in public	✓			
Mingling of the sexes in public	✓			
Mixed bathing in public swimming pools	✓			
Distributing religious pamphlets (literature) in public/side streets	✓			

AUSTRIA

	Is customary Is allowed Is permissible Is used. Is OK	**Is not customary Is frowned upon**	**Is disallowed Is forbidden Is a crime**	**(See last page for comments on items referenced here)**
Dancing on side street		✓		
Nude bathing	✓			3
Littering			✓	
Binge Drinking	✓			
hitchhiking	✓			
Jaywalking			✓	
Drunk driving			✓	4
Speeding			✓	
Skating on side streets (side-walk)	✓			
Graffiti painting			✓	
Pilfering			✓	
Prostitution	✓			5
Haggling in the market place	✓			
Consumption of alcoholic beverages in bars and restaurants	✓			
Gambling	✓			
Possession of pornographic materials	✓			6
Possession of the Christian Bible	✓			
Possession of the Moslem Koran	✓			
Possession of bullet-proof vest		✓		
Possession of toy gun	✓			
Possession of fire crackers and fireworks			✓	7
Possession of prescription drugs (without doctor's note)			✓	
Possession of regulated drugs (narcotics)			✓	
Possession of firearms (by foreigners)	✓			8
Possession of pocket knife in public	✓			
Using walkie talkies	✓			9
Using of "boom boxes"(loud sounding stereo system)		✓		
Using "walkman" (very small radio/cassettes with ear plugs) in public places	✓			
Using "walkman" (very small radio/cassettes with ear plugs) while driving or riding		✓		

AUSTRIA

	Is customary Is allowed Is permissible Is used Is OK	Is not customary Is frowned upon	Is disallowed Is forbidden Is a crime	(See last page for comments on items referenced here)
Use of cellular phone	✓			
Use of binoculars/periscopes other than in sports arena		✓		
Taking photographs of people (without their permission)	✓			
Taking photographs at airports, train and bus stations	✓			
Taking photographs of airports	✓			
Taking photographs of churches and synagogues	✓			
Taking photographs of religious statues	✓			
Taking photographs of public buildings	✓			
Taking photographs of bridges	✓			
Tipping (gratuity)	✓			
Tipping (when service is rendered)	✓			
Tipping (when service is not rendered)	✓			
Tipping waiters/waitresses at restaurants and hotels	✓			
Tipping taxi/cab drivers	✓			
Tipping baggage handlers, porters, door persons	✓			
Tipping of hair dressers/barbers	✓			
Overtipping	✓			
Undertipping		✓		
Spilling cigarette butt (ash) on side streets/on the floor	✓			
Men wearing lipstick		✓		
Wearing visible tattoo marks	✓			
Men painting/coloring their finger or toe nails		✓		
Cross dressing (men dressed like women & vice versa)			✓	
Walking in public without a shirt (i.e. with the upper half of the body naked)		✓		
Men wearing braided hair	✓			
Men wearing earrings	✓			
Men wearing dreadlock hair style	✓			
Homosexuality	✓			
Lesbianism	✓			

AUSTRIA

	Is customary Is allowed Is permissible Is used Is OK	Is not customary Is frowned upon	Is disallowed Is forbidden Is a crime	(See last page for comments on items referenced here)
Females covering their hair (wearing headgear) in public		✓		
Females exposing their full face in public	✓			
Females driving automobiles	✓			
Females riding motorcycles	✓			
Females riding bicycles	✓			
Females smoking in public	✓			
Women wearing bras (braziers) in public	✓			
Use of lipstick by women	✓			
A woman extending her hands first when introduced	✓			
Female bashing			✓	
Females wearing trousers	✓			
Females wearing minis (short dresses)	✓			
Females wearing bikinis	✓			
Females wearing shorts	✓			
Persons of opposite sex holding hands in public	✓			
Persons of same sex holding hands in public		✓		
Handshake between opposite sex	✓			
Hugging in public by same sex		✓		
Hugging in public by opposite sex	✓			
Men and women walking side by side in public	✓			
Man walking ahead (in public), with the woman following		✓		
Woman walking ahead (in public), with the man following		✓		
Men opening doors for women	✓			
Sitting with legs crossed in the presence of elders	✓			
Talking to an elderly person with one's hat/cap on		✓		
Talking to an elderly person with hands positioned on both sides of one's waist	✓			
Blowing one's nose in public	✓			
Blowing one's nose in the presence of others		✓		
Addressing people by their title	✓			

AUSTRIA

	Is customary Is allowed Is permissible Is used. Is OK	Is not customary Is frowned upon	Is disallowed Is forbidden Is a crime	(See last page for comments on items referenced here)
Addressing people by their family name/surname/last name/given name	✓			
Addressing people by their first name/ given name	✓			
Women going through doors first	✓			
Men helping women with their coats	✓			
Men extending their hands to women first during greetings	✓			
Taking off one's hat when entering a private home	✓			
Removing one's shoes when entering a private home	✓			
Invited guests bringing food at social gatherings	✓			
Guests bringing drinks at social gatherings	✓			
Shaking hands when leaving a small group	✓			
Shaking hands with everyone present, upon arrival at a social gathering		✓		
Eating with the right hand	✓			
Eating with the left hand	✓			
Eating with both hands		✓		
Presenting a gift or passing on an object with the left hand	✓			
Asking a man about his wife	✓			
Asking a woman about her husband	✓			
Making prior appointments before a meeting or visit	✓			
Addressing an audience with one or both hands in the pocket			✓	
Carrying on conversation during meals		✓		
Females sitting with legs crossed	✓			
People discussing their wealth	✓			
Asking someone his or her age, or how old the person is		✓		
Complementing someone on his/her physical looks	✓			
Complementing someone on his/her attire	✓			
Use of both hands in handshake		✓		
In greeting, a handshake accompanied by a slight bow	✓			

AUSTRIA

	Is customary Is allowed Is permissible Is used. Is OK	Is not customary Is frowned upon	Is disallowed Is forbidden Is a crime	(See last page for comments on items referenced here)
Salutations such as "Good morning", "Good afternoon", "Good evening"	✓			
The completion of a business deal with a handshake	✓			
Starting a negotiation session with a handshake	✓			
A gift for the host/hostess	✓			
Giving a business gift	✓			
A gift of money (use of money as gift)		✓		
Use of flowers as a gift	✓			
Use of business cards	✓			
Accepting/presenting gifts with both hands	✓			
Burning of the country's flag			✓	
Mutilation of the national currency			✓	
Casual wearing of clothings made with colors & marks of the national flag	✓			
Wearing of look-alike military (camouflage) fatigues (attire)	✓			
Sitting on the floor (on floor mats)		✓		
Discussion of religion	✓			
Discussion of politics	✓			
Discussion of sex	✓			
Patting/slapping someone on the buttocks		✓		
Patting/slapping someone on the back		✓		
Touching or patting someone's head/hair		✓		
Casual touching of any part of someone's body	✓			
Drinking directly out of a bottle/can	✓			10
Placing one's leg(s) on the table or chair		✓		

AUSTRIA

	Is customary Is allowed Is permissible Is used. Is OK	Is not customary Is frowned upon	Is disallowed Is forbidden Is a crime	(See last page for comments on items referenced here)
Showing the sole of one's foot (feet)		✓		
People standing very close when talking	✓			
Maintaining steady eye contact (direct gaze) when talking to someone	✓			
Kissing or exchange of kisses on the cheek	✓			
Counting money (change) in someone's palm		✓		
Finger pointing in public (in a daring manner)		✓		
Seeking attention by winking the eyes	✓			
Tapping the head to indicate someone is crazy	✓			
Twirling the head to indicate someone is crazy		✓		
Whistling as a way of requesting something/seeking attention		✓		
Using "thumbs-up" sign to mean OK	✓			
Forming a circle with the thumb and index finger (forefinger) to mean OK	✓			
Using the fingers to make a "V" sign for victory		✓		
Beckoning to someone with the index finger (forefinger)			✓	
The left to right waving of the hand with open palms facing outward to indicate "Good bye"	✓			
The use of a nod to show acknowledgement	✓			
Stopping/beckoning a taxi using a stretched hand with the thumb pointing upward	✓			
Using the thumb finger pointed to a direction, to request a ride or a hike	✓			
Raising one's hand/waving with an open fist to summon a taxi	✓			
Tapping one's foot/feet on the floor in a public gathering		✓		
Wiggling one's leg(s) when in a sitting position		✓		
Use of the hand (by motorists and cyclists) to signal direction of traffic	✓			

AUSTRIA

		(See last page for comments on items referenced here)
Foreign tourists are welcome in the country.	yes	
The use of seat belt is mandatory.	yes	
International driving license is accepted.	yes	
U.S. driver's license is accepted.	yes	11
It is considered impolite to yawn in public.	yes	
Death penalty for drug trafficking is the law.	no	
Life imprisonment for drug trafficking is the law.	no	
Guilty until proven innocent in court is the law.	no	
Innocent until proven guilty in court is the law.	yes	
Pedestrians always have right of way.	no	
Exit visas are required of visitors.	no	
Crash helmet is mandatory for motor cyclist.	yes	
Hanging is used as a form of legal punishment.	no	
Decapitation of a limb is used as a form of punishment.	no	
Caning is used as a form of legal punishment.	no	
Electric shock is used as a form of legal punishment.	none	
One is expected to stand up during the playing of the national anthem.	yes	
Crash helmet is mandatory for bicyclists.	no	
Guests are expected to eat every thing on their plates.	yes	
Table manners are very informal.	no	
One is expected to cover one's mouth when laughing.	no	
A vertical nod of the head means YES (OK).	yes	
A horizontal shaking of the head means NO (Not OK).	no	
Prostitution is allowed only in designated areas.	yes	
One is expected to take off one's hat during playing of national anthem.	yes	
Separate seating arrangements (between sexes) are maintained at movies.	no	
Separate seating arrangements (between sexes) are maintained at churches.	no	
Uninvited visitors or guests may not be welcome, even among acquaintances.	no	
Pets (e.g. cats, dog) are allowed in some hotels and restaurants.	yes	
Couples invited for a meal may be separated during meals according to their sex.	no	
Punctuality is the order of business.	yes	
Automobiles are driven with headlights always turned on.	no	12
Motorcycles are driven with headlights always turned on.	no	13
Visitors with expired visa face mandatory jail time.	yes	
Visitors without exit visa face jail time.	no	
Visitors without entry visa face mandatory (automatic) jail time.	n/a	14

ADDITIONAL COUNTRY INFORMATION

(A)	**The types of gifts to avoid:**	cactus, soap
(B)	**Appropriate gifts for a foreigner to give:**	chocolate, flowers (odd #),typical gifts from the country of origin
(C)	**Best time to present gifts (at the beginning or at the end of a visit?):**	at the beginning
(D)	**Best time to present gifts (on initial or later visits?):**	initial visit
(E)	**Best place to present gifts (in private or in public?):**	in private
(F)	**Number(s) with certain connotations and/or myths attached to them:**	good luck: 7, birth day bad luck: 13
(G)	**Basic shape(s) with negative connotations:**	n/a
(H)	**Basic color(s) with negative connotations:**	black, brown
(I)	**Traditional greeting methods include:**	handshake, kiss
(J)	**Safe topics for discussion include:**	weather, fashion, travel, art, family, food, sports
(K)	**Best time for conversations (before, during, after meals?):**	before/after meals
(L)	**Forms of legal punishment:**	jailing
(M)	**Approximately length of time one could be detained by law and order authorities before being charged in court:**	one could be detained for 48 hours by policemen
(N)	**January 15, 1999, for example, will normally be written as:**	15.1.99
(O)	**Emergency code number**:	114 ambulance, 133 police, 122 fire-brigade 141 first aid doc.
(P)	**Ambulance code Number**:	144
(Q)	**Police code number:**	133
(R)	**Telephone (country) code:**	0043
(S)	**Telex (country) code:**	0043
(T)	**Electricity requirements**:	220-v
(U)	**Legal drinking age:**	16
(V)	**Systems of weights and measures:**	kg. meters
(W)	**Legal age of incarceration**:	14
(X)	**Driving side of the road:**	right
(Y)	**Minimum expenditure expected of foreign visitors? $**	US - $100
(Z)	**Name of currency**:	Austrian schilling
(Za)	**Some places 0ff-limits to foreign visitors:**	private sites and premises, military areas
(Zb)	**Some places, structures and items prohibited from being photographed:**	military installations

ENDNOTES

Item Number: COMMENTS/EXPLANATIONS

n/a: Not applicable/Not available/No response

(1) Smoking in public buildings (schools, offices, authorities, museums is forbidden by law.

(2) Only in park.

(3) In designation areas.

(4) Drunk driving is also forbidden by law and may cost your driving license!

(5) Generally prostitution is allowed everywhere, except in specified areas, e.g. near churches.

(6) The possession of pornographic materials is forbidden by law.

(7) Forbidden by law are some kinds of them, as they are classified according to the danger.

(8) Must have a gun license.

(9) Must be regulations

(10) But not in restaurants.

(11) The U.S. driver's license is accepted only for one year, presupposed that the driver is 18 years old.

(12) It is not obligatory to always turn on headlights when driving automobiles or motorcycles, but it will be appreciated by the policemen and it raises your own security.

(13) It is not obligatory to always turn on headlights when driving automobiles or motorcycles, but it will be appreciated by the policemen and it raises your own security.

(14) It depends on the circumstances.

BELGIUM	Is customary Is allowed Is permissible Is used. Is OK	Is not customary Is frowned upon	Is disallowed Is forbidden Is a crime	(See last page for comments on items referenced here)
Smoking in public			✓	
Eating in public	✓			
Not flushing public toilet	✓			
Spitting in public		✓		
Feeding animals & birds in public	✓			
Whistling in public	✓			
Drinking alcohol in public	✓			
Kissing in public	✓			
Breast feeding in public		✓		
Drunkenness (in public)		✓		
Cursing in public		✓		
Religious preaching in public		✓		
Begging (panhandling) in public		✓		
Giving money to beggars/panhandlers	✓			
Giving food/drink to beggars/panhandlers	✓			
Brushing teeth in public (other than in restrooms)		✓		
Strolling with pets in major public roads/streets	✓			
Chewing gum in public	✓			
Chewing gum in government offices		✓		
Combing hair in public (other than in toilets/restrooms)		✓		
Undressing/dressing in public		✓		
Wearing of dark glasses indoors in public places	✓			
Public display of wealth		✓		
Praying openly in public in non-designated areas		✓		
Walking bare feet in public		✓		
Chewing tobacco in public	✓			
Trimming one's finger or toe nails in public		✓		
Laughing aloud in public	✓			
Mingling of the sexes in public			✓	
Mixed bathing in public swimming pools			✓	
Distributing religious pamphlets (literature) in public/side streets		✓		

BELGIUM

	Is customary Is allowed Is permissible Is used. Is OK	Is not customary Is frowned upon	Is disallowed Is forbidden Is a crime	(See last page for comments on items referenced here)
Dancing on side street		✓		
Nude bathing		✓		
Littering		✓		
Binge Drinking	✓			
hitchhiking	✓			
Jaywalking			✓	
Drunk driving			✓	
Speeding			✓	
Skating on side streets (side-walk)	✓			
Graffiti painting			✓	
Pilfering			✓	
Prostitution			✓	
Haggling in the market place		✓		
Consumption of alcoholic beverages in bars and restaurants				n/a
Gambling	✓			1
Possession of pornographic materials	✓			2
Possession of the Christian Bible	✓			
Possession of the Moslem Koran	✓			
Possession of bullet-proof vest	✓			
Possession of toy gun	✓			
Possession of fire crackers and fireworks	✓			
Possession of prescription drugs (without doctor's note)		✓		
Possession of regulated drugs (narcotics)			✓	
Possession of firearms (by foreigners)			✓	3
Possession of pocket knife in public	✓			
Using walkie talkies	✓			
Using of "boom boxes"(loud sounding stereo system)		✓		
Using "walkman" (very small radio/cassettes with ear plugs) in public places	✓			
Using "walkman" (very small radio/cassettes with ear plugs) while driving or riding		✓		

BELGIUM

	Is customary Is allowed Is permissible Is used Is OK	Is not customary Is frowned upon	Is disallowed Is forbidden Is a crime	(See last page for comments on items referenced here)
Use of cellular phone	✓			
Use of binoculars/periscopes other than in sports arena	✓			
Taking photographs of people (without their permission)	✓			
Taking photographs at airports, train and bus stations	✓			
Taking photographs of airports	✓			
Taking photographs of churches and synagogues	✓			
Taking photographs of religious statues	✓			
Taking photographs of public buildings				n/a
Taking photographs of bridges				n/a
Tipping (gratuity)	✓			
Tipping (when service is rendered)	✓			
Tipping (when service is not rendered)	✓			
Tipping waiters/waitresses at restaurants and hotels				n/a
Tipping taxi/cab drivers				n/a
Tipping baggage handlers, porters, door persons				n/a
Tipping of hair dressers/barbers				n/a
Overtipping	✓			
Undertipping	✓			
Spilling cigarette butt (ash) on side streets/on the floor		✓		
Men wearing lipstick		✓		
Wearing visible tattoo marks	✓			
Men painting/coloring their finger or toe nails		✓		
Cross dressing (men dressed like women & vice versa)		✓		
Walking in public without a shirt (i.e. with the upper half of the body naked)				n/a
Men wearing braided hair		✓		
Men wearing earrings		✓		
Men wearing dreadlock hair style	✓			
Homosexuality		✓		
Lesbianism		✓		

BELGIUM

	Is customary Is allowed Is permissible Is used Is OK	Is not customary Is frowned upon	Is disallowed Is forbidden Is a crime	(See last page for comments on items referenced here)
Females covering their hair (wearing headgear) in public	✓			
Females exposing their full face in public	✓			
Females driving automobiles	✓			
Females riding motorcycles	✓			
Females riding bicycles	✓			
Females smoking in public				n/a
Women wearing bras (braziers) in public		✓		
Use of lipstick by women	✓			
A woman extending her hands first when introduced	✓			
Female bashing		✓		
Females wearing trousers	✓			
Females wearing minis (short dresses)	✓			
Females wearing bikinis	✓			
Females wearing shorts	✓			
Persons of opposite sex holding hands in public	✓			
Persons of same sex holding hands in public	✓			
Handshake between opposite sex	✓			
Hugging in public by same sex	✓			
Hugging in public by opposite sex	✓			
Men and women walking side by side in public				n/a
Man walking ahead (in public), with the woman following				n/a
Woman walking ahead (in public), with the man following				n/a
Men opening doors for women	✓			
Sitting with legs crossed in the presence of elders	✓			
Talking to an elderly person with one's hat/cap on				n/a
Talking to an elderly person with hands positioned on both sides of one's waist				n/a
Blowing one's nose in public	✓			
Blowing one's nose in the presence of others	✓			
Addressing people by their title	✓			

BELGIUM

	Is customary Is allowed Is permissible Is used. Is OK	Is not customary Is frowned upon	Is disallowed Is forbidden Is a crime	(See last page for comments on items referenced here)
Addressing people by their family name/surname/last name/given name	✓			
Addressing people by their first name/ given name		✓		
Women going through doors first	✓			
Men helping women with their coats	✓			
Men extending their hands to women first during greetings	✓			
Taking off one's hat when entering a private home	✓			
Removing one's shoes when entering a private home				n/a
Invited guests bringing food at social gatherings		✓		
Guests bringing drinks at social gatherings		✓		
Shaking hands when leaving a small group	✓			
Shaking hands with everyone present, upon arrival at a social gathering	✓			
Eating with the right hand	✓			
Eating with the left hand		✓		
Eating with both hands				n/a
Presenting a gift or passing on an object with the left hand		✓		
Asking a man about his wife	✓			
Asking a woman about her husband	✓			
Making prior appointments before a meeting or visit	✓			
Addressing an audience with one or both hands in the pocket	✓			
Carrying on conversation during meals				n/a
Females sitting with legs crossed	✓			
People discussing their wealth		✓		
Asking someone his or her age, or how old the person is				n/a
Complementing someone on his/her physical looks				n/a
Complementing someone on his/her attire				n/a
Use of both hands in handshake		✓		144
In greeting, a handshake accompanied by a slight bow	✓			

BELGIUM

	Is customary Is allowed Is permissible Is used. Is OK	Is not customary Is frowned upon	Is disallowed Is forbidden Is a crime	(See last page for comments on items referenced here)
Salutations such as "Good morning", "Good afternoon", "Good evening"	✓			
The completion of a business deal with a handshake				n/a
Starting a negotiation session with a handshake				n/a
A gift for the host/hostess	✓			
Giving a business gift	✓			4
A gift of money (use of money as gift)		✓		
Use of flowers as a gift	✓			
Use of business cards	✓			
Accepting/presenting gifts with both hands	✓			
Burning of the country's flag			✓	
Mutilation of the national currency			✓	
Casual wearing of clothings made with colors & marks of the national flag				n/a
Wearing of look-alike military (camouflage) fatigues (attire)	✓			
Sitting on the floor (on floor mats)		✓		
Discussion of religion	✓			
Discussion of politics	✓			
Discussion of sex		✓		
Patting/slapping someone on the buttocks		✓		
Patting/slapping someone on the back	✓			
Touching or patting someone's head/hair	✓			
Casual touching of any part of someone's body				n/a
Drinking directly out of a bottle/can	✓			
Placing one's leg(s) on the table or chair		✓		

BELGIUM

	Is customary Is allowed Is permissible Is used. Is OK	Is not customary Is frowned upon	Is disallowed Is forbidden Is a crime	(See last page for comments on items referenced here)
Showing the sole of one's foot (feet)				n/a
People standing very close when talking		✓		
Maintaining steady eye contact (direct gaze) when talking to someone	✓			
Kissing or exchange of kisses on the cheek	✓			
Counting money (change) in someone's palm				n/a
Finger pointing in public (in a daring manner)		✓		
Seeking attention by winking the eyes				n/a
Tapping the head to indicate someone is crazy				n/a
Twirling the head to indicate someone is crazy				n/a
Whistling as a way of requesting something/seeking attention				n/a
Using "thumbs-up" sign to mean OK				n/a
Forming a circle with the thumb and index finger (forefinger) to mean OK				n/a
Using the fingers to make a "V" sign for victory				n/a
Beckoning to someone with the index finger (forefinger)				n/a
The left to right waving of the hand with open palms facing outward to indicate "Good bye"				n/a
The use of a nod to show acknowledgement				n/a
Stopping/beckoning a taxi using a stretched hand with the thumb pointing upward				n/a
Using the thumb finger pointed to a direction, to request a ride or a hike				n/a
Raising one's hand/waving with an open fist to summon a taxi				n/a
Tapping one's foot/feet on the floor in a public gathering				n/a
Wiggling one's leg(s) when in a sitting position				n/a
Use of the hand (by motorists and cyclists) to signal direction of traffic				n/a

BELGIUM

		(See last page for comments on items referenced here)
Foreign tourists are welcome in the country.	yes	
The use of seat belt is mandatory.	yes	
International driving license is accepted.	yes	
U.S. driver's license is accepted.	yes	
It is considered impolite to yawn in public.	no	
Death penalty for drug trafficking is the law.	no	
Life imprisonment for drug trafficking is the law.	no	
Guilty until proven innocent in court is the law.	no	
Innocent until proven guilty in court is the law.	yes	
Pedestrians always have right of way.	no	
Exit visas are required of visitors.	no	
Crash helmet is mandatory for motor cyclist.	yes	
Hanging is used as a form of legal punishment.	no	
Decapitation of a limb is used as a form of punishment.	no	
Caning is used as a form of legal punishment.	no	
Electric shock is used as a form of legal punishment.	no	
One is expected to stand up during the playing of the national anthem.	no	
Crash helmet is mandatory for bicyclists.	no	
Guests are expected to eat every thing on their plates.	yes	
Table manners are very informal.	no	
One is expected to cover one's mouth when laughing.	no	
A vertical nod of the head means YES (OK).	yes	
A horizontal shaking of the head means NO (Not OK).	yes	
Prostitution is allowed only in designated areas.	no	
One is expected to take off one's hat during playing of national anthem.	yes	
Separate seating arrangements (between sexes) are maintained at movies.	no	
Separate seating arrangements (between sexes) are maintained at churches.	no	
Uninvited visitors or guests may not be welcome, even among acquaintances.	yes	
Pets (e.g. cats, dog) are allowed in some hotels and restaurants.	yes	
Couples invited for a meal may be separated during meals according to their sex.	yes	
Punctuality is the order of business.	yes	
Automobiles are driven with headlights always turned on.	n/a	
Motorcycles are driven with headlights always turned on.	n/a	
Visitors with expired visa face mandatory jail time.	no	6
Visitors without exit visa face jail time.	no	
Visitors without entry visa face mandatory (automatic) jail time.	no	7

ADDITIONAL COUNTRY INFORMATION

(A)	**The types of gifts to avoid:**	Chrysanthemums
(B)	**Appropriate gifts for a foreigner to give:**	something typical of their country of origin.
(C)	**Best time to present gifts (at the beginning or at the end of a visit?):**	beginning
(D)	**Best time to present gifts (on initial or later visits?):**	n/a
(E)	**Best place to present gifts (in private or in public?):**	n/a
(F)	**Number(s) with certain connotations and/or myths attached to them:**	n/a
(G)	**Basic shape(s) with negative connotations:**	n/a
(H)	**Basic color(s) with negative connotations:**	n/a
(I)	**Traditional greeting methods include:**	n/a
(J)	**Safe topics for discussion include:**	these are not forbidden
(K)	**Best time for conversations (before, during, after meals?):**	n/a
(L)	**Forms of legal punishment:**	jailing
(M)	**Approximately length of time one could be detained by law and order authorities before being charged in court:**	n/a
(N)	**January 15, 1999, for example, will normally be written as:**	15/1/99
(O)	**Emergency code number**:	100/101 see below
(P)	**Ambulance code Number**:	100 medical/fire emergencies
(Q)	**Police code number:**	101 police
(R)	**Telephone (country) code:**	32
(S)	**Telex (country) code:**	846
(T)	**Electricity requirements**:	220/50
(U)	**Legal drinking age:**	none
(V)	**Systems of weights and measures:**	metric
(W)	**Legal age of incarceration**:	16 years
(X)	**Driving side of the road:**	right
(Y)	**Minimum expenditure expected of foreign visitors? $**	n/a
(Z)	**Name of currency**:	franc (Belgian franc)
(Za)	**Some places 0ff-limits to foreign visitors:**	n/a
(Zb)	**Some places, structures and items prohibited from being photographed:**	n/a

ENDNOTES

Item Number: COMMENTS/EXPLANATIONS

n/a: Not applicable/Not available/No response

(1) It is legal in the framework organized by the state and if you are at least 18 years of age.

(2) It is allowed as long as you are over 18 years of age.

(3) You need a permit to possess firearms.

(4) Usually the right cheek

(5) OK to an extent, but may be construed as bribery.

(6) but may face deportation

(7) but may face deportation

BULGARIA	Is customary Is allowed Is permissible Is used. Is OK	Is not customary Is frowned upon	Is disallowed Is forbidden Is a crime	(See last page for comments on items referenced here)
Smoking in public	✓			
Eating in public		✓		
Not flushing public toilet	✓			
Spitting in public			✓	
Feeding animals & birds in public	✓			
Whistling in public				n/a
Drinking alcohol in public	✓			
Kissing in public	✓			
Breast feeding in public		✓		
Drunkenness (in public)		✓		
Cursing in public			✓	
Religious preaching in public			✓	
Begging (panhandling) in public		✓		
Giving money to beggars/panhandlers		✓		
Giving food/drink to beggars/panhandlers		✓		
Brushing teeth in public (other than in restrooms)		✓		
Strolling with pets in major public roads/streets		✓		
Chewing gum in public		✓		
Chewing gum in government offices			✓	
Combing hair in public (other than in toilets/restrooms)		✓		
Undressing/dressing in public		✓		
Wearing of dark glasses indoors in public places	✓			
Public display of wealth		✓		
Praying openly in public in non-designated areas			✓	
Walking bare feet in public		✓		
Chewing tobacco in public		✓		
Trimming one's finger or toe nails in public		✓		
Laughing aloud in public	✓			
Mingling of the sexes in public				n/a
Mixed bathing in public swimming pools				n/a
Distributing religious pamphlets (literature) in public/side streets				n/a

BULGARIA

	Is customary Is allowed Is permissible Is used. Is OK	Is not customary Is frowned upon	Is disallowed Is forbidden Is a crime	(See last page for comments on items referenced here)
Dancing on side street		✓		
Nude bathing		✓		
Littering			✓	
Binge Drinking		✓		
hitchhiking			✓	
Jaywalking			✓	
Drunk driving		✓		
Speeding			✓	
Skating on side streets (side-walk)		✓		
Graffiti painting		✓		
Pilfering			✓	
Prostitution			✓	
Haggling in the market place				n/a
Consumption of alcoholic beverages in bars and restaurants				n/a
Gambling		✓		
Possession of pornographic materials		✓		
Possession of the Christian Bible		✓		
Possession of the Moslem Koran		✓		
Possession of bullet-proof vest		✓		
Possession of toy gun		✓		
Possession of fire crackers and fireworks		✓		
Possession of prescription drugs (without doctor's note)			✓	
Possession of regulated drugs (narcotics)			✓	
Possession of firearms (by foreigners)			✓	
Possession of pocket knife in public		✓		
Using walkie talkies		✓		
Using of "boom boxes"(loud sounding stereo system)			✓	
Using "walkman" (very small radio/cassettes with ear plugs) in public places		✓		
Using "walkman" (very small radio/cassettes with ear plugs) while driving or riding				n/a

BULGARIA

	Is customary Is allowed Is permissible Is used Is OK	Is not customary Is frowned upon	Is disallowed Is forbidden Is a crime	(See last page for comments on items referenced here)
Use of cellular phone		✓		
Use of binoculars/periscopes other than in sports arena		✓		
Taking photographs of people (without their permission)		✓		
Taking photographs at airports, train and bus stations	✓			
Taking photographs of airports	✓			
Taking photographs of churches and synagogues	✓			
Taking photographs of religious statues	✓			
Taking photographs of public buildings				n/a
Taking photographs of bridges				n/a
Tipping (gratuity)		✓		
Tipping (when service is rendered)		✓		
Tipping (when service is not rendered)		✓		
Tipping waiters/waitresses at restaurants and hotels				n/a
Tipping taxi/cab drivers				n/a
Tipping baggage handlers, porters, door persons				n/a
Tipping of hair dressers/barbers				n/a
Overtipping				n/a
Undertipping			✓	
Spilling cigarette butt (ash) on side streets/on the floor			✓	
Men wearing lipstick		✓		
Wearing visible tattoo marks		✓		
Men painting/coloring their finger or toe nails		✓		
Cross dressing (men dressed like women & vice versa)			✓	
Walking in public without a shirt (i.e. with the upper half of the body naked)				n/a
Men wearing braided hair		✓		
Men wearing earrings		✓		
Men wearing dreadlock hair style		✓		
Homosexuality			✓	
Lesbianism			✓	

BULGARIA

	Is customary Is allowed Is permissible Is used Is OK	Is not customary Is frowned upon	Is disallowed Is forbidden Is a crime	(See last page for comments on items referenced here)
Females covering their hair (wearing headgear) in public		✓		
Females exposing their full face in public	✓			
Females driving automobiles	✓			
Females riding motorcycles	✓			
Females riding bicycles	✓			
Females smoking in public				n/a
Women wearing bras (braziers) in public			✓	
Use of lipstick by women	✓			
A woman extending her hands first when introduced	✓			
Female bashing			✓	
Females wearing trousers	✓			
Females wearing minis (short dresses)	✓			
Females wearing bikinis	✓			
Females wearing shorts		✓		
Persons of opposite sex holding hands in public		✓		
Persons of same sex holding hands in public		✓		
Handshake between opposite sex	✓			
Hugging in public by same sex		✓		
Hugging in public by opposite sex		✓		
Men and women walking side by side in public				n/a
Man walking ahead (in public), with the woman following				n/a
Woman walking ahead (in public), with the man following				n/a
Men opening doors for women	✓			
Sitting with legs crossed in the presence of elders	✓			
Talking to an elderly person with one's hat/cap on				n/a
Talking to an elderly person with hands positioned on both sides of one's waist				n/a
Blowing one's nose in public		✓		
Blowing one's nose in the presence of others		✓		
Addressing people by their title		✓		

BULGARIA

	Is customary Is allowed Is permissible Is used. Is OK	Is not customary Is frowned upon	Is disallowed Is forbidden Is a crime	(See last page for comments on items referenced here)
Addressing people by their family name/surname/last name/given name	✓			
Addressing people by their first name/ given name	✓			
Women going through doors first	✓			
Men helping women with their coats	✓			
Men extending their hands to women first during greetings	✓			
Taking off one's hat when entering a private home	✓			
Removing one's shoes when entering a private home				n/a
Invited guests bringing food at social gatherings		✓		
Guests bringing drinks at social gatherings	✓			
Shaking hands when leaving a small group	✓			
Shaking hands with everyone present, upon arrival at a social gathering		✓		
Eating with the right hand	✓			
Eating with the left hand		✓		
Eating with both hands		✓		
Presenting a gift or passing on an object with the left hand		✓		
Asking a man about his wife	✓			
Asking a woman about her husband	✓			
Making prior appointments before a meeting or visit	✓			
Addressing an audience with one or both hands in the pocket		✓		
Carrying on conversation during meals				n/a
Females sitting with legs crossed	✓			
People discussing their wealth		✓		
Asking someone his or her age, or how old the person is				n/a
Complementing someone on his/her physical looks				n/a
Complementing someone on his/her attire				n/a
Use of both hands in handshake		✓		
In greeting, a handshake accompanied by a slight bow	✓			

BULGARIA

	Is customary Is allowed Is permissible Is used. Is OK	Is not customary Is frowned upon	Is disallowed Is forbidden Is a crime	(See last page for comments on items referenced here)
Salutations such as "Good morning", "Good afternoon", "Good evening"	✓			
The completion of a business deal with a handshake				n/a
Starting a negotiation session with a handshake				n/a
A gift for the host/hostess	✓			
Giving a business gift		✓		
A gift of money (use of money as gift)		✓		
Use of flowers as a gift	✓			
Use of business cards		✓		
Accepting/presenting gifts with both hands	✓			
Burning of the country's flag			✓	
Mutilation of the national currency			✓	
Casual wearing of clothings made with colors & marks of the national flag				n/a
Wearing of look-alike military (camouflage) fatigues (attire)		✓		
Sitting on the floor (on floor mats)		✓		
Discussion of religion		✓		
Discussion of politics	✓			
Discussion of sex	✓			
Patting/slapping someone on the buttocks			✓	
Patting/slapping someone on the back		✓		
Touching or patting someone's head/hair		✓		
Casual touching of any part of someone's body				n/a
Drinking directly out of a bottle/can		✓		
Placing one's leg(s) on the table or chair		✓		

BULGARIA

	Is customary Is allowed Is permissible Is used. Is OK	Is not customary Is frowned upon	Is disallowed Is forbidden Is a crime	(See last page for comments on items referenced here)
Showing the sole of one's foot (feet)				n/a
People standing very close when talking		✓		
Maintaining steady eye contact (direct gaze) when talking to someone	✓			
Kissing or exchange of kisses on the cheek		✓		
Counting money (change) in someone's palm				n/a
Finger pointing in public (in a daring manner)		✓		
Seeking attention by winking the eyes				n/a
Tapping the head to indicate someone is crazy				n/a
Twirling the head to indicate someone is crazy				n/a
Whistling as a way of requesting something/seeking attention				n/a
Using "thumbs-up" sign to mean OK				n/a
Forming a circle with the thumb and index finger (forefinger) to mean OK				n/a
Using the fingers to make a "V" sign for victory				n/a
Beckoning to someone with the index finger (forefinger)				n/a
The left to right waving of the hand with open palms facing outward to indicate "Good bye"				n/a
The use of a nod to show acknowledgement				n/a
Stopping/beckoning a taxi using a stretched hand with the thumb pointing upward				n/a
Using the thumb finger pointed to a direction, to request a ride or a hike				n/a
Raising one's hand/waving with an open fist to summon a taxi				n/a
Tapping one's foot/feet on the floor in a public gathering				n/a
Wiggling one's leg(s) when in a sitting position				n/a
Use of the hand (by motorists and cyclists) to signal direction of traffic				n/a

BULGARIA

		(See last page for comments on items referenced here)
Foreign tourists are welcome in the country.	yes	
The use of seat belt is mandatory.	yes	
International driving license is accepted.	no	
U.S. driver's license is accepted.	yes	
It is considered impolite to yawn in public.	yes	
Death penalty for drug trafficking is the law.	no	
Life imprisonment for drug trafficking is the law.	no	
Guilty until proven innocent in court is the law.	yes	
Innocent until proven guilty in court is the law.	yes	
Pedestrians always have right of way.	no	
Exit visas are required of visitors.	no	
Crash helmet is mandatory for motor cyclist.	yes	
Hanging is used as a form of legal punishment.	no	
Decapitation of a limb is used as a form of punishment.	no	
Caning is used as a form of legal punishment.	no	
Electric shock is used as a form of legal punishment.	no	
One is expected to stand up during the playing of the national anthem.	yes	
Crash helmet is mandatory for bicyclists.	yes	
Guests are expected to eat every thing on their plates.	yes	
Table manners are very informal.	yes & no	
One is expected to cover one's mouth when laughing.	no	
A vertical nod of the head means YES (OK).	no	
A horizontal shaking of the head means NO (Not OK).	no	
Prostitution is allowed only in designated areas.	yes	
One is expected to take off one's hat during playing of national anthem.	yes	
Separate seating arrangements (between sexes) are maintained at movies.	no	
Separate seating arrangements (between sexes) are maintained at churches.	no	
Uninvited visitors or guests may not be welcome, even among acquaintances.	no	
Pets (e.g. cats, dog) are allowed in some hotels and restaurants.	no	
Couples invited for a meal may be separated during meals according to their sex.	no	
Punctuality is the order of business.	yes	
Automobiles are driven with headlights always turned on.		n/a
Motorcycles are driven with headlights always turned on.		n/a
Visitors with expired visa face mandatory jail time.	no	
Visitors without exit visa face jail time.	no	
Visitors without entry visa face mandatory (automatic) jail time.	no	

ADDITIONAL COUNTRY INFORMATION

(A)	**The types of gifts to avoid:**	n/a
(B)	**Appropriate gifts for a foreigner to give:**	flowers, candy, wine, small presents
(C)	**Best time to present gifts (at the beginning or at the end of a visit?):**	at the beginning
(D)	**Best time to present gifts (on initial or later visits?):**	n/a
(E)	**Best place to present gifts (in private or in public?):**	n/a
(F)	**Number(s) with certain connotations and/or myths attached to them:**	n/a
(G)	**Basic shape(s) with negative connotations:**	n/a
(H)	**Basic color(s) with negative connotations:**	n/a
(I)	**Traditional greeting methods include:**	n/a
(J)	**Safe topics for discussion include:**	All topics. It depends on the parties involved.
(K)	**Best time for conversations (before, during, after meals?):**	n/a
(L)	**Forms of legal punishment:**	jailing
(M)	**Approximately length of time one could be detained by law and order authorities before being charged in court:**	n/a
(N)	**January 15, 1999, for example, will normally be written as:**	15/01/99
(O)	**Emergency code number:**	146
(P)	**Ambulance code Number:**	150
(Q)	**Police code number:**	166
(R)	**Telephone (country) code:**	359
(S)	**Telex (country) code:**	865
(T)	**Electricity requirements:**	220/50
(U)	**Legal drinking age:**	21
(V)	**Systems of weights and measures:**	Metric
(W)	**Legal age of incarceration:**	n/a
(X)	**Driving side of the road:**	right
(Y)	**Minimum expenditure expected of foreign visitors? $**	yes, 500 U.S. dollars
(Z)	**Name of currency:**	Lev
(Za)	**Some places 0ff-limits to foreign visitors:**	n/a
(Zb)	**Some places, structures and items prohibited from being photographed:**	n/a

REPUBLIC OF CROATIA	**Is customary Is allowed Is permissible Is used. Is OK**	**Is not customary Is frowned upon**	**Is disallowed Is forbidden Is a crime**	**(See last page for comments on items referenced here)**
Smoking in public			✓	
Eating in public	✓			
Not flushing public toilet			✓	
Spitting in public			✓	
Feeding animals & birds in public			✓	
Whistling in public	✓			
Drinking alcohol in public	✓			
Kissing in public	✓			
Breast feeding in public		✓		
Drunkenness (in public)		✓		
Cursing in public		✓		
Religious preaching in public	✓			
Begging (panhandling) in public	✓			
Giving money to beggars/panhandlers	✓			
Giving food/drink to beggars/panhandlers		✓		
Brushing teeth in public (other than in restrooms)		✓		
Strolling with pets in major public roads/streets	✓			
Chewing gum in public	✓			
Chewing gum in government offices		✓		
Combing hair in public (other than in toilets/restrooms)		✓		
Undressing/dressing in public		✓		
Wearing of dark glasses indoors in public places	✓			
Public display of wealth		✓		
Praying openly in public in non-designated areas	✓			
Walking bare feet in public	✓			
Chewing tobacco in public	✓			
Trimming one's finger or toe nails in public		✓		
Laughing aloud in public	✓			
Mingling of the sexes in public				n/a
Mixed bathing in public swimming pools				n/a
Distributing religious pamphlets (literature) in public/side streets				n/a

CROATIA

	Is customary Is allowed Is permissible Is used. Is OK	Is not customary Is frowned upon	Is disallowed Is forbidden Is a crime	(See last page for comments on items referenced here)
Dancing on side street	✓			
Nude bathing				1
Littering			✓	
Binge Drinking		✓		
hitchhiking		✓		
Jaywalking			✓	
Drunk driving			✓	
Speeding			✓	
Skating on side streets (side-walk)	✓			
Graffiti painting			✓	
Pilfering			✓	
Prostitution			✓	
Haggling in the market place				n/a
Consumption of alcoholic beverages in bars and restaurants				n/a
Gambling	✓			
Possession of pornographic materials		✓		
Possession of the Christian Bible	✓			
Possession of the Moslem Koran	✓			
Possession of bullet-proof vest	✓			
Possession of toy gun	✓			
Possession of fire crackers and fireworks			✓	
Possession of prescription drugs (without doctor's note)			✓	
Possession of regulated drugs (narcotics)			✓	
Possession of firearms (by foreigners)			✓	
Possession of pocket knife in public		✓		
Using walkie talkies			✓	2
Using of "boom boxes"(loud sounding stereo system)	✓			
Using "walkman" (very small radio/cassettes with ear plugs) in public places	✓			
Using "walkman" (very small radio/cassettes with ear plugs) while driving or riding				n/a

CROATIA

	Is customary Is allowed Is permissible Is used Is OK	Is not customary Is frowned upon	Is disallowed Is forbidden Is a crime	(See last page for comments on items referenced here)
Use of cellular phone	✓			
Use of binoculars/periscopes other than in sports arena	✓			
Taking photographs of people (without their permission)	✓			
Taking photographs at airports, train and bus stations			✓	
Taking photographs of airports			✓	
Taking photographs of churches and synagogues			✓	
Taking photographs of religious statues			✓	
Taking photographs of public buildings				n/a
Taking photographs of bridges				n/a
Tipping (gratuity)	✓			
Tipping (when service is rendered)	✓			
Tipping (when service is not rendered)		✓		
Tipping waiters/waitresses at restaurants and hotels				n/a
Tipping taxi/cab drivers				n/a
Tipping baggage handlers, porters, door persons				n/a
Tipping of hair dressers/barbers				n/a
Overtipping	✓			
Undertipping		✓		
Spilling cigarette butt (ash) on side streets/on the floor		✓		
Men wearing lipstick		✓		
Wearing visible tattoo marks	✓			
Men painting/coloring their finger or toe nails		✓		
Cross dressing (men dressed like women & vice versa)		✓		
Walking in public without a shirt (i.e. with the upper half of the body naked)				n/a
Men wearing braided hair	✓			
Men wearing earrings	✓			
Men wearing dreadlock hair style	✓			
Homosexuality	✓			
Lesbianism	✓			

CROATIA

	Is customary Is allowed Is permissible Is used Is OK	Is not customary Is frowned upon	Is disallowed Is forbidden Is a crime	(See last page for comments on items referenced here)
Females covering their hair (wearing headgear) in public	✓			
Females exposing their full face in public		✓		
Females driving automobiles	✓			
Females riding motorcycles	✓			
Females riding bicycles	✓			
Females smoking in public	✓			
Women wearing bras (braziers) in public				n/a
Use of lipstick by women		✓		
A woman extending her hands first when introduced	✓			
Female bashing	✓			
Females wearing trousers		✓		
Females wearing minis (short dresses)	✓			
Females wearing bikinis	✓			
Females wearing shorts				3
Persons of opposite sex holding hands in public	✓			
Persons of same sex holding hands in public	✓			
Handshake between opposite sex	✓			
Hugging in public by same sex	✓			
Hugging in public by opposite sex	✓			
Men and women walking side by side in public				n/a
Man walking ahead (in public), with the woman following				n/a
Woman walking ahead (in public), with the man following				n/a
Men opening doors for women	✓			
Sitting with legs crossed in the presence of elders	✓			
Talking to an elderly person with one's hat/cap on				n/a
Talking to an elderly person with hands positioned on both sides of one's waist				n/a
Blowing one's nose in public	✓			
Blowing one's nose in the presence of others	✓			
Addressing people by their title	✓			4

CROATIA

	Is customary Is allowed Is permissible Is used. Is OK	Is not customary Is frowned upon	Is disallowed Is forbidden Is a crime	(See last page for comments on items referenced here)
Addressing people by their family name/surname/last name/given name	✓			5
Addressing people by their first name/ given name				n/a
Women going through doors first	✓			
Men helping women with their coats	✓			
Men extending their hands to women first during greetings		✓		
Taking off one's hat when entering a private home	✓			
Removing one's shoes when entering a private home				n/a
Invited guests bringing food at social gatherings		✓		
Guests bringing drinks at social gatherings		✓		
Shaking hands when leaving a small group	✓			
Shaking hands with everyone present, upon arrival at a social gathering	✓			
Eating with the right hand	✓			
Eating with the left hand	✓			
Eating with both hands		✓		
Presenting a gift or passing on an object with the left hand		✓		
Asking a man about his wife	✓			
Asking a woman about her husband	✓			
Making prior appointments before a meeting or visit	✓			
Addressing an audience with one or both hands in the pocket		✓		
Carrying on conversation during meals				n/a
Females sitting with legs crossed		✓		
People discussing their wealth		✓		
Asking someone his or her age, or how old the person is	✓			
Complementing someone on his/her physical looks	✓			
Complementing someone on his/her attire	✓			
Use of both hands in handshake				n/a
In greeting, a handshake accompanied by a slight bow				n/a

CROATIA

	Is customary Is allowed Is permissible Is used. Is OK	Is not customary Is frowned upon	Is disallowed Is forbidden Is a crime	(See last page for comments on items referenced here)
Salutations such as "Good morning", "Good afternoon", "Good evening"	✓			
The completion of a business deal with a handshake	✓			
Starting a negotiation session with a handshake		✓		
A gift for the host/hostess	✓			
Giving a business gift	✓			
A gift of money (use of money as gift)	✓			
Use of flowers as a gift		✓		
Use of business cards	✓			
Accepting/presenting gifts with both hands	✓			
Burning of the country's flag	✓			
Mutilation of the national currency			✓	
Casual wearing of clothings made with colors & marks of the national flag			✓	
Wearing of look-alike military (camouflage) fatigues (attire)				n/a
Sitting on the floor (on floor mats)		✓		
Discussion of religion		✓		
Discussion of politics	✓			
Discussion of sex	✓			
Patting/slapping someone on the buttocks		✓		
Patting/slapping someone on the back	✓			
Touching or patting someone's head/hair	✓			
Casual touching of any part of someone's body				n/a
Drinking directly out of a bottle/can		✓		
Placing one's leg(s) on the table or chair		✓		

CROATIA

	Is customary Is allowed Is permissible Is used. Is OK	Is not customary Is frowned upon	Is disallowed Is forbidden Is a crime	(See last page for comments on items referenced here)
Showing the sole of one's foot (feet)				n/a
People standing very close when talking		✓		
Maintaining steady eye contact (direct gaze) when talking to someone	✓			
Kissing or exchange of kisses on the cheek	✓			
Counting money (change) in someone's palm				n/a
Finger pointing in public (in a daring manner)		✓		
Seeking attention by winking the eyes				n/a
Tapping the head to indicate someone is crazy				n/a
Twirling the head to indicate someone is crazy				n/a
Whistling as a way of requesting something/seeking attention				n/a
Using "thumbs-up" sign to mean OK				n/a
Forming a circle with the thumb and index finger (forefinger) to mean OK				n/a
Using the fingers to make a "V" sign for victory				n/a
Beckoning to someone with the index finger (forefinger)				n/a
The left to right waving of the hand with open palms facing outward to indicate "Good bye"				n/a
The use of a nod to show acknowledgement				n/a
Stopping/beckoning a taxi using a stretched hand with the thumb pointing upward				n/a
Using the thumb finger pointed to a direction, to request a ride or a hike				n/a
Raising one's hand/waving with an open fist to summon a taxi				n/a
Tapping one's foot/feet on the floor in a public gathering				n/a
Wiggling one's leg(s) when in a sitting position				n/a
Use of the hand (by motorists and cyclists) to signal direction of traffic				n/a

CROATIA

		(See last page for comments on items referenced here)
Foreign tourists are welcome in the country.	yes	
The use of seat belt is mandatory.	yes	
International driving license is accepted.	yes	
U.S. driver's license is accepted.	yes	
It is considered impolite to yawn in public.	yes	
Death penalty for drug trafficking is the law.	no	
Life imprisonment for drug trafficking is the law.	no	
Guilty until proven innocent in court is the law.	no	
Innocent until proven guilty in court is the law.	yes	
Pedestrians always have right of way.	yes	
Exit visas are required of visitors.	no	
Crash helmet is mandatory for motor cyclist.	yes	
Hanging is used as a form of legal punishment.	no	
Decapitation of a limb is used as a form of punishment.	no	
Caning is used as a form of legal punishment.	no	
Electric shock is used as a form of legal punishment.	no	
One is expected to stand up during the playing of the national anthem.	yes	
Crash helmet is mandatory for bicyclists.		n/a
Guests are expected to eat every thing on their plates.	no	
Table manners are very informal.	no	
One is expected to cover one's mouth when laughing.	no	
A vertical nod of the head means YES (OK).	yes	
A horizontal shaking of the head means NO (Not OK).	yes	
Prostitution is allowed only in designated areas.	no	
One is expected to take off one's hat during playing of national anthem.	yes	
Separate seating arrangements (between sexes) are maintained at movies.	no	
Separate seating arrangements (between sexes) are maintained at churches.	no	
Uninvited visitors or guests may not be welcome, even among acquaintances.	no	
Pets (e.g. cats, dog) are allowed in some hotels and restaurants.	yes	
Couples invited for a meal may be separated during meals according to their sex.		6
Punctuality is the order of business.	yes	
Automobiles are driven with headlights always turned on.		n/a
Motorcycles are driven with headlights always turned on.		n/a
Visitors with expired visa face mandatory jail time.	no	
Visitors without exit visa face jail time.	no	
Visitors without entry visa face mandatory (automatic) jail time.	no	

ADDITIONAL COUNTRY INFORMATION

(A)	**The types of gifts to avoid:**	n/a
(B)	**Appropriate gifts for a foreigner to give:**	souvenirs, monographs from the visitor's country.
(C)	**Best time to present gifts (at the beginning or at the end of a visit?):**	in the beginning
(D)	**Best time to present gifts (on initial or later visits?):**	n/a
(E)	**Best place to present gifts (in private or in public?):**	n/a
(F)	**Number(s) with certain connotations and/or myths attached to them:**	n/a
(G)	**Basic shape(s) with negative connotations:**	n/a
(H)	**Basic color(s) with negative connotations:**	n/a
(I)	**Traditional greeting methods include:**	n/a
(J)	**Safe topics for discussion include:**	weather, travel, family, religion, domestic politics, sports international politics, social conditions.
(K)	**Best time for conversations (before, during, after meals?):**	n/a
(L)	**Forms of legal punishment:**	fines, jailing
(M)	**Approximately length of time one could be detained by law and order authorities before being charged in court:**	48 hours
(N)	**January 15, 1999, for example, will normally be written as:**	15/01/99
(O)	**Emergency code number:**	93
(P)	**Ambulance code Number:**	94
(Q)	**Police code number:**	92
(R)	**Telephone (country) code:**	387
(S)	**Telex (country) code:**	n/a
(T)	**Electricity requirements:**	n/a
(U)	**Legal drinking age:**	18
(V)	**Systems of weights and measures:**	n/a
(W)	**Legal age of incarceration:**	18
(X)	**Driving side of the road:**	right
(Y)	**Minimum expenditure expected of foreign visitors? $**	yes
(Z)	**Name of currency:**	kuna
(Za)	**Some places 0ff-limits to foreign visitors:**	n/a
(Zb)	**Some places, structures and items prohibited from being photographed:**	n/a

ENDNOTES

Item Number: COMMENTS/EXPLANATIONS

n/a: Not applicable/Not available/No response

(1) Nude bathing is allowed only at nudist camp.
(2) only with permission
(3) depends
(4) depends
(5) usually, when official
(6) depends

CYPRUS	Is customary Is allowed Is permissible Is used. Is OK	Is not customary Is frowned upon	Is disallowed Is forbidden Is a crime	(See last page for comments on items referenced here)
Smoking in public	✓			
Eating in public	✓			
Not flushing public toilet		✓		
Spitting in public		✓		
Feeding animals & birds in public	✓			
Whistling in public	✓			
Drinking alcohol in public	✓			
Kissing in public	✓			
Breast feeding in public	✓			
Drunkenness (in public)		✓		
Cursing in public		✓		
Religious preaching in public	✓			
Begging (panhandling) in public		✓		
Giving money to beggars/panhandlers	✓			
Giving food/drink to beggars/panhandlers	✓			
Brushing teeth in public (other than in restrooms)		✓		
Strolling with pets in major public roads/streets	✓			
Chewing gum in public	✓			
Chewing gum in government offices		✓		
Combing hair in public (other than in toilets/restrooms)	✓			
Undressing/dressing in public		✓		
Wearing of dark glasses indoors in public places	✓			
Public display of wealth	✓			
Praying openly in public in non-designated areas		✓		
Walking bare feet in public		✓		
Chewing tobacco in public	✓			
Trimming one's finger or toe nails in public		✓		
Laughing aloud in public	✓			
Mingling of the sexes in public	✓			
Mixed bathing in public swimming pools	✓			
Distributing religious pamphlets (literature) in public/side streets	✓			

CYPRUS

	Is customary Is allowed Is permissible Is used. Is OK	Is not customary Is frowned upon	Is disallowed Is forbidden Is a crime	(See last page for comments on items referenced here)
Dancing on side street	✓			
Nude bathing		✓		
Littering			✓	
Binge Drinking		✓		
hitchhiking	✓			
Jaywalking		✓		
Drunk driving			✓	
Speeding			✓	
Skating on side streets (side-walk)	✓			
Graffiti painting			✓	
Pilfering			✓	
Prostitution		✓		
Haggling in the market place	✓			
Consumption of alcoholic beverages in bars and restaurants	✓			
Gambling			✓	
Possession of pornographic materials		✓		
Possession of the Christian Bible	✓			
Possession of the Moslem Koran	✓			
Possession of bullet-proof vest	✓			
Possession of toy gun	✓			
Possession of fire crackers and fireworks			✓	
Possession of prescription drugs (without doctor's note)			✓	
Possession of regulated drugs (narcotics)			✓	
Possession of firearms (by foreigners)			✓	
Possession of pocket knife in public	✓			
Using walkie talkies	✓			
Using of "boom boxes"(loud sounding stereo system)		✓		
Using "walkman" (very small radio/cassettes with ear plugs) in public places	✓			
Using "walkman" (very small radio/cassettes with ear plugs) while driving or riding			✓	

CYPRUS

	Is customary Is allowed Is permissible Is used Is OK	Is not customary Is frowned upon	Is disallowed Is forbidden Is a crime	(See last page for comments on items referenced here)
Use of cellular phone	✓			
Use of binoculars/periscopes other than in sports arena		✓		
Taking photographs of people (without their permission)			✓	
Taking photographs at airports, train and bus stations			✓	
Taking photographs of airports	✓			
Taking photographs of churches and synagogues	✓			
Taking photographs of religious statues	✓			
Taking photographs of public buildings	✓			
Taking photographs of bridges	✓			
Tipping (gratuity)	✓			
Tipping (when service is rendered)	✓			
Tipping (when service is not rendered)	✓			
Tipping waiters/waitresses at restaurants and hotels	✓			
Tipping taxi/cab drivers	✓			
Tipping baggage handlers, porters, door persons	✓			
Tipping of hair dressers/barbers	✓			
Overtipping	✓			
Undertipping		✓		
Spilling cigarette butt (ash) on side streets/on the floor		✓		
Men wearing lipstick		✓		
Wearing visible tattoo marks		✓		
Men painting/coloring their finger or toe nails		✓		
Cross dressing (men dressed like women & vice versa)		✓		
Walking in public without a shirt (i.e. with the upper half of the body naked)		✓		
Men wearing braided hair		✓		
Men wearing earrings	✓			
Men wearing dreadlock hair style	✓			
Homosexuality		✓		
Lesbianism		✓		

CYPRUS

	Is customary Is allowed Is permissible Is used Is OK	Is not customary Is frowned upon	Is disallowed Is forbidden Is a crime	(See last page for comments on items referenced here)
Females covering their hair (wearing headgear) in public	✓			
Females exposing their full face in public	✓			
Females driving automobiles	✓			
Females riding motorcycles	✓			
Females riding bicycles	✓			
Females smoking in public	✓			
Women wearing bras (braziers) in public		✓		
Use of lipstick by women	✓			
A woman extending her hands first when introduced	✓			
Female bashing			✓	
Females wearing trousers	✓			
Females wearing minis (short dresses)	✓			
Females wearing bikinis	✓			
Females wearing shorts	✓			
Persons of opposite sex holding hands in public	✓			
Persons of same sex holding hands in public		✓		
Handshake between opposite sex	✓			
Hugging in public by same sex		✓		
Hugging in public by opposite sex	✓			
Men and women walking side by side in public	✓			
Man walking ahead (in public), with the woman following		✓		
Woman walking ahead (in public), with the man following		✓		
Men opening doors for women	✓			
Sitting with legs crossed in the presence of elders	✓			
Talking to an elderly person with one's hat/cap on		✓		
Talking to an elderly person with hands positioned on both sides of one's waist		✓		
Blowing one's nose in public	✓			
Blowing one's nose in the presence of others	✓			
Addressing people by their title	✓			

CYPRUS

	Is customary Is allowed Is permissible Is used. Is OK	Is not customary Is frowned upon	Is disallowed Is forbidden Is a crime	(See last page for comments on items referenced here)
Addressing people by their family name/surname/last name/given name	✓			
Addressing people by their first name/ given name	✓			
Women going through doors first	✓			
Men helping women with their coats	✓			
Men extending their hands to women first during greetings	✓			
Taking off one's hat when entering a private home	✓			
Removing one's shoes when entering a private home		✓		
Invited guests bringing food at social gatherings	✓			
Guests bringing drinks at social gatherings	✓			
Shaking hands when leaving a small group	✓			
Shaking hands with everyone present, upon arrival at a social gathering	✓			
Eating with the right hand	✓			
Eating with the left hand	✓			
Eating with both hands		✓		
Presenting a gift or passing on an object with the left hand	✓			
Asking a man about his wife	✓			
Asking a woman about her husband	✓			
Making prior appointments before a meeting or visit	✓			
Addressing an audience with one or both hands in the pocket	✓			
Carrying on conversation during meals	✓			
Females sitting with legs crossed	✓			
People discussing their wealth		✓		
Asking someone his or her age, or how old the person is	✓			
Complementing someone on his/her physical looks	✓			
Complementing someone on his/her attire	✓			
Use of both hands in handshake		✓		
In greeting, a handshake accompanied by a slight bow		✓		

CYPRUS

	Is customary Is allowed Is permissible Is used. Is OK	Is not customary Is frowned upon	Is disallowed Is forbidden Is a crime	(See last page for comments on items referenced here)
Salutations such as "Good morning", "Good afternoon", "Good evening"	✓			
The completion of a business deal with a handshake	✓			
Starting a negotiation session with a handshake	✓			
A gift for the host/hostess	✓			
Giving a business gift	✓			
A gift of money (use of money as gift)	✓			
Use of flowers as a gift	✓			
Use of business cards	✓			
Accepting/presenting gifts with both hands	✓			
Burning of the country's flag			✓	
Mutilation of the national currency		✓		
Casual wearing of clothings made with colors & marks of the national flag	✓			
Wearing of look-alike military (camouflage) fatigues (attire)	✓			
Sitting on the floor (on floor mats)		✓		
Discussion of religion	✓			
Discussion of politics	✓			
Discussion of sex	✓			
Patting/slapping someone on the buttocks		✓		
Patting/slapping someone on the back	✓			
Touching or patting someone's head/hair	✓			
Casual touching of any part of someone's body		✓		
Drinking directly out of a bottle/can	✓			
Placing one's leg(s) on the table or chair		✓		

CYPRUS

	Is customary Is allowed Is permissible Is used. Is OK	Is not customary Is frowned upon	Is disallowed Is forbidden Is a crime	(See last page for comments on items referenced here)
Showing the sole of one's foot (feet)	✓			
People standing very close when talking	✓			
Maintaining steady eye contact (direct gaze) when talking to someone	✓			
Kissing or exchange of kisses on the cheek	✓			
Counting money (change) in someone's palm	✓			
Finger pointing in public (in a daring manner)		✓		
Seeking attention by winking the eyes		✓		
Tapping the head to indicate someone is crazy	✓			
Twirling the head to indicate someone is crazy	✓			
Whistling as a way of requesting something/seeking attention		✓		
Using "thumbs-up" sign to mean OK	✓			
Forming a circle with the thumb and index finger (forefinger) to mean OK	✓			
Using the fingers to make a "V" sign for victory	✓			
Beckoning to someone with the index finger (forefinger)	✓			
The left to right waving of the hand with open palms facing outward to indicate "Good bye"	✓			
The use of a nod to show acknowledgement	✓			
Stopping/beckoning a taxi using a stretched hand with the thumb pointing upward	✓			
Using the thumb finger pointed to a direction, to request a ride or a hike	✓			
Raising one's hand/waving with an open fist to summon a taxi	✓			
Tapping one's foot/feet on the floor in a public gathering	✓			
Wiggling one's leg(s) when in a sitting position	✓			
Use of the hand (by motorists and cyclists) to signal direction of traffic	✓			

CYPRUS

		(See last page for comments on items referenced here)
Foreign tourists are welcome in the country.	yes	
The use of seat belt is mandatory.	yes	
International driving license is accepted.	yes	
U.S. driver's license is accepted.	yes	
It is considered impolite to yawn in public.	yes	
Death penalty for drug trafficking is the law.	no	
Life imprisonment for drug trafficking is the law.	no	
Guilty until proven innocent in court is the law.	no	
Innocent until proven guilty in court is the law.	yes	
Pedestrians always have right of way.	yes	
Exit visas are required of visitors.	no	
Crash helmet is mandatory for motor cyclist.	yes	
Hanging is used as a form of legal punishment.	no	
Decapitation of a limb is used as a form of punishment.	no	
Caning is used as a form of legal punishment.	no	
Electric shock is used as a form of legal punishment.	no	
One is expected to stand up during the playing of the national anthem.	yes	
Crash helmet is mandatory for bicyclists.	no	
Guests are expected to eat every thing on their plates.	no	
Table manners are very informal.	yes	
One is expected to cover one's mouth when laughing.	no	
A vertical nod of the head means YES (OK).	yes	
A horizontal shaking of the head means NO (Not OK).	yes	
Prostitution is allowed only in designated areas.	yes	
One is expected to take off one's hat during playing of national anthem.	yes	
Separate seating arrangements (between sexes) are maintained at movies.	no	
Separate seating arrangements (between sexes) are maintained at churches.	no	
Uninvited visitors or guests may not be welcome, even among acquaintances.	no	
Pets (e.g. cats, dog) are allowed in some hotels and restaurants.	yes	
Couples invited for a meal may be separated during meals according to their sex.	no	
Punctuality is the order of business.	no	
Automobiles are driven with headlights always turned on.	no	
Motorcycles are driven with headlights always turned on.	no	
Visitors with expired visa face mandatory jail time.	no	
Visitors without exit visa face jail time.	no	
Visitors without entry visa face mandatory (automatic) jail time.	no	

ADDITIONAL COUNTRY INFORMATION

(A)	**The types of gifts to avoid:**	n/a
(B)	**Appropriate gifts for a foreigner to give:**	souvenir flowers
(C)	**Best time to present gifts (at the beginning or at the end of a visit?):**	at the beginning
(D)	**Best time to present gifts (on initial or later visits?):**	initial visit
(E)	**Best place to present gifts (in private or in public?):**	n/a
(F)	**Number(s) with certain connotations and/or myths attached to them:**	13: bad luck
(G)	**Basic shape(s) with negative connotations:**	n/a
(H)	**Basic color(s) with negative connotations:**	black = death
(I)	**Traditional greeting methods include:**	handshake, hug, kiss patting the other's back
(J)	**Safe topics for discussion include:**	weather, fashion, travel, art, family, religion, domestic politics, food, sport, international politics, social conditions, money and personal wealth sex.
(K)	**Best time for conversations (before, during, after meals?):**	anytime
(L)	**Forms of legal punishment:**	jailing
(M)	**Approximately length of time one could be detained by law and order authorities before being charged in court:**	depends upon case
(N)	**January 15, 1999, for example, will normally be written as:**	15/1/99
(O)	**Emergency code number**:	199
(P)	**Ambulance code Number**:	199
(Q)	**Police code number:**	199
(R)	**Telephone (country) code:**	357
(S)	**Telex (country) code:**	357
(T)	**Electricity requirements**:	220
(U)	**Legal drinking age:**	n/a
(V)	**Systems of weights and measures:**	Metric/Imperial
(W)	**Legal age of incarceration**:	n/a
(X)	**Driving side of the road:**	left
(Y)	**Minimum expenditure expected of foreign visitors? $**	n/a
(Z)	**Name of currency**:	Cyprus Pound
(Za)	**Some places 0ff-limits to foreign visitors:**	military campus installations
(Zb)	**Some places, structures and items prohibited from being photographed:**	military campus installation

CZECH REPUBLIC	Is customary Is allowed Is permissible Is used. Is OK	Is not customary Is frowned upon	Is disallowed Is forbidden Is a crime	(See last page for comments on items referenced here)
Smoking in public	✓			1
Eating in public	✓			
Not flushing public toilet		✓		
Spitting in public	✓			
Feeding animals & birds in public	✓			1
Whistling in public	✓			
Drinking alcohol in public	✓			
Kissing in public	✓			
Breast feeding in public		✓		
Drunkenness (in public)		✓		
Cursing in public		✓		
Religious preaching in public				
Begging (panhandling) in public	✓			
Giving money to beggars/panhandlers	✓			
Giving food/drink to beggars/panhandlers	✓			
Brushing teeth in public (other than in restrooms)		✓		
Strolling with pets in major public roads/streets	✓			
Chewing gum in public	✓			
Chewing gum in government offices	✓			
Combing hair in public (other than in toilets/restrooms)	✓			
Undressing/dressing in public		✓		
Wearing of dark glasses indoors in public places	✓			
Public display of wealth	✓			
Praying openly in public in non-designated areas	✓			
Walking bare feet in public		✓		
Chewing tobacco in public		✓		
Trimming one's finger or toe nails in public		✓		
Laughing aloud in public	✓			
Mingling of the sexes in public	✓			
Mixed bathing in public swimming pools	✓			
Distributing religious pamphlets (literature) in public/side streets	✓			

CZECH REPUBLIC

	Is customary Is allowed Is permissible Is used. Is OK	Is not customary Is frowned upon	Is disallowed Is forbidden Is a crime	(See last page for comments on items referenced here)
Dancing on side street	✓			
Nude bathing	✓			2
Littering			✓	
Binge Drinking	✓			
hitchhiking	✓			
Jaywalking			✓	
Drunk driving			✓	
Speeding			✓	
Skating on side streets (side-walk)			✓	
Graffiti painting			✓	
Pilfering			✓	
Prostitution	✓			
Haggling in the market place		✓		
Consumption of alcoholic beverages in bars and restaurants	✓			
Gambling	✓			
Possession of pornographic materials	✓			
Possession of the Christian Bible	✓			
Possession of the Moslem Koran	✓			
Possession of bullet-proof vest	✓			
Possession of toy gun	✓			
Possession of fire crackers and fireworks	✓			3
Possession of prescription drugs (without doctor's note)	✓			
Possession of regulated drugs (narcotics)			✓	
Possession of firearms (by foreigners)	✓			
Possession of pocket knife in public	✓			
Using walkie talkies	✓			4
Using of "boom boxes"(loud sounding stereo system)	✓			
Using "walkman" (very small radio/cassettes with ear plugs) in public places	✓			
Using "walkman" (very small radio/cassettes with ear plugs) while driving or riding			✓	

CZECH REPUBLIC

	Is customary Is allowed Is permissible Is used Is OK	Is not customary Is frowned upon	Is disallowed Is forbidden Is a crime	(See last page for comments on items referenced here)
Use of cellular phone	✓			
Use of binoculars/periscopes other than in sports arena	✓			
Taking photographs of people (without their permission)	✓			
Taking photographs at airports, train and bus stations	✓			
Taking photographs of airports	✓			
Taking photographs of churches and synagogues	✓			
Taking photographs of religious statues	✓			
Taking photographs of public buildings	✓			
Taking photographs of bridges	✓			
Tipping (gratuity)	✓			
Tipping (when service is rendered)	✓			
Tipping (when service is not rendered)	✓			
Tipping waiters/waitresses at restaurants and hotels	✓			
Tipping taxi/cab drivers	✓			
Tipping baggage handlers, porters, door persons	✓			
Tipping of hair dressers/barbers	✓			
Overtipping	✓			
Undertipping		✓		
Spilling cigarette butt (ash) on side streets/on the floor		✓		
Men wearing lipstick		✓		
Wearing visible tattoo marks	✓			
Men painting/coloring their finger or toe nails		✓		
Cross dressing (men dressed like women & vice versa)		✓		
Walking in public without a shirt (i.e. with the upper half of the body naked)		✓		
Men wearing braided hair	✓			
Men wearing earrings	✓			
Men wearing dreadlock hair style	✓			
Homosexuality	✓			
Lesbianism	✓			

CZECH REPUBLIC

	Is customary Is allowed Is permissible Is used Is OK	Is not customary Is frowned upon	Is disallowed Is forbidden Is a crime	(See last page for comments on items referenced here)
Females covering their hair (wearing headgear) in public		✓		
Females exposing their full face in public	✓			
Females driving automobiles	✓			
Females riding motorcycles	✓			
Females riding bicycles	✓			
Females smoking in public	✓			
Women wearing bras (braziers) in public	✓			
Use of lipstick by women	✓			
A woman extending her hands first when introduced	✓			
Female bashing		✓		
Females wearing trousers	✓			
Females wearing minis (short dresses)	✓			
Females wearing bikinis	✓			
Females wearing shorts	✓			
Persons of opposite sex holding hands in public	✓			
Persons of same sex holding hands in public	✓			
Handshake between opposite sex	✓			
Hugging in public by same sex	✓			
Hugging in public by opposite sex	✓			
Men and women walking side by side in public	✓			
Man walking ahead (in public), with the woman following				n/a
Woman walking ahead (in public), with the man following				n/a
Men opening doors for women	✓			
Sitting with legs crossed in the presence of elders	✓			
Talking to an elderly person with one's hat/cap on				n/a
Talking to an elderly person with hands positioned on both sides of one's waist				n/a
Blowing one's nose in public	✓			5
Blowing one's nose in the presence of others				6
Addressing people by their title	✓			

CZECH REPUBLIC

	Is customary Is allowed Is permissible Is used. Is OK	Is not customary Is frowned upon	Is disallowed Is forbidden Is a crime	(See last page for comments on items referenced here)
Addressing people by their family name/surname/last name/given name	✓			
Addressing people by their first name/ given name	✓			
Women going through doors first	✓			
Men helping women with their coats	✓			
Men extending their hands to women first during greetings				7
Taking off one's hat when entering a private home	✓			
Removing one's shoes when entering a private home	✓			
Invited guests bringing food at social gatherings		✓		
Guests bringing drinks at social gatherings	✓			
Shaking hands when leaving a small group	✓			
Shaking hands with everyone present, upon arrival at a social gathering	✓			
Eating with the right hand	✓			
Eating with the left hand	✓			
Eating with both hands	✓			
Presenting a gift or passing on an object with the left hand	✓			
Asking a man about his wife	✓			
Asking a woman about her husband				8
Making prior appointments before a meeting or visit	✓			
Addressing an audience with one or both hands in the pocket	✓			
Carrying on conversation during meals	✓			
Females sitting with legs crossed	✓			
People discussing their wealth	✓			
Asking someone his or her age, or how old the person is	✓			
Complementing someone on his/her physical looks	✓			
Complementing someone on his/her attire	✓			
Use of both hands in handshake		✓		
In greeting, a handshake accompanied by a slight bow		✓		

CZECH REPUBLIC

	Is customary Is allowed Is permissible Is used. Is OK	Is not customary Is frowned upon	Is disallowed Is forbidden Is a crime	(See last page for comments on items referenced here)
Salutations such as "Good morning", "Good afternoon", "Good evening"	✓			
The completion of a business deal with a handshake				n/a
Starting a negotiation session with a handshake				n/a
A gift for the host/hostess	✓			
Giving a business gift	✓			
A gift of money (use of money as gift)	✓			
Use of flowers as a gift	✓			
Use of business cards	✓			
Accepting/presenting gifts with both hands	✓			
Burning of the country's flag		✓		
Mutilation of the national currency			✓	
Casual wearing of clothings made with colors & marks of the national flag	✓			
Wearing of look-alike military (camouflage) fatigues (attire)	✓			
Sitting on the floor (on floor mats)				9
Discussion of religion	✓			
Discussion of politics	✓			
Discussion of sex	✓			
Patting/slapping someone on the buttocks	✓			
Patting/slapping someone on the back	✓			
Touching or patting someone's head/hair	✓			
Casual touching of any part of someone's body				n/a
Drinking directly out of a bottle/can	✓			
Placing one's leg(s) on the table or chair		✓		

CZECH REPUBLIC

	Is customary Is allowed Is permissible Is used. Is OK	Is not customary Is frowned upon	Is disallowed Is forbidden Is a crime	(See last page for comments on items referenced here)
Showing the sole of one's foot (feet)				n/a
People standing very close when talking				10
Maintaining steady eye contact (direct gaze) when talking to someone	✓			
Kissing or exchange of kisses on the cheek	✓			
Counting money (change) in someone's palm	✓			
Finger pointing in public (in a daring manner)				n/a
Seeking attention by winking the eyes		✓		
Tapping the head to indicate someone is crazy		✓		
Twirling the head to indicate someone is crazy		✓		
Whistling as a way of requesting something/seeking attention		✓		
Using "thumbs-up" sign to mean OK	✓			
Forming a circle with the thumb and index finger (forefinger) to mean OK		✓		
Using the fingers to make a "V" sign for victory	✓			
Beckoning to someone with the index finger (forefinger)	✓			
The left to right waving of the hand with open palms facing outward to indicate "Good bye"	✓			
The use of a nod to show acknowledgement	✓			
Stopping/beckoning a taxi using a stretched hand with the thumb pointing upward				n/a
Using the thumb finger pointed to a direction, to request a ride or a hike		✓		
Raising one's hand/waving with an open fist to summon a taxi	✓			
Tapping one's foot/feet on the floor in a public gathering				n/a
Wiggling one's leg(s) when in a sitting position				n/a
Use of the hand (by motorists and cyclists) to signal direction of traffic	✓			

CZECH REPUBLIC

		(See last page for comments on items referenced here)
Foreign tourists are welcome in the country.	yes	
The use of seat belt is mandatory.	yes	
International driving license is accepted.	yes	
U.S. driver's license is accepted.	no	
It is considered impolite to yawn in public.	yes	
Death penalty for drug trafficking is the law.		11
Life imprisonment for drug trafficking is the law.	no	
Guilty until proven innocent in court is the law.	no	
Innocent until proven guilty in court is the law.	yes	
Pedestrians always have right of way.		12
Exit visas are required of visitors.		13
Crash helmet is mandatory for motor cyclist.	yes	
Hanging is used as a form of legal punishment.	no	
Decapitation of a limb is used as a form of punishment.	no	
Caning is used as a form of legal punishment.	no	
Electric shock is used as a form of legal punishment.	no	
One is expected to stand up during the playing of the national anthem.	yes	
Crash helmet is mandatory for bicyclists.	no	
Guests are expected to eat every thing on their plates.	no	
Table manners are very informal.	no	
One is expected to cover one's mouth when laughing.	no	
A vertical nod of the head means YES (OK).	yes	
A horizontal shaking of the head means NO (Not OK).	yes	
Prostitution is allowed only in designated areas.	yes	
One is expected to take off one's hat during playing of national anthem.	yes	
Separate seating arrangements (between sexes) are maintained at movies.	no	
Separate seating arrangements (between sexes) are maintained at churches.		14
Uninvited visitors or guests may not be welcome, even among acquaintances.		n/a
Pets (e.g. cats, dog) are allowed in some hotels and restaurants.	yes	
Couples invited for a meal may be separated during meals according to their sex.	no	
Punctuality is the order of business.	yes	
Automobiles are driven with headlights always turned on.	no	
Motorcycles are driven with headlights always turned on.	no	
Visitors with expired visa face mandatory jail time.	no	
Visitors without exit visa face jail time.	no	
Visitors without entry visa face mandatory (automatic) jail time.	no	

ADDITIONAL COUNTRY INFORMATION

(A)	**The types of gifts to avoid:**	n/a
(B)	**Appropriate gifts for a foreigner to give:**	flowers, chocolates, liquor, wine, books
(C)	**Best time to present gifts (at the beginning or at the end of a visit?):**	beginning - special occasions - birthdays days etc.
(D)	**Best time to present gifts (on initial or later visits?):**	n/a
(E)	**Best place to present gifts (in private or in public?):**	n/a
(F)	**Number(s) with certain connotations and/or myths attached to them:**	13 unlucky
(G)	**Basic shape(s) with negative connotations:**	none
(H)	**Basic color(s) with negative connotations:**	n/a
(I)	**Traditional greeting methods include:**	handshake
(J)	**Safe topics for discussion include:**	any - depending on the circumstances, sports
(K)	**Best time for conversations (before, during, after meals?):**	n/a
(L)	**Forms of legal punishment:**	fire imprisonment
(M)	**Approximately length of time one could be detained by law and order authorities before being charged in court:**	3 days (it is currently being discussed to changed the law)
(N)	**January 15, 1999, for example, will normally be written as:**	15/1/99
(O)	**Emergency code number:**	158
(P)	**Ambulance code Number:**	373333 (car) 155 (doctor)
(Q)	**Police code number:**	158
(R)	**Telephone (country) code:**	42
(S)	**Telex (country) code:**	849
(T)	**Electricity requirements:**	220 volt
(U)	**Legal drinking age:**	18
(V)	**Systems of weights and measures:**	metric
(W)	**Legal age of incarceration:**	18
(X)	**Driving side of the road:**	right
(Y)	**Minimum expenditure expected of foreign visitors? $**	no
(Z)	**Name of currency:**	Koruna
(Za)	**Some places 0ff-limits to foreign visitors:**	n/a
(Zb)	**Some places, structures and items prohibited from being photographed:**	n/a

ENDNOTES

Item Number: COMMENTS/EXPLANATIONS

n/a: Not applicable/Not available/No response

(1) In some places

(2) In some places

(3) With permit

(4) On special occasions

(5) With handkerchief

(6) With handkerchief

(7) Women extend hands first

(8) It is ok, but depends on the circumstances

(9) It is allowed, not customary

(10) In some places

(11) No death penalty

(12) Not always

(13) Entry visas are requested for some

(14) Depends on the faith (religion)

DENMARK	Is customary Is allowed Is permissible Is used. Is OK	Is not customary Is frowned upon	Is disallowed Is forbidden Is a crime	(See last page for comments on items referenced here)
Smoking in public	✓			
Eating in public	✓			
Not flushing public toilet		✓		
Spitting in public		✓		
Feeding animals & birds in public	✓			
Whistling in public	✓			
Drinking alcohol in public	✓			
Kissing in public	✓			
Breast feeding in public	✓			
Drunkenness (in public)	✓			
Cursing in public	✓			
Religious preaching in public	✓			
Begging (panhandling) in public				1
Giving money to beggars/panhandlers		✓		
Giving food/drink to beggars/panhandlers		✓		
Brushing teeth in public (other than in restrooms)		✓		
Strolling with pets in major public roads/streets	✓			
Chewing gum in public	✓			
Chewing gum in government offices	✓			
Combing hair in public (other than in toilets/restrooms)	✓			
Undressing/dressing in public	✓			
Wearing of dark glasses indoors in public places	✓			
Public display of wealth	✓			2
Praying openly in public in non-designated areas	✓			
Walking bare feet in public	✓			
Chewing tobacco in public	✓			
Trimming one's finger or toe nails in public		✓		
Laughing aloud in public	✓			
Mingling of the sexes in public	✓			
Mixed bathing in public swimming pools		✓		
Distributing religious pamphlets (literature) in public/side streets	✓			

DENMARK

	Is customary Is allowed Is permissible Is used. Is OK	Is not customary Is frowned upon	Is disallowed Is forbidden Is a crime	(See last page for comments on items referenced here)
Dancing on side street	✓			
Nude bathing	✓			3
Littering			✓	
Binge Drinking	✓			
hitchhiking	✓			
Jaywalking			✓	
Drunk driving			✓	
Speeding			✓	
Skating on side streets (side-walk)			✓	
Graffiti painting			✓	4
Pilfering			✓	5
Prostitution			✓	
Haggling in the market place		✓		
Consumption of alcoholic beverages in bars and restaurants	✓			
Gambling	✓			6
Possession of pornographic materials	✓			
Possession of the Christian Bible	✓			
Possession of the Moslem Koran	✓			
Possession of bullet-proof vest	✓			
Possession of toy gun	✓			
Possession of fire crackers and fireworks		✓		
Possession of prescription drugs (without doctor's note)			✓	
Possession of regulated drugs (narcotics)			✓	
Possession of firearms (by foreigners)		✓		
Possession of pocket knife in public		✓		
Using walkie talkies		✓		
Using of "boom boxes"(loud sounding stereo system)	✓			
Using "walkman" (very small radio/cassettes with ear plugs) in public places	✓			
Using "walkman" (very small radio/cassettes with ear plugs) while driving or riding	✓			

DENMARK

	Is customary Is allowed Is permissible Is used Is OK	Is not customary Is frowned upon	Is disallowed Is forbidden Is a crime	(See last page for comments on items referenced here)
Use of cellular phone	✓			
Use of binoculars/periscopes other than in sports arena	✓			
Taking photographs of people (without their permission)		✓		
Taking photographs at airports, train and bus stations	✓			
Taking photographs of airports		✓		
Taking photographs of churches and synagogues	✓			
Taking photographs of religious statues	✓			
Taking photographs of public buildings	✓			
Taking photographs of bridges	✓			
Tipping (gratuity)		✓		7
Tipping (when service is rendered)		✓		
Tipping (when service is not rendered)		✓		
Tipping waiters/waitresses at restaurants and hotels		✓		
Tipping taxi/cab drivers		✓		
Tipping baggage handlers, porters, door persons		✓		
Tipping of hair dressers/barbers		✓		
Overtipping		✓		
Undertipping		✓		
Spilling cigarette butt (ash) on side streets/on the floor	✓			
Men wearing lipstick		✓		8
Wearing visible tattoo marks	✓			
Men painting/coloring their finger or toe nails		✓		
Cross dressing (men dressed like women & vice versa)		✓		9
Walking in public without a shirt (i.e. with the upper half of the body naked)		✓		
Men wearing braided hair		✓		
Men wearing earrings	✓			
Men wearing dreadlock hair style		✓		
Homosexuality	✓			
Lesbianism	✓			

DENMARK

	Is customary Is allowed Is permissible Is used Is OK	Is not customary Is frowned upon	Is disallowed Is forbidden Is a crime	(See last page for comments on items referenced here)
Females covering their hair (wearing headgear) in public	✓			
Females exposing their full face in public	✓			
Females driving automobiles	✓			
Females riding motorcycles	✓			
Females riding bicycles	✓			
Females smoking in public	✓			
Women wearing bras (braziers) in public	✓			
Use of lipstick by women	✓			
A woman extending her hands first when introduced	✓			
Female bashing	✓			
Females wearing trousers	✓			
Females wearing minis (short dresses)	✓			
Females wearing bikinis	✓			
Females wearing shorts	✓			
Persons of opposite sex holding hands in public	✓			
Persons of same sex holding hands in public	✓			
Handshake between opposite sex	✓			
Hugging in public by same sex	✓			
Hugging in public by opposite sex	✓			
Men and women walking side by side in public	✓			
Man walking ahead (in public), with the woman following		✓		
Woman walking ahead (in public), with the man following		✓		
Men opening doors for women		✓		
Sitting with legs crossed in the presence of elders	✓			
Talking to an elderly person with one's hat/cap on		✓		
Talking to an elderly person with hands positioned on both sides of one's waist	✓			
Blowing one's nose in public	✓			
Blowing one's nose in the presence of others	✓			
Addressing people by their title		✓		

DENMARK

	Is customary Is allowed Is permissible Is used. Is OK	Is not customary Is frowned upon	Is disallowed Is forbidden Is a crime	(See last page for comments on items referenced here)
Addressing people by their family name/surname/last name/given name	✓			
Addressing people by their first name/ given name	✓			
Women going through doors first	✓			
Men helping women with their coats	✓			
Men extending their hands to women first during greetings	✓			
Taking off one's hat when entering a private home	✓			
Removing one's shoes when entering a private home		✓		
Invited guests bringing food at social gatherings	✓			
Guests bringing drinks at social gatherings	✓			
Shaking hands when leaving a small group	✓			
Shaking hands with everyone present, upon arrival at a social gathering	✓			
Eating with the right hand	✓			
Eating with the left hand	✓			
Eating with both hands	✓			
Presenting a gift or passing on an object with the left hand	✓			
Asking a man about his wife	✓			
Asking a woman about her husband	✓			
Making prior appointments before a meeting or visit	✓			
Addressing an audience with one or both hands in the pocket	✓			
Carrying on conversation during meals	✓			
Females sitting with legs crossed	✓			
People discussing their wealth	✓			
Asking someone his or her age, or how old the person is	✓			
Complementing someone on his/her physical looks	✓			
Complementing someone on his/her attire	✓			
Use of both hands in handshake	✓			
In greeting, a handshake accompanied by a slight bow	✓			

DENMARK

	Is customary Is allowed Is permissible Is used. Is OK	Is not customary Is frowned upon	Is disallowed Is forbidden Is a crime	(See last page for comments on items referenced here)
Salutations such as "Good morning", "Good afternoon", "Good evening"	✓			
The completion of a business deal with a handshake	✓			
Starting a negotiation session with a handshake	✓			
A gift for the host/hostess	✓			
Giving a business gift	✓			
A gift of money (use of money as gift)	✓			
Use of flowers as a gift	✓			
Use of business cards	✓			
Accepting/presenting gifts with both hands		✓		
Burning of the country's flag		✓		10
Mutilation of the national currency	✓			
Casual wearing of clothings made with colors & marks of the national flag	✓			
Wearing of look-alike military (camouflage) fatigues (attire)	✓			
Sitting on the floor (on floor mats)		✓		
Discussion of religion	✓			
Discussion of politics	✓			
Discussion of sex	✓			
Patting/slapping someone on the buttocks		✓		
Patting/slapping someone on the back	✓			
Touching or patting someone's head/hair		✓		
Casual touching of any part of someone's body		✓		
Drinking directly out of a bottle/can	✓			
Placing one's leg(s) on the table or chair		✓		

DENMARK

	Is customary Is allowed Is permissible Is used. Is OK	Is not customary Is frowned upon	Is disallowed Is forbidden Is a crime	(See last page for comments on items referenced here)
Showing the sole of one's foot (feet)	✓			
People standing very close when talking	✓			
Maintaining steady eye contact (direct gaze) when talking to someone	✓			
Kissing or exchange of kisses on the cheek	✓			
Counting money (change) in someone's palm		✓		
Finger pointing in public (in a daring manner)		✓		
Seeking attention by winking the eyes		✓		
Tapping the head to indicate someone is crazy	✓			
Twirling the head to indicate someone is crazy		✓		
Whistling as a way of requesting something/seeking attention		✓		
Using "thumbs-up" sign to mean OK	✓			
Forming a circle with the thumb and index finger (forefinger) to mean OK	✓			
Using the fingers to make a "V" sign for victory	✓			
Beckoning to someone with the index finger (forefinger)	✓			
The left to right waving of the hand with open palms facing outward to indicate "Good bye"	✓			
The use of a nod to show acknowledgement	✓			
Stopping/beckoning a taxi using a stretched hand with the thumb pointing upward	✓			
Using the thumb finger pointed to a direction, to request a ride or a hike	✓			
Raising one's hand/waving with an open fist to summon a taxi	✓			
Tapping one's foot/feet on the floor in a public gathering	✓			
Wiggling one's leg(s) when in a sitting position	✓			
Use of the hand (by motorists and cyclists) to signal direction of traffic	✓			

DENMARK

		(See last page for comments on items referenced here)
Foreign tourists are welcome in the country.	yes	
The use of seat belt is mandatory.	yes	
International driving license is accepted.	yes	
U.S. driver's license is accepted.	yes	
It is considered impolite to yawn in public.	no	
Death penalty for drug trafficking is the law.	no	
Life imprisonment for drug trafficking is the law.	no	
Guilty until proven innocent in court is the law.	no	
Innocent until proven guilty in court is the law.	yes	
Pedestrians always have right of way.	yes	
Exit visas are required of visitors.	no	
Crash helmet is mandatory for motor cyclist.	yes	
Hanging is used as a form of legal punishment.	no	
Decapitation of a limb is used as a form of punishment.	no	
Caning is used as a form of legal punishment.	no	
Electric shock is used as a form of legal punishment.	no	
One is expected to stand up during the playing of the national anthem.	no	
Crash helmet is mandatory for bicyclists.	no	
Guests are expected to eat every thing on their plates.	no	
Table manners are very informal.	yes	
One is expected to cover one's mouth when laughing.	no	
A vertical nod of the head means YES (OK).	yes	
A horizontal shaking of the head means NO (Not OK).	yes	
Prostitution is allowed only in designated areas.	no	
One is expected to take off one's hat during playing of national anthem.	no	
Separate seating arrangements (between sexes) are maintained at movies.	no	
Separate seating arrangements (between sexes) are maintained at churches.	no	
Uninvited visitors or guests may not be welcome, even among acquaintances.	no	
Pets (e.g. cats, dog) are allowed in some hotels and restaurants.	no	
Couples invited for a meal may be separated during meals according to their sex.	no	
Punctuality is the order of business.	yes	
Automobiles are driven with headlights always turned on.	yes	
Motorcycles are driven with headlights always turned on.	yes	
Visitors with expired visa face mandatory jail time.	no	
Visitors without exit visa face jail time.	no	
Visitors without entry visa face mandatory (automatic) jail time.	no	

ADDITIONAL COUNTRY INFORMATION

(A)	**The types of gifts to avoid:**	best to stick to flowers, wine, chocolate
(B)	**Appropriate gifts for a foreigner to give:**	flowers, wine, chocolate
(C)	**Best time to present gifts (at the beginning or at the end of a visit?):**	at the beginning
(D)	**Best time to present gifts (on initial or later visits?):**	at the beginning
(E)	**Best place to present gifts (in private or in public?):**	on a table
(F)	**Number(s) with certain connotations and/or myths attached to them:**	13
(G)	**Basic shape(s) with negative connotations:**	signs from hitler germany
(H)	**Basic color(s) with negative connotations:**	black
(I)	**Traditional greeting methods include:**	handshake
(J)	**Safe topics for discussion include:**	weather, fashion, travel, art, family, religion, domestic politics, food, sports, international politics, social conditions, money, sex
(K)	**Best time for conversations (before, during, after meals?):**	when you meet. depends on the occasion.
(L)	**Forms of legal punishment:**	jailing, fines
(M)	**Approximately length of time one could be detained by law and order authorities before being charged in court:**	24 hrs.
(N)	**January 15, 1999, for example, will normally be written as:**	15/1/99
(O)	**Emergency code number:**	112
(P)	**Ambulance code Number:**	112
(Q)	**Police code number:**	112
(R)	**Telephone (country) code:**	45
(S)	**Telex (country) code:**	855
(T)	**Electricity requirements:**	220 volts
(U)	**Legal drinking age:**	18
(V)	**Systems of weights and measures:**	metric
(W)	**Legal age of incarceration:**	18
(X)	**Driving side of the road:**	right
(Y)	**Minimum expenditure expected of foreign visitors? $**	enough to pay for food and lodging
(Z)	**Name of currency:**	Danish Kroner
(Za)	**Some places 0ff-limits to foreign visitors:**	military bases
(Zb)	**Some places, structures and items prohibited from being photographed:**	n/a

ENDNOTES

Item Number: COMMENTS/EXPLANATIONS

n/a: Not applicable/Not available/No response
(1) It's not a problem in Denmark very few beggars
(2) Allowed, but not customary
(3) We do have nude beaches
(4) If you destroy somebody else's or government property, you might, of course be taken to court and end up paying compensation
(5) You can only bet on certain things; only one government controlled betting institution.
(6) We do have casinos
(7) Generally tipping is included in the price, tipping is therefore, not necessary, but may occur to show great gratitude
(8) Allowed, but not customary
(9) Not customary, though, for men to wear dresses
(10) Is not done (does not carry political symbolism to the extent it does in other countries), but is not illegal

Denmark is a very open and accepting country. Women and men are treated alike.

FINLAND	Is customary Is allowed Is permissible Is used. Is OK	Is not customary Is frowned upon	Is disallowed Is forbidden Is a crime	(See last page for comments on items referenced here)
Smoking in public		✓		
Eating in public		✓		
Not flushing public toilet		✓		
Spitting in public		✓		
Feeding animals & birds in public	✓			
Whistling in public		✓		
Drinking alcohol in public			✓	
Kissing in public	✓			
Breast feeding in public		✓		
Drunkenness (in public)		✓		
Cursing in public		✓		
Religious preaching in public		✓		
Begging (panhandling) in public		✓		
Giving money to beggars/panhandlers	✓			
Giving food/drink to beggars/panhandlers	✓			
Brushing teeth in public (other than in restrooms)		✓		
Strolling with pets in major public roads/streets	✓			
Chewing gum in public	✓			
Chewing gum in government offices		✓		
Combing hair in public (other than in toilets/restrooms)	✓			
Undressing/dressing in public			✓	
Wearing of dark glasses indoors in public places	✓			
Public display of wealth		✓		
Praying openly in public in non-designated areas		✓		
Walking bare feet in public		✓		
Chewing tobacco in public		✓		
Trimming one's finger or toe nails in public		✓		
Laughing aloud in public		✓		
Mingling of the sexes in public	✓			
Mixed bathing in public swimming pools	✓			
Distributing religious pamphlets (literature) in public/side streets	✓			

FINLAND

	Is customary Is allowed Is permissible Is used. Is OK	**Is not customary Is frowned upon**	**Is disallowed Is forbidden Is a crime**	**(See last page for comments on items referenced here)**
Dancing on side street		✓		
Nude bathing			✓	
Littering			✓	
Binge Drinking	✓			
hitchhiking		✓		
Jaywalking			✓	
Drunk driving			✓	
Speeding			✓	
Skating on side streets (side-walk)	✓			
Graffiti painting			✓	
Pilfering			✓	
Prostitution			✓	
Haggling in the market place		✓		
Consumption of alcoholic beverages in bars and restaurants	✓			
Gambling	✓			1
Possession of pornographic materials	✓			
Possession of the Christian Bible	✓			
Possession of the Moslem Koran	✓			
Possession of bullet-proof vest	✓			
Possession of toy gun	✓			
Possession of fire crackers and fireworks	✓			
Possession of prescription drugs (without doctor's note)	✓			
Possession of regulated drugs (narcotics)			✓	
Possession of firearms (by foreigners)	✓			
Possession of pocket knife in public	✓			
Using walkie talkies	✓			
Using of "boom boxes"(loud sounding stereo system)	✓			
Using "walkman" (very small radio/cassettes with ear plugs) in public places	✓			
Using "walkman" (very small radio/cassettes with ear plugs) while driving or riding	✓			

FINLAND

	Is customary Is allowed Is permissible Is used Is OK	Is not customary Is frowned upon	Is disallowed Is forbidden Is a crime	(See last page for comments on items referenced here)
Use of cellular phone	✓			
Use of binoculars/periscopes other than in sports arena	✓			
Taking photographs of people (without their permission)	✓			
Taking photographs at airports, train and bus stations	✓			
Taking photographs of airports	✓			
Taking photographs of churches and synagogues	✓			
Taking photographs of religious statues	✓			
Taking photographs of public buildings	✓			
Taking photographs of bridges	✓			
Tipping (gratuity)	✓	✓		2
Tipping (when service is rendered)	✓			
Tipping (when service is not rendered)		✓		
Tipping waiters/waitresses at restaurants and hotels	✓			
Tipping taxi/cab drivers		✓		
Tipping baggage handlers, porters, door persons	✓			
Tipping of hair dressers/barbers		✓		
Overtipping		✓		
Undertipping				
Spilling cigarette butt (ash) on side streets/on the floor		✓		
Men wearing lipstick		✓		
Wearing visible tattoo marks		✓		
Men painting/coloring their finger or toe nails		✓		
Cross dressing (men dressed like women & vice versa)		✓		
Walking in public without a shirt (i.e. with the upper half of the body naked)	✓			
Men wearing braided hair	✓			
Men wearing earrings	✓			
Men wearing dreadlock hair style		✓		
Homosexuality	✓			
Lesbianism	✓			

FINLAND

	Is customary Is allowed Is permissible Is used Is OK	Is not customary Is frowned upon	Is disallowed Is forbidden Is a crime	(See last page for comments on items referenced here)
Females covering their hair (wearing headgear) in public		✓		3
Females exposing their full face in public	✓			
Females driving automobiles	✓			
Females riding motorcycles	✓			
Females riding bicycles	✓			
Females smoking in public	✓			
Women wearing bras (braziers) in public		✓		
Use of lipstick by women	✓			
A woman extending her hands first when introduced	✓			
Female bashing			✓	
Females wearing trousers	✓			
Females wearing minis (short dresses)	✓			
Females wearing bikinis	✓			
Females wearing shorts	✓			
Persons of opposite sex holding hands in public	✓			
Persons of same sex holding hands in public	✓			
Handshake between opposite sex	✓			
Hugging in public by same sex		✓		
Hugging in public by opposite sex	✓			
Men and women walking side by side in public	✓			
Man walking ahead (in public), with the woman following		✓		
Woman walking ahead (in public), with the man following		✓		
Men opening doors for women				
Sitting with legs crossed in the presence of elders	✓			
Talking to an elderly person with one's hat/cap on	✓			
Talking to an elderly person with hands positioned on both sides of one's waist	✓			
Blowing one's nose in public	✓			
Blowing one's nose in the presence of others	✓			
Addressing people by their title	✓			

FINLAND

	Is customary Is allowed Is permissible Is used. Is OK	Is not customary Is frowned upon	Is disallowed Is forbidden Is a crime	(See last page for comments on items referenced here)
Addressing people by their family name/surname/last name/given name	✓			
Addressing people by their first name/ given name	✓			
Women going through doors first	✓			
Men helping women with their coats	✓			
Men extending their hands to women first during greetings	✓			
Taking off one's hat when entering a private home	✓			
Removing one's shoes when entering a private home	✓			
Invited guests bringing food at social gatherings	✓			
Guests bringing drinks at social gatherings	✓			
Shaking hands when leaving a small group	✓			
Shaking hands with everyone present, upon arrival at a social gathering	✓			
Eating with the right hand	✓			
Eating with the left hand	✓			
Eating with both hands	✓			
Presenting a gift or passing on an object with the left hand	✓			
Asking a man about his wife	✓			
Asking a woman about her husband	✓			
Making prior appointments before a meeting or visit	✓			
Addressing an audience with one or both hands in the pocket	✓			
Carrying on conversation during meals	✓			
Females sitting with legs crossed	✓			
People discussing their wealth		✓		
Asking someone his or her age, or how old the person is		✓		
Complementing someone on his/her physical looks	✓			
Complementing someone on his/her attire	✓			
Use of both hands in handshake		✓		
In greeting, a handshake accompanied by a slight bow	✓			

FINLAND

	Is customary Is allowed Is permissible Is used. Is OK	Is not customary Is frowned upon	Is disallowed Is forbidden Is a crime	(See last page for comments on items referenced here)
Salutations such as "Good morning", "Good afternoon", "Good evening"	✓			
The completion of a business deal with a handshake	✓			
Starting a negotiation session with a handshake	✓			
A gift for the host/hostess	✓			
Giving a business gift	✓			
A gift of money (use of money as gift)		✓		
Use of flowers as a gift	✓			
Use of business cards	✓			
Accepting/presenting gifts with both hands	✓			
Burning of the country's flag			✓	
Mutilation of the national currency			✓	
Casual wearing of clothings made with colors & marks of the national flag	✓			
Wearing of look-alike military (camouflage) fatigues (attire)	✓			
Sitting on the floor (on floor mats)	✓			
Discussion of religion		✓		
Discussion of politics	✓			
Discussion of sex		✓		
Patting/slapping someone on the buttocks			✓	
Patting/slapping someone on the back	✓			
Touching or patting someone's head/hair	✓			
Casual touching of any part of someone's body	✓			
Drinking directly out of a bottle/can	✓			
Placing one's leg(s) on the table or chair	✓			

FINLAND

	Is customary Is allowed Is permissible Is used. Is OK	**Is not customary Is frowned upon**	**Is disallowed Is forbidden Is a crime**	**(See last page for comments on items referenced here)**
Showing the sole of one's foot (feet)	✓			
People standing very close when talking	✓			
Maintaining steady eye contact (direct gaze) when talking to someone	✓			
Kissing or exchange of kisses on the cheek	✓			
Counting money (change) in someone's palm				n/a
Finger pointing in public (in a daring manner)		✓		
Seeking attention by winking the eyes	✓			
Tapping the head to indicate someone is crazy	✓			
Twirling the head to indicate someone is crazy	✓			
Whistling as a way of requesting something/seeking attention		✓		
Using "thumbs-up" sign to mean OK	✓			
Forming a circle with the thumb and index finger (forefinger) to mean OK	✓			
Using the fingers to make a "V" sign for victory	✓			
Beckoning to someone with the index finger (forefinger)	✓			
The left to right waving of the hand with open palms facing outward to indicate "Good bye"	✓			
The use of a nod to show acknowledgement	✓			
Stopping/beckoning a taxi using a stretched hand with the thumb pointing upward		✓		
Using the thumb finger pointed to a direction, to request a ride or a hike	✓			
Raising one's hand/waving with an open fist to summon a taxi		✓		
Tapping one's foot/feet on the floor in a public gathering		✓		
Wiggling one's leg(s) when in a sitting position	✓			
Use of the hand (by motorists and cyclists) to signal direction of traffic	✓			

FINLAND

		(See last page for comments on items referenced here)
Foreign tourists are welcome in the country.	yes	
The use of seat belt is mandatory.	yes	
International driving license is accepted.	yes	
U.S. driver's license is accepted.	yes	4
It is considered impolite to yawn in public.	yes	
Death penalty for drug trafficking is the law.	no	
Life imprisonment for drug trafficking is the law.	no	
Guilty until proven innocent in court is the law.	no	
Innocent until proven guilty in court is the law.	yes	
Pedestrians always have right of way.	yes	5
Exit visas are required of visitors.	no	
Crash helmet is mandatory for motor cyclist.	yes	
Hanging is used as a form of legal punishment.	no	
Decapitation of a limb is used as a form of punishment.	no	
Caning is used as a form of legal punishment.	no	
Electric shock is used as a form of legal punishment.	no	
One is expected to stand up during the playing of the national anthem.	yes	
Crash helmet is mandatory for bicyclists.	no	6
Guests are expected to eat every thing on their plates.	yes	
Table manners are very informal.	no	
One is expected to cover one's mouth when laughing.	no	
A vertical nod of the head means YES (OK).	yes	
A horizontal shaking of the head means NO (Not OK).	yes	
Prostitution is allowed only in designated areas.	no	
One is expected to take off one's hat during playing of national anthem.	yes	
Separate seating arrangements (between sexes) are maintained at movies.	no	
Separate seating arrangements (between sexes) are maintained at churches.	no	
Uninvited visitors or guests may not be welcome, even among acquaintances.	yes	
Pets (e.g. cats, dog) are allowed in some hotels and restaurants.	no	7
Couples invited for a meal may be separated during meals according to their sex.	no	
Punctuality is the order of business.	yes	
Automobiles are driven with headlights always turned on.	yes	
Motorcycles are driven with headlights always turned on.	yes	
Visitors with expired visa face mandatory jail time.	no	
Visitors without exit visa face jail time.	no	
Visitors without entry visa face mandatory (automatic) jail time.	no	

ADDITIONAL COUNTRY INFORMATION

(A)	**The types of gifts to avoid:**	very expensive gifts
(B)	**Appropriate gifts for a foreigner to give:**	flowers, music, books
(C)	**Best time to present gifts (at the beginning or at the end of a visit?):**	at the beginning
(D)	**Best time to present gifts (on initial or later visits?):**	none
(E)	**Best place to present gifts (in private or in public?):**	#7 for luck, 13 for accident
(F)	**Number(s) with certain connotations and/or myths attached to them:**	none
(G)	**Basic shape(s) with negative connotations:**	none
(H)	**Basic color(s) with negative connotations:**	none
(I)	**Traditional greeting methods include:**	handshake
(J)	**Safe topics for discussion include:**	weather, fashion, travel, art, food, sports, international politics, hobbies
(K)	**Best time for conversations (before, during, after meals?):**	police can hold a suspect without discharging for up to 7 days.
(L)	**Forms of legal punishment:**	fines, imprisonment
(M)	**Approximately length of time one could be detained by law and order authorities before being charged in court:**	a court has to review the case within 4 days. The court must be notified of the detention within 30 days.
(N)	**January 15, 1999, for example, will normally be written as:**	15.1.1999
(O)	**Emergency code number:**	112
(P)	**Ambulance code Number:**	720-303 (Helsinki)112
(Q)	**Police code number:**	100 22
(R)	**Telephone (country) code:**	358
(S)	**Telex (country) code:**	358
(T)	**Electricity requirements:**	220 v 50 hz
(U)	**Legal drinking age:**	18
(V)	**Systems of weights and measures:**	metric
(W)	**Legal age of incarceration:**	15 - special procedure apply
(X)	**Driving side of the road:**	right
(Y)	**Minimum expenditure expected of foreign visitors? $**	no
(Z)	**Name of currency:**	Markka
(Za)	**Some places 0ff-limits to foreign visitors:**	military
(Zb)	**Some places, structures and items prohibited from being photographed:**	none

ENDNOTES

Item Number: COMMENTS/EXPLANATIONS

n/a: Not applicable/Not available/No response
(1) Restrictions apply
(2) In restaurant
(3) In winter customary
(4) One year
(5) On green light
(6) Recommended
(7) With few exceptions of hotels

FRANCE	Is customary Is allowed Is permissible Is used. Is OK	Is not customary Is frowned upon	Is disallowed Is forbidden Is a crime	(See last page for comments on items referenced here)
Smoking in public	✓			
Eating in public	✓			
Not flushing public toilet		✓		
Spitting in public		✓		
Feeding animals & birds in public	✓			
Whistling in public		✓		
Drinking alcohol in public	✓			
Kissing in public	✓			
Breast feeding in public		✓		
Drunkenness (in public)		✓		
Cursing in public		✓		
Religious preaching in public		✓		
Begging (panhandling) in public		✓		
Giving money to beggars/panhandlers	✓			
Giving food/drink to beggars/panhandlers	✓			
Brushing teeth in public (other than in restrooms)		✓		
Strolling with pets in major public roads/streets	✓			
Chewing gum in public		✓		
Chewing gum in government offices		✓		
Combing hair in public (other than in toilets/restrooms)		✓		
Undressing/dressing in public		✓		
Wearing of dark glasses indoors in public places		✓		
Public display of wealth		✓		
Praying openly in public in non-designated areas		✓		
Walking bare feet in public		✓		
Chewing tobacco in public		✓		
Trimming one's finger or toe nails in public		✓		
Laughing aloud in public		✓		
Mingling of the sexes in public	✓			
Mixed bathing in public swimming pools	✓			
Distributing religious pamphlets (literature) in public/side streets		✓		

FRANCE

	Is customary Is allowed Is permissible Is used. Is OK	Is not customary Is frowned upon	Is disallowed Is forbidden Is a crime	(See last page for comments on items referenced here)
Dancing on side street	✓			
Nude bathing		✓		
Littering		✓		
Binge Drinking		✓		
hitchhiking	✓			
Jaywalking	✓			
Drunk driving		✓		
Speeding	✓			
Skating on side streets (side-walk)		✓		
Graffiti painting		✓		
Pilfering			✓	
Prostitution			✓	
Haggling in the market place			✓	
Consumption of alcoholic beverages in bars and restaurants		✓		
Gambling	✓			
Possession of pornographic materials	✓			
Possession of the Christian Bible	✓			
Possession of the Moslem Koran	✓			
Possession of bullet-proof vest	✓			
Possession of toy gun		✓		
Possession of fire crackers and fireworks		✓		
Possession of prescription drugs (without doctor's note)		✓		
Possession of regulated drugs (narcotics)		✓		
Possession of firearms (by foreigners)			✓	
Possession of pocket knife in public		✓		
Using walkie talkies	✓			
Using of "boom boxes"(loud sounding stereo system)		✓		
Using "walkman" (very small radio/cassettes with ear plugs) in public places	✓			
Using "walkman" (very small radio/cassettes with ear plugs) while driving or riding	✓			

FRANCE

	Is customary Is allowed Is permissible Is used Is OK	Is not customary Is frowned upon	Is disallowed Is forbidden Is a crime	(See last page for comments on items referenced here)
Use of cellular phone	✓			
Use of binoculars/periscopes other than in sports arena	✓			
Taking photographs of people (without their permission)		✓		
Taking photographs at airports, train and bus stations	✓			
Taking photographs of airports	✓			
Taking photographs of churches and synagogues	✓			
Taking photographs of religious statues	✓			
Taking photographs of public buildings	✓			
Taking photographs of bridges	✓			
Tipping (gratuity)	✓			
Tipping (when service is rendered)	✓			
Tipping (when service is not rendered)		✓		
Tipping waiters/waitresses at restaurants and hotels	✓			1
Tipping taxi/cab drivers	✓			
Tipping baggage handlers, porters, door persons	✓			
Tipping of hair dressers/barbers	✓			
Overtipping	✓			
Undertipping	✓			
Spilling cigarette butt (ash) on side streets/on the floor		✓		
Men wearing lipstick		✓		
Wearing visible tattoo marks		✓		
Men painting/coloring their finger or toe nails		✓		
Cross dressing (men dressed like women & vice versa)		✓		
Walking in public without a shirt (i.e. with the upper half of the body naked)		✓		
Men wearing braided hair		✓		
Men wearing earrings		✓		
Men wearing dreadlock hair style		✓		
Homosexuality		✓		
Lesbianism	✓			

FRANCE

	Is customary Is allowed Is permissible Is used Is OK	Is not customary Is frowned upon	Is disallowed Is forbidden Is a crime	(See last page for comments on items referenced here)
Females covering their hair (wearing headgear) in public	✓			
Females exposing their full face in public	✓			
Females driving automobiles	✓			
Females riding motorcycles	✓			
Females riding bicycles	✓			
Females smoking in public	✓			
Women wearing bras (braziers) in public		✓		
Use of lipstick by women	✓			
A woman extending her hands first when introduced	✓			
Female bashing		✓		
Females wearing trousers		✓		
Females wearing minis (short dresses)	✓			
Females wearing bikinis	✓			2
Females wearing shorts	✓			3
Persons of opposite sex holding hands in public	✓			
Persons of same sex holding hands in public	✓			
Handshake between opposite sex	✓			
Hugging in public by same sex		✓		
Hugging in public by opposite sex		✓		
Men and women walking side by side in public	✓			
Man walking ahead (in public), with the woman following	✓			
Woman walking ahead (in public), with the man following		✓		
Men opening doors for women	✓			
Sitting with legs crossed in the presence of elders	✓			
Talking to an elderly person with one's hat/cap on		✓		
Talking to an elderly person with hands positioned on both sides of one's waist	✓			
Blowing one's nose in public		✓		
Blowing one's nose in the presence of others		✓		
Addressing people by their title	✓			

FRANCE

	Is customary Is allowed Is permissible Is used. Is OK	Is not customary Is frowned upon	Is disallowed Is forbidden Is a crime	(See last page for comments on items referenced here)
Addressing people by their family name/surname/last name/given name		✓		
Addressing people by their first name/ given name	✓			4
Women going through doors first	✓			
Men helping women with their coats	✓			
Men extending their hands to women first during greetings	✓			
Taking off one's hat when entering a private home	✓			
Removing one's shoes when entering a private home		✓		
Invited guests bringing food at social gatherings		✓		
Guests bringing drinks at social gatherings		✓		
Shaking hands when leaving a small group	✓			
Shaking hands with everyone present, upon arrival at a social gathering	✓			
Eating with the right hand	✓			
Eating with the left hand	✓			
Eating with both hands	✓			
Presenting a gift or passing on an object with the left hand	✓			
Asking a man about his wife	✓			
Asking a woman about her husband	✓			
Making prior appointments before a meeting or visit	✓			
Addressing an audience with one or both hands in the pocket	✓			
Carrying on conversation during meals	✓			
Females sitting with legs crossed	✓			
People discussing their wealth		✓		
Asking someone his or her age, or how old the person is		✓		
Complementing someone on his/her physical looks	✓			
Complementing someone on his/her attire	✓			
Use of both hands in handshake		✓		
In greeting, a handshake accompanied by a slight bow		✓		

FRANCE

	Is customary Is allowed Is permissible Is used. Is OK	Is not customary Is frowned upon	Is disallowed Is forbidden Is a crime	(See last page for comments on items referenced here)
Salutations such as "Good morning", "Good afternoon", "Good evening"	✓			
The completion of a business deal with a handshake	✓			
Starting a negotiation session with a handshake	✓			
A gift for the host/hostess	✓			
Giving a business gift	✓			
A gift of money (use of money as gift)	✓			
Use of flowers as a gift	✓			
Use of business cards			✓	
Accepting/presenting gifts with both hands	✓			
Burning of the country's flag		✓		
Mutilation of the national currency		✓		
Casual wearing of clothings made with colors & marks of the national flag		✓		
Wearing of look-alike military (camouflage) fatigues (attire)		✓		
Sitting on the floor (on floor mats)		✓		
Discussion of religion	✓			
Discussion of politics	✓			
Discussion of sex		✓		
Patting/slapping someone on the buttocks		✓		
Patting/slapping someone on the back		✓		
Touching or patting someone's head/hair		✓		
Casual touching of any part of someone's body		✓		
Drinking directly out of a bottle/can		✓		
Placing one's leg(s) on the table or chair		✓		

FRANCE

	Is customary Is allowed Is permissible Is used. Is OK	Is not customary Is frowned upon	Is disallowed Is forbidden Is a crime	(See last page for comments on items referenced here)
Showing the sole of one's foot (feet)		✓		
People standing very close when talking	✓			
Maintaining steady eye contact (direct gaze) when talking to someone	✓			
Kissing or exchange of kisses on the cheek	✓			
Counting money (change) in someone's palm	✓			
Finger pointing in public (in a daring manner)		✓		
Seeking attention by winking the eyes	✓			
Tapping the head to indicate someone is crazy	✓			
Twirling the head to indicate someone is crazy		✓		
Whistling as a way of requesting something/seeking attention		✓		
Using "thumbs-up" sign to mean OK		✓		
Forming a circle with the thumb and index finger (forefinger) to mean OK		✓		
Using the fingers to make a "V" sign for victory		✓		
Beckoning to someone with the index finger (forefinger)	✓			
The left to right waving of the hand with open palms facing outward to indicate "Good bye"	✓			
The use of a nod to show acknowledgement	✓			
Stopping/beckoning a taxi using a stretched hand with the thumb pointing upward	✓			
Using the thumb finger pointed to a direction, to request a ride or a hike	✓			
Raising one's hand/waving with an open fist to summon a taxi	✓			
Tapping one's foot/feet on the floor in a public gathering		✓		
Wiggling one's leg(s) when in a sitting position	✓			
Use of the hand (by motorists and cyclists) to signal direction of traffic	✓			

FRANCE

		(See last page for comments on items referenced here)
Foreign tourists are welcome in the country.	yes	
The use of seat belt is mandatory.	yes	
International driving license is accepted.	yes	
U.S. driver's license is accepted.	yes	
It is considered impolite to yawn in public.	yes	5
Death penalty for drug trafficking is the law.	no	
Life imprisonment for drug trafficking is the law.	no	
Guilty until proven innocent in court is the law.	no	
Innocent until proven guilty in court is the law.	yes	
Pedestrians always have right of way.	yes	
Exit visas are required of visitors.	no	
Crash helmet is mandatory for motor cyclist.	yes	
Hanging is used as a form of legal punishment.	no	
Decapitation of a limb is used as a form of punishment.	no	
Caning is used as a form of legal punishment.	no	
Electric shock is used as a form of legal punishment.	no	
One is expected to stand up during the playing of the national anthem.	yes	
Crash helmet is mandatory for bicyclists.	no	
Guests are expected to eat every thing on their plates.	yes	
Table manners are very informal.	no	
One is expected to cover one's mouth when laughing.	no	
A vertical nod of the head means YES (OK).	yes	
A horizontal shaking of the head means NO (Not OK).	yes	
Prostitution is allowed only in designated areas.	no	
One is expected to take off one's hat during playing of national anthem.	yes	
Separate seating arrangements (between sexes) are maintained at movies.	no	
Separate seating arrangements (between sexes) are maintained at churches.	no	
Uninvited visitors or guests may not be welcome, even among acquaintances.	yes	
Pets (e.g. cats, dog) are allowed in some hotels and restaurants.	yes	
Couples invited for a meal may be separated during meals according to their sex.	no	
Punctuality is the order of business.	no	
Automobiles are driven with headlights always turned on.	no	
Motorcycles are driven with headlights always turned on.	no	
Visitors with expired visa face mandatory jail time.	no	6
Visitors without exit visa face jail time.	no	7
Visitors without entry visa face mandatory (automatic) jail time.	no	8

ADDITIONAL COUNTRY INFORMATION

(A)	**The types of gifts to avoid:**	chrysanthemums
(B)	**Appropriate gifts for a foreigner to give:**	books, flowers, chocolate
(C)	**Best time to present gifts (at the beginning or at the end of a visit?):**	beginning
(D)	**Best time to present gifts (on initial or later visits?):**	initial
(E)	**Best place to present gifts (in private or in public?):**	either
(F)	**Number(s) with certain connotations and/or myths attached to them:**	13
(G)	**Basic shape(s) with negative connotations:**	n/a
(H)	**Basic color(s) with negative connotations:**	n/a
(I)	**Traditional greeting methods include:**	handshake, kiss
(J)	**Safe topics for discussion include:**	weather, fashion, travel, art, family, food, sports
(K)	**Best time for conversations (before, during, after meals?):**	before meals, during meals, after meal
(L)	**Forms of legal punishment:**	jailing
(M)	**Approximately length of time one could be detained by law and order authorities before being charged in court:**	month
(N)	**January 15, 1999, for example, will normally be written as:**	15/01/99
(O)	**Emergency code number:**	17
(P)	**Ambulance code Number:**	15
(Q)	**Police code number:**	17
(R)	**Telephone (country) code:**	33
(S)	**Telex (country) code:**	842
(T)	**Electricity requirements:**	220v
(U)	**Legal drinking age:**	none
(V)	**Systems of weights and measures:**	metric
(W)	**Legal age of incarceration:**	16
(X)	**Driving side of the road:**	right
(Y)	**Minimum expenditure expected of foreign visitors? $**	no
(Z)	**Name of currency:**	franc
(Za)	**Some places 0ff-limits to foreign visitors:**	none
(Zb)	**Some places, structures and items prohibited from being photographed:**	military establishments/installations.

ENDNOTES

Item Number: COMMENTS/EXPLANATIONS

n/a: Not applicable/Not available/No response
(1) Tip is usually included in service charge
(2) Not in city
(3) Not in city
(4) Only if invited to, use first name
(5) For a limited period (tourists only)
(6) Deportation is the punishment
(7) Deportation is the punishment
(8) Deportation is the punishment

GERMANY	Is customary Is allowed Is permissible Is used. Is OK	Is not customary Is frowned upon	Is disallowed Is forbidden Is a crime	(See last page for comments on items referenced here)
Smoking in public	✓			
Eating in public		✓		
Not flushing public toilet			✓	
Spitting in public		✓		
Feeding animals & birds in public	✓			
Whistling in public	✓			
Drinking alcohol in public		✓		
Kissing in public	✓			
Breast feeding in public		✓		
Drunkenness (in public)		✓		
Cursing in public		✓		
Religious preaching in public		✓		
Begging (panhandling) in public		✓		
Giving money to beggars/panhandlers	✓			
Giving food/drink to beggars/panhandlers	✓			
Brushing teeth in public (other than in restrooms)		✓		
Strolling with pets in major public roads/streets				1
Chewing gum in public	✓			
Chewing gum in government offices		✓		
Combing hair in public (other than in toilets/restrooms)		✓		
Undressing/dressing in public		✓		
Wearing of dark glasses indoors in public places		✓		
Public display of wealth		✓		
Praying openly in public in non-designated areas		✓		
Walking bare feet in public		✓		
Chewing tobacco in public		✓		
Trimming one's finger or toe nails in public			✓	
Laughing aloud in public	✓			
Mingling of the sexes in public	✓			
Mixed bathing in public swimming pools	✓			
Distributing religious pamphlets (literature) in public/side streets	✓			

GERMANY

	Is customary Is allowed Is permissible Is used. Is OK	Is not customary Is frowned upon	Is disallowed Is forbidden Is a crime	(See last page for comments on items referenced here)
Dancing on side street	✓			
Nude bathing		✓		
Littering			✓	
Binge Drinking			✓	
hitchhiking	✓			
Jaywalking			✓	
Drunk driving			✓	
Speeding		✓		
Skating on side streets (side-walk)		✓		
Graffiti painting			✓	
Pilfering			✓	
Prostitution		✓		
Haggling in the market place		✓		
Consumption of alcoholic beverages in bars and restaurants	✓			
Gambling	✓			
Possession of pornographic materials		✓		
Possession of the Christian Bible	✓			
Possession of the Moslem Koran	✓			
Possession of bullet-proof vest		✓		
Possession of toy gun	✓			
Possession of fire crackers and fireworks	✓			
Possession of prescription drugs (without doctor's note)			✓	
Possession of regulated drugs (narcotics)			✓	
Possession of firearms (by foreigners)				2
Possession of pocket knife in public	✓			
Using walkie talkies	✓			
Using of "boom boxes"(loud sounding stereo system)			✓	
Using "walkman" (very small radio/cassettes with ear plugs) in public places	✓			
Using "walkman" (very small radio/cassettes with ear plugs) while driving or riding		✓		

GERMANY

	Is customary Is allowed Is permissible Is used Is OK	Is not customary Is frowned upon	Is disallowed Is forbidden Is a crime	(See last page for comments on items referenced here)
Use of cellular phone	✓			
Use of binoculars/periscopes other than in sports arena	✓			
Taking photographs of people (without their permission)		✓		
Taking photographs at airports, train and bus stations	✓			3
Taking photographs of airports	✓			
Taking photographs of churches and synagogues	✓			4
Taking photographs of religious statues				
Taking photographs of public buildings	✓			
Taking photographs of bridges	✓			
Tipping (gratuity)	✓			
Tipping (when service is rendered)	✓			
Tipping (when service is not rendered)		✓		
Tipping waiters/waitresses at restaurants and hotels	✓			
Tipping taxi/cab drivers	✓			
Tipping baggage handlers, porters, door persons	✓			
Tipping of hair dressers/barbers	✓			
Overtipping		✓		
Undertipping		✓		
Spilling cigarette butt (ash) on side streets/on the floor		✓		
Men wearing lipstick		✓		
Wearing visible tattoo marks	✓			
Men painting/coloring their finger or toe nails		✓		
Cross dressing (men dressed like women & vice versa)		✓		
Walking in public without a shirt (i.e. with the upper half of the body naked)		✓		
Men wearing braided hair		✓		
Men wearing earrings	✓			
Men wearing dreadlock hair style	✓			
Homosexuality	✓			
Lesbianism	✓			

GERMANY

	Is customary Is allowed Is permissible Is used Is OK	Is not customary Is frowned upon	Is disallowed Is forbidden Is a crime	(See last page for comments on items referenced here)
Females covering their hair (wearing headgear) in public	✓			
Females exposing their full face in public	✓			
Females driving automobiles	✓			
Females riding motorcycles	✓			
Females riding bicycles	✓			
Females smoking in public	✓			
Women wearing bras (braziers) in public		✓		
Use of lipstick by women	✓			
A woman extending her hands first when introduced	✓			
Female bashing			✓	
Females wearing trousers	✓			
Females wearing minis (short dresses)	✓			
Females wearing bikinis	✓			5
Females wearing shorts	✓			
Persons of opposite sex holding hands in public	✓			
Persons of same sex holding hands in public	✓			
Handshake between opposite sex	✓			
Hugging in public by same sex	✓			
Hugging in public by opposite sex	✓			
Men and women walking side by side in public	✓			
Man walking ahead (in public), with the woman following	✓			
Woman walking ahead (in public), with the man following	✓			
Men opening doors for women	✓			
Sitting with legs crossed in the presence of elders		✓		
Talking to an elderly person with one's hat/cap on		✓		
Talking to an elderly person with hands positioned on both sides of one's waist		✓		
Blowing one's nose in public	✓			6
Blowing one's nose in the presence of others	✓			7
Addressing people by their title	✓			

GERMANY

	Is customary Is allowed Is permissible Is used. Is OK	Is not customary Is frowned upon	Is disallowed Is forbidden Is a crime	(See last page for comments on items referenced here)
Addressing people by their family name/surname/last name/given name	✓			
Addressing people by their first name/ given name	✓			8
Women going through doors first	✓			
Men helping women with their coats	✓			
Men extending their hands to women first during greetings	✓			
Taking off one's hat when entering a private home	✓			
Removing one's shoes when entering a private home		✓		
Invited guests bringing food at social gatherings	✓			
Guests bringing drinks at social gatherings	✓			
Shaking hands when leaving a small group	✓			
Shaking hands with everyone present, upon arrival at a social gathering	✓			
Eating with the right hand	✓			
Eating with the left hand	✓			
Eating with both hands	✓			
Presenting a gift or passing on an object with the left hand	✓			
Asking a man about his wife	✓			
Asking a woman about her husband	✓			
Making prior appointments before a meeting or visit	✓			
Addressing an audience with one or both hands in the pocket		✓		
Carrying on conversation during meals	✓			
Females sitting with legs crossed	✓			9
People discussing their wealth	✓			
Asking someone his or her age, or how old the person is		✓		
Complementing someone on his/her physical looks	✓			
Complementing someone on his/her attire	✓			
Use of both hands in handshake		✓		
In greeting, a handshake accompanied by a slight bow	✓			

GERMANY

	Is customary Is allowed Is permissible Is used. Is OK	Is not customary Is frowned upon	Is disallowed Is forbidden Is a crime	(See last page for comments on items referenced here)
Salutations such as "Good morning", "Good afternoon", "Good evening"	✓			
The completion of a business deal with a handshake	✓			
Starting a negotiation session with a handshake	✓			
A gift for the host/hostess	✓			
Giving a business gift		✓		10
A gift of money (use of money as gift)	✓			11
Use of flowers as a gift	✓			
Use of business cards	✓			
Accepting/presenting gifts with both hands		✓		
Burning of the country's flag			✓	
Mutilation of the national currency		✓		12
Casual wearing of clothings made with colors & marks of the national flag		✓		
Wearing of look-alike military (camouflage) fatigues (attire)		✓		
Sitting on the floor (on floor mats)		✓		
Discussion of religion	✓			
Discussion of politics	✓			
Discussion of sex	✓			
Patting/slapping someone on the buttocks		✓		
Patting/slapping someone on the back	✓			
Touching or patting someone's head/hair	✓			
Casual touching of any part of someone's body		✓		
Drinking directly out of a bottle/can	✓			
Placing one's leg(s) on the table or chair		✓		

GERMANY

	Is customary Is allowed Is permissible Is used. Is OK	Is not customary Is frowned upon	Is disallowed Is forbidden Is a crime	(See last page for comments on items referenced here)
Showing the sole of one's foot (feet)		✓		
People standing very close when talking	✓			
Maintaining steady eye contact (direct gaze) when talking to someone	✓			
Kissing or exchange of kisses on the cheek	✓			
Counting money (change) in someone's palm	✓			
Finger pointing in public (in a daring manner)		✓		
Seeking attention by winking the eyes		✓		
Tapping the head to indicate someone is crazy		✓		
Twirling the head to indicate someone is crazy		✓		
Whistling as a way of requesting something/seeking attention		✓		
Using "thumbs-up" sign to mean OK	✓			
Forming a circle with the thumb and index finger (forefinger) to mean OK		✓		
Using the fingers to make a "V" sign for victory	✓			
Beckoning to someone with the index finger (forefinger)		✓		
The left to right waving of the hand with open palms facing outward to indicate "Good bye"		✓		
The use of a nod to show acknowledgement	✓			
Stopping/beckoning a taxi using a stretched hand with the thumb pointing upward	✓			
Using the thumb finger pointed to a direction, to request a ride or a hike	✓			
Raising one's hand/waving with an open fist to summon a taxi		✓		
Tapping one's foot/feet on the floor in a public gathering		✓		
Wiggling one's leg(s) when in a sitting position		✓		
Use of the hand (by motorists and cyclists) to signal direction of traffic		✓		

GERMANY

		(See last page for comments on items referenced here)
Foreign tourists are welcome in the country.	yes	
The use of seat belt is mandatory.	yes	
International driving license is accepted.	yes	
U.S. driver's license is accepted.	yes	
It is considered impolite to yawn in public.	yes	
Death penalty for drug trafficking is the law.	no	
Life imprisonment for drug trafficking is the law.	yes	
Guilty until proven innocent in court is the law.	yes	
Innocent until proven guilty in court is the law.	no	
Pedestrians always have right of way.	yes/no	13
Exit visas are required of visitors.	no	
Crash helmet is mandatory for motor cyclist.	yes	
Hanging is used as a form of legal punishment.	no	
Decapitation of a limb is used as a form of punishment.	no	
Caning is used as a form of legal punishment.	no	
Electric shock is used as a form of legal punishment.	no	
One is expected to stand up during the playing of the national anthem.	yes	
Crash helmet is mandatory for bicyclists.	no	14
Guests are expected to eat every thing on their plates.	yes	
Table manners are very informal.	no	
One is expected to cover one's mouth when laughing.	no	
A vertical nod of the head means YES (OK).	yes	
A horizontal shaking of the head means NO (Not OK).	yes	
Prostitution is allowed only in designated areas.	yes	
One is expected to take off one's hat during playing of national anthem.	yes	
Separate seating arrangements (between sexes) are maintained at movies.	no	
Separate seating arrangements (between sexes) are maintained at churches.	no	
Uninvited visitors or guests may not be welcome, even among acquaintances.	yes/no	
Pets (e.g. cats, dog) are allowed in some hotels and restaurants.	yes	
Couples invited for a meal may be separated during meals according to their sex.	no	
Punctuality is the order of business.	yes	
Automobiles are driven with headlights always turned on.	no	
Motorcycles are driven with headlights always turned on.	no	
Visitors with expired visa face mandatory jail time.	no	
Visitors without exit visa face jail time.	no	
Visitors without entry visa face mandatory (automatic) jail time.		

ADDITIONAL COUNTRY INFORMATION

(A)	**The types of gifts to avoid:**	n/a
(B)	**Appropriate gifts for a foreigner to give:**	flowers (except odd number flowers)
(C)	**Best time to present gifts (at the beginning or at the end of a visit?):**	beginning
(D)	**Best time to present gifts (on initial or later visits?):**	initial
(E)	**Best place to present gifts (in private or in public?):**	private
(F)	**Number(s) with certain connotations and/or myths attached to them:**	n/a
(G)	**Basic shape(s) with negative connotations:**	n/a
(H)	**Basic color(s) with negative connotations:**	n/a
(I)	**Traditional greeting methods include:**	handshake
(J)	**Safe topics for discussion include:**	hobbies, sports
(K)	**Best time for conversations (before, during, after meals?):**	all times
(L)	**Forms of legal punishment:**	n/a
(M)	**Approximately length of time one could be detained by law and order authorities before being charged in court:**	n/a
(N)	**January 15, 1999, for example, will normally be written as:**	15/01/99
(O)	**Emergency code number:**	110
(P)	**Ambulance code Number:**	110
(Q)	**Police code number:**	110
(R)	**Telephone (country) code:**	49
(S)	**Telex (country) code:**	841
(T)	**Electricity requirements:**	220 volt
(U)	**Legal drinking age:**	18
(V)	**Systems of weights and measures:**	metric system
(W)	**Legal age of incarceration:**	n/a
(X)	**Driving side of the road:**	right
(Y)	**Minimum expenditure expected of foreign visitors? $**	n/a
(Z)	**Name of currency:**	Deutsche Mark (D.M.)
(Za)	**Some places 0ff-limits to foreign visitors:**	n/a
(Zb)	**Some places, structures and items prohibited from being photographed:**	n/a

ENDNOTES

Item Number: COMMENTS/EXPLANATIONS

n/a: Not applicable/Not available/No response

(1) On side-walk only

(2) Only by license.

(3) Unless stated otherwise.

(4) Unless stated otherwise.

(5) Only in swimming pools.

(6) Only with handkerchief.

(7) Only with handkerchief.

(8) Among friends/relatives.

(9) On chair.

(10) Unless with publicity.

(11) Only among friends and relatives.

(12) Is considered foolish.

(13) No if traffic light is red.

(14) No, but recommended

GREECE	Is customary Is allowed Is permissible Is used. Is OK	Is not customary Is frowned upon	Is disallowed Is forbidden Is a crime	(See last page for comments on items referenced here)
Smoking in public	✓			
Eating in public	✓			
Not flushing public toilet			✓	
Spitting in public			✓	
Feeding animals & birds in public	✓			
Whistling in public		✓		
Drinking alcohol in public	✓			
Kissing in public	✓			
Breast feeding in public		✓		
Drunkenness (in public)			✓	
Cursing in public			✓	
Religious preaching in public			✓	
Begging (panhandling) in public			✓	
Giving money to beggars/panhandlers	✓			
Giving food/drink to beggars/panhandlers	✓			
Brushing teeth in public (other than in restrooms)			✓	
Strolling with pets in major public roads/streets	✓			
Chewing gum in public	✓			
Chewing gum in government offices		✓		
Combing hair in public (other than in toilets/restrooms)		✓		
Undressing/dressing in public			✓	
Wearing of dark glasses indoors in public places		✓		
Public display of wealth		✓		
Praying openly in public in non-designated areas	✓			
Walking bare feet in public		✓		
Chewing tobacco in public	✓			
Trimming one's finger or toe nails in public		✓		
Laughing aloud in public	✓			
Mingling of the sexes in public	✓			
Mixed bathing in public swimming pools	✓			
Distributing religious pamphlets (literature) in public/side streets	✓			

DO'S AND DON'TS AROUND THE WORLD: A COUNTRY GUIDE TO CULTURAL AND SOCIAL TABOOS AND ETIQUETTE

GREECE

	Is customary Is allowed Is permissible Is used. Is OK	Is not customary Is frowned upon	Is disallowed Is forbidden Is a crime	(See last page for comments on items referenced here)
Dancing on side street	✓			
Nude bathing	`	✓		1
Littering			✓	
Binge Drinking	✓			
hitchhiking	✓			
Jaywalking			✓	
Drunk driving			✓	
Speeding	✓			
Skating on side streets (side-walk)			✓	
Graffiti painting			✓	
Pilfering			✓	
Prostitution	✓			
Haggling in the market place	✓			
Consumption of alcoholic beverages in bars and restaurants			✓	
Gambling	✓			2
Possession of pornographic materials	✓			
Possession of the Christian Bible	✓			
Possession of the Moslem Koran	✓			
Possession of bullet-proof vest	✓			
Possession of toy gun	✓			
Possession of fire crackers and fireworks			✓	
Possession of prescription drugs (without doctor's note)			✓	
Possession of regulated drugs (narcotics)			✓	
Possession of firearms (by foreigners)			✓	
Possession of pocket knife in public			✓	
Using walkie talkies	✓			3
Using of "boom boxes"(loud sounding stereo system)	✓			
Using "walkman" (very small radio/cassettes with ear plugs) in public places	✓			
Using "walkman" (very small radio/cassettes with ear plugs) while driving or riding			✓	

GREECE

	Is customary Is allowed Is permissible Is used Is OK	Is not customary Is frowned upon	Is disallowed Is forbidden Is a crime	(See last page for comments on items referenced here)
Use of cellular phone	✓			4
Use of binoculars/periscopes other than in sports arena	✓			5
Taking photographs of people (without their permission)		✓		
Taking photographs at airports, train and bus stations	✓			
Taking photographs of airports			✓	
Taking photographs of churches and synagogues	✓			
Taking photographs of religious statues	✓			
Taking photographs of public buildings	✓			
Taking photographs of bridges	✓			
Tipping (gratuity)	✓			
Tipping (when service is rendered)	✓			
Tipping (when service is not rendered)	✓			
Tipping waiters/waitresses at restaurants and hotels	✓			
Tipping taxi/cab drivers	✓			
Tipping baggage handlers, porters, door persons	✓			
Tipping of hair dressers/barbers	✓			
Overtipping	✓			
Undertipping	✓			
Spilling cigarette butt (ash) on side streets/on the floor			✓	
Men wearing lipstick		✓		
Wearing visible tattoo marks	✓			
Men painting/coloring their finger or toe nails		✓		
Cross dressing (men dressed like women & vice versa)	✓			
Walking in public without a shirt (i.e. with the upper half of the body naked)	✓			
Men wearing braided hair	✓			
Men wearing earrings	✓			
Men wearing dreadlock hair style	✓			
Homosexuality	✓			6
Lesbianism	✓			7

GREECE

	Is customary Is allowed Is permissible Is used Is OK	Is not customary Is frowned upon	Is disallowed Is forbidden Is a crime	(See last page for comments on items referenced here)
Females covering their hair (wearing headgear) in public		✓		
Females exposing their full face in public	✓			
Females driving automobiles	✓			
Females riding motorcycles	✓			
Females riding bicycles	✓			
Females smoking in public	✓			
Women wearing bras (braziers) in public	✓			
Use of lipstick by women	✓			
A woman extending her hands first when introduced	✓			
Female bashing			✓	
Females wearing trousers	✓			
Females wearing minis (short dresses)	✓			
Females wearing bikinis	✓			
Females wearing shorts	✓			
Persons of opposite sex holding hands in public	✓			
Persons of same sex holding hands in public	✓			
Handshake between opposite sex	✓			
Hugging in public by same sex	✓			8
Hugging in public by opposite sex	✓			
Men and women walking side by side in public	✓			
Man walking ahead (in public), with the woman following	✓			9
Woman walking ahead (in public), with the man following	✓			10
Men opening doors for women	✓			
Sitting with legs crossed in the presence of elders	✓			
Talking to an elderly person with one's hat/cap on	✓			
Talking to an elderly person with hands positioned on both sides of one's waist	✓			
Blowing one's nose in public	✓			
Blowing one's nose in the presence of others	✓			
Addressing people by their title	✓			

GREECE

	Is customary Is allowed Is permissible Is used. Is OK	Is not customary Is frowned upon	Is disallowed Is forbidden Is a crime	(See last page for comments on items referenced here)
Addressing people by their family name/surname/last name/given name	✓			
Addressing people by their first name/ given name	✓			
Women going through doors first	✓			
Men helping women with their coats	✓			
Men extending their hands to women first during greetings	✓			
Taking off one's hat when entering a private home	✓			
Removing one's shoes when entering a private home			✓	
Invited guests bringing food at social gatherings			✓	
Guests bringing drinks at social gatherings	✓			
Shaking hands when leaving a small group	✓			
Shaking hands with everyone present, upon arrival at a social gathering	✓			
Eating with the right hand	✓			
Eating with the left hand	✓			
Eating with both hands	✓			
Presenting a gift or passing on an object with the left hand	✓			
Asking a man about his wife	✓			
Asking a woman about her husband	✓			
Making prior appointments before a meeting or visit	✓			
Addressing an audience with one or both hands in the pocket			✓	
Carrying on conversation during meals	✓			
Females sitting with legs crossed	✓			
People discussing their wealth	✓			
Asking someone his or her age, or how old the person is		✓		
Complementing someone on his/her physical looks	✓			
Complementing someone on his/her attire	✓			
Use of both hands in handshake	✓			
In greeting, a handshake accompanied by a slight bow			✓	

GREECE

	Is customary Is allowed Is permissible Is used. Is OK	Is not customary Is frowned upon	Is disallowed Is forbidden Is a crime	(See last page for comments on items referenced here)
Salutations such as "Good morning", "Good afternoon", "Good evening"	✓			
The completion of a business deal with a handshake	✓			
Starting a negotiation session with a handshake	✓			
A gift for the host/hostess	✓			
Giving a business gift	✓			
A gift of money (use of money as gift)			✓	
Use of flowers as a gift	✓			
Use of business cards	✓			
Accepting/presenting gifts with both hands	✓			
Burning of the country's flag			✓	
Mutilation of the national currency			✓	
Casual wearing of clothings made with colors & marks of the national flag	✓			
Wearing of look-alike military (camouflage) fatigues (attire)	✓			
Sitting on the floor (on floor mats)	✓			
Discussion of religion	✓			
Discussion of politics	✓			
Discussion of sex	✓			
Patting/slapping someone on the buttocks	✓			
Patting/slapping someone on the back	✓			
Touching or patting someone's head/hair	✓			
Casual touching of any part of someone's body	✓			
Drinking directly out of a bottle/can	✓			
Placing one's leg(s) on the table or chair		✓		

GREECE

	Is customary Is allowed Is permissible Is used. Is OK	Is not customary Is frowned upon	Is disallowed Is forbidden Is a crime	(See last page for comments on items referenced here)
Showing the sole of one's foot (feet)		✓		
People standing very close when talking	✓			
Maintaining steady eye contact (direct gaze) when talking to someone	✓			
Kissing or exchange of kisses on the cheek	✓			
Counting money (change) in someone's palm		✓		
Finger pointing in public (in a daring manner)		✓		
Seeking attention by winking the eyes	✓			
Tapping the head to indicate someone is crazy		✓		
Twirling the head to indicate someone is crazy		✓		
Whistling as a way of requesting something/seeking attention		✓		
Using "thumbs-up" sign to mean OK		✓		
Forming a circle with the thumb and index finger (forefinger) to mean OK		✓		
Using the fingers to make a "V" sign for victory		✓		
Beckoning to someone with the index finger (forefinger)	✓			
The left to right waving of the hand with open palms facing outward to indicate "Good bye"		✓		
The use of a nod to show acknowledgement	✓			
Stopping/beckoning a taxi using a stretched hand with the thumb pointing upward		✓		
Using the thumb finger pointed to a direction, to request a ride or a hike	✓			
Raising one's hand/waving with an open fist to summon a taxi	✓			
Tapping one's foot/feet on the floor in a public gathering		✓		
Wiggling one's leg(s) when in a sitting position	✓			
Use of the hand (by motorists and cyclists) to signal direction of traffic	✓			

GREECE

		(See last page for comments on items referenced here)
Foreign tourists are welcome in the country.	yes	
The use of seat belt is mandatory.	yes	
International driving license is accepted.	yes	
U.S. driver's license is accepted.	no	
It is considered impolite to yawn in public.	yes	
Death penalty for drug trafficking is the law.	no	
Life imprisonment for drug trafficking is the law.	no	11
Guilty until proven innocent in court is the law.	no	
Innocent until proven guilty in court is the law.	yes	
Pedestrians always have right of way.	yes	12
Exit visas are required of visitors.	no	
Crash helmet is mandatory for motor cyclist.	yes	
Hanging is used as a form of legal punishment.	no	
Decapitation of a limb is used as a form of punishment.	no	
Caning is used as a form of legal punishment.	no	
Electric shock is used as a form of legal punishment.	no	
One is expected to stand up during the playing of the national anthem.	yes	
Crash helmet is mandatory for bicyclists.	no	
Guests are expected to eat every thing on their plates.	no	
Table manners are very informal.	yes	
One is expected to cover one's mouth when laughing.	no	
A vertical nod of the head means YES (OK).	yes	
A horizontal shaking of the head means NO (Not OK).	no	
Prostitution is allowed only in designated areas.	no	13
One is expected to take off one's hat during playing of national anthem.	yes	
Separate seating arrangements (between sexes) are maintained at movies.	no	
Separate seating arrangements (between sexes) are maintained at churches.	no	
Uninvited visitors or guests may not be welcome, even among acquaintances.	no	
Pets (e.g. cats, dog) are allowed in some hotels and restaurants.	yes	
Couples invited for a meal may be separated during meals according to their sex.	no	
Punctuality is the order of business.	yes	
Automobiles are driven with headlights always turned on.	no	
Motorcycles are driven with headlights always turned on.	no	
Visitors with expired visa face mandatory jail time.	yes	14
Visitors without exit visa face jail time.	no	
Visitors without entry visa face mandatory (automatic) jail time.	yes	14

ADDITIONAL COUNTRY INFORMATION

(A)	**The types of gifts to avoid:**	n/a
(B)	**Appropriate gifts for a foreigner to give:**	flowers, cake, something typical from the visitor's country of origin
(C)	**Best time to present gifts (at the beginning or at the end of a visit?):**	beginning
(D)	**Best time to present gifts (on initial or later visits?):**	initial visit
(E)	**Best place to present gifts (in private or in public?):**	it doesn't matter
(F)	**Number(s) with certain connotations and/or myths attached to them:**	13: bad luck
(G)	**Basic shape(s) with negative connotations:**	none
(H)	**Basic color(s) with negative connotations:**	black
(I)	**Traditional greeting methods include:**	handshake, hug, kiss, nod, patting the other's back.
(J)	**Safe topics for discussion include:**	weather, fashion, travel, art, family, religion, domestic politics, food, sports,international politics, social conditions, money and personal wealth, sex
(K)	**Best time for conversations (before, during, after meals?):**	anytime
(L)	**Forms of legal punishment:**	jailing
(M)	**Approximately length of time one could be detained by law and order authorities before being charged in court:**	n/a (See note #M)
(N)	**January 15, 1999, for example, will normally be written as:**	15/1/99
(O)	**Emergency code number:**	100
(P)	**Ambulance code Number:**	166
(Q)	**Police code number:**	100
(R)	**Telephone (country) code:**	30
(S)	**Telex (country) code:**	601
(T)	**Electricity requirements:**	220v
(U)	**Legal drinking age:**	18 (in bars)
(V)	**Systems of weights and measures:**	kilos - meters
(W)	**Legal age of incarceration:**	18 (See note #W)
(X)	**Driving side of the road:**	right
(Y)	**Minimum expenditure expected of foreign visitors? $**	no
(Z)	**Name of currency:**	Drachmas
(Za)	**Some places 0ff-limits to foreign visitors:**	military facilities
(Zb)	**Some places, structures and items prohibited from being photographed:**	military facilities

ENDNOTES

Item Number: COMMENTS/EXPLANATIONS

n/a: Not applicable/Not available/No response

(1) Allowed only in specified beaches. Topless bathing, on the other hand, is rather common.

(2) Gambling is allowed in casinos and specially licensed establishments.

(3) Under special license.

(4) They should not be used while driving.

(5) It is however frowned upon when someone uses them in order to spy upon someone else's private life.

(6) Homosexuality and lesbianism are permissible, however homophobia is rather common. Homosexuals may become subjects of mockery.

(7) Homosexuality and lesbianism are permissible, however homophobia is rather common. Homosexuals may become subjects of mockery.

(8) Hugging between men may often be misinterpreted. i.e. in a market place. On the contrary, when in a club, such an act is less provocative. Hugging between women is an acceptable form of sociability and does not necessarily imply lesbianism.

(9) Men and women walk side by side.

(10) Men and women walk side by side.

(11) It depends on the quantity and on possible previous offenses of drug trafficking.

(12) Caution, however is needed.

(13) Prostitution is generally illegal.

(14) Violators face fine and/or deportation

(M) It depends on the degree of the offence (petty offence, misdemeanor, felony and whether the wrongdoer is caught red handed or not.

(W) Minors (under 18) are treated with leniency and placed in special institutions.

HUNGARY	Is customary Is allowed Is permissible Is used. Is OK	Is not customary Is frowned upon	Is disallowed Is forbidden Is a crime	(See last page for comments on items referenced here)
Smoking in public	✓			
Eating in public		✓		
Not flushing public toilet		✓		
Spitting in public			✓	
Feeding animals & birds in public	✓			
Whistling in public	✓			
Drinking alcohol in public	✓			
Kissing in public	✓			
Breast feeding in public		✓		
Drunkenness (in public)		✓		
Cursing in public	✓			
Religious preaching in public	✓			
Begging (panhandling) in public	✓			
Giving money to beggars/panhandlers	✓			
Giving food/drink to beggars/panhandlers		✓		
Brushing teeth in public (other than in restrooms)		✓		
Strolling with pets in major public roads/streets	✓			
Chewing gum in public	✓			
Chewing gum in government offices	✓			
Combing hair in public (other than in toilets/restrooms)		✓		
Undressing/dressing in public		✓		
Wearing of dark glasses indoors in public places	✓			
Public display of wealth	✓			
Praying openly in public in non-designated areas		✓		
Walking bare feet in public	✓			
Chewing tobacco in public		✓		
Trimming one's finger or toe nails in public		✓		
Laughing aloud in public	✓			
Mingling of the sexes in public	✓			
Mixed bathing in public swimming pools	✓			
Distributing religious pamphlets (literature) in public/side streets	✓			

HUNGARY

	Is customary Is allowed Is permissible Is used. Is OK	Is not customary Is frowned upon	Is disallowed Is forbidden Is a crime	(See last page for comments on items referenced here)
Dancing on side street		✓		
Nude bathing		✓		
Littering			✓	
Binge Drinking	✓			
hitchhiking	✓			
Jaywalking	✓			
Drunk driving			✓	
Speeding			✓	
Skating on side streets (side-walk)		✓		
Graffiti painting			✓	
Pilfering			✓	
Prostitution			✓	
Haggling in the market place	✓			
Consumption of alcoholic beverages in bars and restaurants	✓			
Gambling	✓			
Possession of pornographic materials	✓			
Possession of the Christian Bible	✓			
Possession of the Moslem Koran	✓			
Possession of bullet-proof vest	✓			
Possession of toy gun	✓			
Possession of fire crackers and fireworks			✓	
Possession of prescription drugs (without doctor's note)	✓			
Possession of regulated drugs (narcotics)			✓	
Possession of firearms (by foreigners)	✓			
Possession of pocket knife in public	✓			
Using walkie talkies	✓			
Using of "boom boxes"(loud sounding stereo system)		✓		
Using "walkman" (very small radio/cassettes with ear plugs) in public places	✓			
Using "walkman" (very small radio/cassettes with ear plugs) while driving or riding	✓			

HUNGARY

	Is customary Is allowed Is permissible Is used Is OK	Is not customary Is frowned upon	Is disallowed Is forbidden Is a crime	(See last page for comments on items referenced here)
Use of cellular phone	✓			
Use of binoculars/periscopes other than in sports arena	✓			
Taking photographs of people (without their permission)		✓		
Taking photographs at airports, train and bus stations	✓			
Taking photographs of airports	✓			
Taking photographs of churches and synagogues	✓			
Taking photographs of religious statues	✓			
Taking photographs of public buildings	✓			
Taking photographs of bridges	✓			
Tipping (gratuity)	✓			
Tipping (when service is rendered)	✓			
Tipping (when service is not rendered)	✓			
Tipping waiters/waitresses at restaurants and hotels	✓			
Tipping taxi/cab drivers	✓			
Tipping baggage handlers, porters, door persons	✓			
Tipping of hair dressers/barbers	✓			
Overtipping		✓		
Undertipping		✓		
Spilling cigarette butt (ash) on side streets/on the floor	✓			
Men wearing lipstick		✓		
Wearing visible tattoo marks	✓			
Men painting/coloring their finger or toe nails		✓		
Cross dressing (men dressed like women & vice versa)	✓			
Walking in public without a shirt (i.e. with the upper half of the body naked)		✓		
Men wearing braided hair		✓		
Men wearing earrings		✓		
Men wearing dreadlock hair style		✓		
Homosexuality	✓			
Lesbianism	✓			

HUNGARY

	Is customary Is allowed Is permissible Is used Is OK	Is not customary Is frowned upon	Is disallowed Is forbidden Is a crime	(See last page for comments on items referenced here)
Females covering their hair (wearing headgear) in public		✓		
Females exposing their full face in public	✓			
Females driving automobiles	✓			
Females riding motorcycles	✓			
Females riding bicycles	✓			
Females smoking in public	✓			
Women wearing bras (braziers) in public		✓		
Use of lipstick by women	✓			
A woman extending her hands first when introduced	✓			
Female bashing		✓		
Females wearing trousers	✓			
Females wearing minis (short dresses)	✓			
Females wearing bikinis	✓			
Females wearing shorts	✓			
Persons of opposite sex holding hands in public	✓			
Persons of same sex holding hands in public		✓		
Handshake between opposite sex	✓			
Hugging in public by same sex		✓		
Hugging in public by opposite sex	✓			
Men and women walking side by side in public	✓			
Man walking ahead (in public), with the woman following		✓		
Woman walking ahead (in public), with the man following		✓		
Men opening doors for women	✓			
Sitting with legs crossed in the presence of elders	✓			
Talking to an elderly person with one's hat/cap on	✓			
Talking to an elderly person with hands positioned on both sides of one's waist	✓			
Blowing one's nose in public	✓			
Blowing one's nose in the presence of others	✓			
Addressing people by their title	✓			

HUNGARY

	Is customary Is allowed Is permissible Is used. Is OK	Is not customary Is frowned upon	Is disallowed Is forbidden Is a crime	(See last page for comments on items referenced here)
Addressing people by their family name/surname/last name/given name	✓			
Addressing people by their first name/ given name	✓			
Women going through doors first	✓			
Men helping women with their coats	✓			
Men extending their hands to women first during greetings		✓		
Taking off one's hat when entering a private home	✓			
Removing one's shoes when entering a private home		✓		
Invited guests bringing food at social gatherings		✓		
Guests bringing drinks at social gatherings	✓			
Shaking hands when leaving a small group	✓			
Shaking hands with everyone present, upon arrival at a social gathering	✓			
Eating with the right hand	✓			
Eating with the left hand		✓		
Eating with both hands	✓			
Presenting a gift or passing on an object with the left hand		✓		
Asking a man about his wife	✓			
Asking a woman about her husband	✓			
Making prior appointments before a meeting or visit	✓			
Addressing an audience with one or both hands in the pocket		✓		
Carrying on conversation during meals	✓			
Females sitting with legs crossed	✓			
People discussing their wealth		✓		
Asking someone his or her age, or how old the person is	✓			
Complementing someone on his/her physical looks	✓			
Complementing someone on his/her attire	✓			
Use of both hands in handshake		✓		
In greeting, a handshake accompanied by a slight bow		✓		

HUNGARY

	Is customary Is allowed Is permissible Is used. Is OK	Is not customary Is frowned upon	Is disallowed Is forbidden Is a crime	(See last page for comments on items referenced here)
Salutations such as "Good morning", "Good afternoon", "Good evening"	✓			
The completion of a business deal with a handshake	✓			
Starting a negotiation session with a handshake	✓			
A gift for the host/hostess	✓			
Giving a business gift	✓			
A gift of money (use of money as gift)		✓		
Use of flowers as a gift	✓			
Use of business cards	✓			
Accepting/presenting gifts with both hands	✓			
Burning of the country's flag			✓	
Mutilation of the national currency			✓	
Casual wearing of clothings made with colors & marks of the national flag			✓	
Wearing of look-alike military (camouflage) fatigues (attire)		✓		
Sitting on the floor (on floor mats)		✓		
Discussion of religion	✓			
Discussion of politics	✓			
Discussion of sex	✓			
Patting/slapping someone on the buttocks		✓		
Patting/slapping someone on the back	✓			
Touching or patting someone's head/hair	✓			
Casual touching of any part of someone's body	✓			
Drinking directly out of a bottle/can		✓		
Placing one's leg(s) on the table or chair		✓		

HUNGARY

	Is customary Is allowed Is permissible Is used. Is OK	Is not customary Is frowned upon	Is disallowed Is forbidden Is a crime	(See last page for comments on items referenced here)
Showing the sole of one's foot (feet)		✓		
People standing very close when talking		✓		
Maintaining steady eye contact (direct gaze) when talking to someone	✓			
Kissing or exchange of kisses on the cheek	✓			
Counting money (change) in someone's palm	✓			
Finger pointing in public (in a daring manner)		✓		
Seeking attention by winking the eyes	✓			
Tapping the head to indicate someone is crazy	✓			
Twirling the head to indicate someone is crazy	✓			
Whistling as a way of requesting something/seeking attention	✓			
Using "thumbs-up" sign to mean OK	✓			
Forming a circle with the thumb and index finger (forefinger) to mean OK		✓		
Using the fingers to make a "V" sign for victory		✓		
Beckoning to someone with the index finger (forefinger)		✓		
The left to right waving of the hand with open palms facing outward to indicate "Good bye"		✓		
The use of a nod to show acknowledgement	✓			
Stopping/beckoning a taxi using a stretched hand with the thumb pointing upward		✓		
Using the thumb finger pointed to a direction, to request a ride or a hike	✓			
Raising one's hand/waving with an open fist to summon a taxi	✓			
Tapping one's foot/feet on the floor in a public gathering		✓		
Wiggling one's leg(s) when in a sitting position		✓		
Use of the hand (by motorists and cyclists) to signal direction of traffic	✓			

HUNGARY

		(See last page for comments on items referenced here)
Foreign tourists are welcome in the country.	yes	
The use of seat belt is mandatory.	yes	
International driving license is accepted.	yes	
U.S. driver's license is accepted.	yes	
It is considered impolite to yawn in public.	yes	
Death penalty for drug trafficking is the law.	no	1
Life imprisonment for drug trafficking is the law.	no	
Guilty until proven innocent in court is the law.	no	
Innocent until proven guilty in court is the law.	yes	
Pedestrians always have right of way.	no	
Exit visas are required of visitors.	no	
Crash helmet is mandatory for motor cyclist.	yes	
Hanging is used as a form of legal punishment.	no	
Decapitation of a limb is used as a form of punishment.	no	
Caning is used as a form of legal punishment.	no	
Electric shock is used as a form of legal punishment.	no	
One is expected to stand up during the playing of the national anthem.	yes	
Crash helmet is mandatory for bicyclists.	no	
Guests are expected to eat every thing on their plates.	no	
Table manners are very informal.	yes	
One is expected to cover one's mouth when laughing.	no	
A vertical nod of the head means YES (OK).	yes	
A horizontal shaking of the head means NO (Not OK).	yes	
Prostitution is allowed only in designated areas.	yes	
One is expected to take off one's hat during playing of national anthem.	yes	
Separate seating arrangements (between sexes) are maintained at movies.	no	
Separate seating arrangements (between sexes) are maintained at churches.	no	2
Uninvited visitors or guests may not be welcome, even among acquaintances.	no	
Pets (e.g. cats, dog) are allowed in some hotels and restaurants.	yes	3
Couples invited for a meal may be separated during meals according to their sex.	no	
Punctuality is the order of business.	yes	
Automobiles are driven with headlights always turned on.	no	4
Motorcycles are driven with headlights always turned on.	yes	
Visitors with expired visa face mandatory jail time.	no	
Visitors without exit visa face jail time.	no	
Visitors without entry visa face mandatory (automatic) jail time.	no	

ADDITIONAL COUNTRY INFORMATION

(A)	**The types of gifts to avoid:**	none
(B)	**Appropriate gifts for a foreigner to give:**	men - drink, women - flower
(C)	**Best time to present gifts (at the beginning or at the end of a visit?):**	at the at the beginning or at the end of a visit
(D)	**Best time to present gifts (on initial or later visits?):**	initial visit
(E)	**Best place to present gifts (in private or in public?):**	in private or in public
(F)	**Number(s) with certain connotations and/or myths attached to them:**	13 is considered unlucky
(G)	**Basic shape(s) with negative connotations:**	none
(H)	**Basic color(s) with negative connotations:**	
(I)	**Traditional greeting methods include:**	handshake, kiss, nod, bow
(J)	**Safe topics for discussion include:**	weather, fashion, travel, art, family, religion, domestic politics, food, sports, international politics, social conditions, money and personal wealth, sex.
(K)	**Best time for conversations (before, during, after meals?):**	indifferent
(L)	**Forms of legal punishment:**	jailing
(M)	**Approximately length of time one could be detained by law and order authorities before being charged in court:**	unlimited but decided by court
(N)	**January 15, 1999, for example, will normally be written as:**	1999/01/15
(O)	**Emergency code number:**	n/a
(P)	**Ambulance code Number:**	04
(Q)	**Police code number:**	07
(R)	**Telephone (country) code:**	36
(S)	**Telex (country) code:**	861
(T)	**Electricity requirements:**	220v/50hz
(U)	**Legal drinking age:**	18
(V)	**Systems of weights and measures:**	metric
(W)	**Legal age of incarceration:**	18/18-19 youth jail
(X)	**Driving side of the road:**	right
(Y)	**Minimum expenditure expected of foreign visitors? $**	50$/day
(Z)	**Name of currency:**	forint
(Za)	**Some places 0ff-limits to foreign visitors:**	none
(Zb)	**Some places, structures and items prohibited from being photographed:**	none

ENDNOTES

Item Number: ***COMMENTS/EXPLANATIONS***

n/a: Not applicable/Not available/No response

(1) No death penalty at all

(2) Certain churches, as orthodox, yes

(3) Legally there are no such areas

(4) Only outside cities

ICELAND	Is customary Is allowed Is permissible Is used. Is OK	Is not customary Is frowned upon	Is disallowed Is forbidden Is a crime	(See last page for comments on items referenced here)
Smoking in public	✓			
Eating in public	✓			
Not flushing public toilet		✓		
Spitting in public			✓	
Feeding animals & birds in public		✓		
Whistling in public	✓			
Drinking alcohol in public	✓			
Kissing in public	✓			
Breast feeding in public		✓		
Drunkenness (in public)	✓			
Cursing in public	✓			
Religious preaching in public	✓			
Begging (panhandling) in public		✓		
Giving money to beggars/panhandlers		✓		
Giving food/drink to beggars/panhandlers		✓		
Brushing teeth in public (other than in restrooms)	✓			
Strolling with pets in major public roads/streets	✓			
Chewing gum in public	✓			
Chewing gum in government offices	✓			
Combing hair in public (other than in toilets/restrooms)	✓			
Undressing/dressing in public		✓		
Wearing of dark glasses indoors in public places	✓			
Public display of wealth		✓		
Praying openly in public in non-designated areas	✓			
Walking bare feet in public		✓		
Chewing tobacco in public	✓			
Trimming one's finger or toe nails in public	✓			
Laughing aloud in public	✓			
Mingling of the sexes in public	✓			
Mixed bathing in public swimming pools	✓			
Distributing religious pamphlets (literature) in public/side streets	✓			

DO'S AND DON'TS AROUND THE WORLD: A COUNTRY GUIDE TO CULTURAL AND SOCIAL TABOOS AND ETIQUETTE

ICELAND

	Is customary Is allowed Is permissible Is used. Is OK	Is not customary Is frowned upon	Is disallowed Is forbidden Is a crime	(See last page for comments on items referenced here)
Dancing on side street	✓			
Nude bathing			✓	
Littering			✓	
Binge Drinking	✓			
hitchhiking		✓		
Jaywalking	✓			
Drunk driving			✓	
Speeding			✓	
Skating on side streets (side-walk)	✓			
Graffiti painting			✓	
Pilfering	✓			
Prostitution			✓	
Haggling in the market place		✓		
Consumption of alcoholic beverages in bars and restaurants	✓			
Gambling			✓	
Possession of pornographic materials		✓		
Possession of the Christian Bible	✓			
Possession of the Moslem Koran	✓			
Possession of bullet-proof vest		✓		
Possession of toy gun	✓			
Possession of fire crackers and fireworks	✓			
Possession of prescription drugs (without doctor's note)	✓			
Possession of regulated drugs (narcotics)			✓	
Possession of firearms (by foreigners)			✓	
Possession of pocket knife in public	✓			
Using walkie talkies	✓			
Using of "boom boxes"(loud sounding stereo system)	✓			
Using "walkman" (very small radio/cassettes with ear plugs) in public places	✓			
Using "walkman" (very small radio/cassettes with ear plugs) while driving or riding			✓	

ICELAND

	Is customary Is allowed Is permissible Is used Is OK	Is not customary Is frowned upon	Is disallowed Is forbidden Is a crime	(See last page for comments on items referenced here)
Use of cellular phone	✓			
Use of binoculars/periscopes other than in sports arena	✓			
Taking photographs of people (without their permission)	✓			
Taking photographs at airports, train and bus stations	✓			
Taking photographs of airports	✓			
Taking photographs of churches and synagogues	✓			
Taking photographs of religious statues	✓			
Taking photographs of public buildings	✓			
Taking photographs of bridges	✓			
Tipping (gratuity)		✓		
Tipping (when service is rendered)		✓		
Tipping (when service is not rendered)		✓		
Tipping waiters/waitresses at restaurants and hotels		✓		
Tipping taxi/cab drivers		✓		
Tipping baggage handlers, porters, door persons		✓		
Tipping of hair dressers/barbers		✓		
Overtipping		✓		
Undertipping		✓		
Spilling cigarette butt (ash) on side streets/on the floor	✓			
Men wearing lipstick		✓		
Wearing visible tattoo marks	✓			
Men painting/coloring their finger or toe nails		✓		
Cross dressing (men dressed like women & vice versa)		✓		
Walking in public without a shirt (i.e. with the upper half of the body naked)		✓		
Men wearing braided hair	✓			
Men wearing earrings	✓			
Men wearing dreadlock hair style	✓			
Homosexuality	✓			
Lesbianism	✓			

ICELAND

	Is customary Is allowed Is permissible Is used Is OK	Is not customary Is frowned upon	Is disallowed Is forbidden Is a crime	(See last page for comments on items referenced here)
Females covering their hair (wearing headgear) in public		✓		
Females exposing their full face in public	✓			
Females driving automobiles	✓			
Females riding motorcycles	✓			
Females riding bicycles	✓			
Females smoking in public	✓			
Women wearing bras (braziers) in public	✓			
Use of lipstick by women	✓			
A woman extending her hands first when introduced	✓			
Female bashing		✓		
Females wearing trousers	✓			
Females wearing minis (short dresses)	✓			
Females wearing bikinis	✓			
Females wearing shorts	✓			
Persons of opposite sex holding hands in public	✓			
Persons of same sex holding hands in public	✓			
Handshake between opposite sex	✓			
Hugging in public by same sex	✓			
Hugging in public by opposite sex	✓			
Men and women walking side by side in public	✓			
Man walking ahead (in public), with the woman following		✓		
Woman walking ahead (in public), with the man following		✓		
Men opening doors for women	✓			
Sitting with legs crossed in the presence of elders	✓			
Talking to an elderly person with one's hat/cap on	✓			
Talking to an elderly person with hands positioned on both sides of one's waist	✓			
Blowing one's nose in public	✓			
Blowing one's nose in the presence of others	✓			
Addressing people by their title		✓		

ICELAND

	Is customary Is allowed Is permissible Is used. Is OK	Is not customary Is frowned upon	Is disallowed Is forbidden Is a crime	(See last page for comments on items referenced here)
Addressing people by their family name/surname/last name/given name	✓			
Addressing people by their first name/ given name	✓			
Women going through doors first	✓			
Men helping women with their coats	✓			
Men extending their hands to women first during greetings	✓			
Taking off one's hat when entering a private home	✓			
Removing one's shoes when entering a private home	✓			
Invited guests bringing food at social gatherings	✓			
Guests bringing drinks at social gatherings	✓			
Shaking hands when leaving a small group	✓			
Shaking hands with everyone present, upon arrival at a social gathering		✓		
Eating with the right hand	✓			
Eating with the left hand	✓			
Eating with both hands	✓			
Presenting a gift or passing on an object with the left hand	✓			
Asking a man about his wife	✓			
Asking a woman about her husband	✓			
Making prior appointments before a meeting or visit	✓			
Addressing an audience with one or both hands in the pocket	✓			
Carrying on conversation during meals	✓			
Females sitting with legs crossed	✓			
People discussing their wealth		✓		
Asking someone his or her age, or how old the person is	✓			
Complementing someone on his/her physical looks	✓			
Complementing someone on his/her attire	✓			
Use of both hands in handshake		✓		
In greeting, a handshake accompanied by a slight bow	✓			

ICELAND

	Is customary Is allowed Is permissible Is used. Is OK	Is not customary Is frowned upon	Is disallowed Is forbidden Is a crime	(See last page for comments on items referenced here)
Salutations such as "Good morning", "Good afternoon", "Good evening"	✓			
The completion of a business deal with a handshake	✓			
Starting a negotiation session with a handshake	✓			
A gift for the host/hostess	✓			
Giving a business gift	✓			
A gift of money (use of money as gift)	✓			
Use of flowers as a gift	✓			
Use of business cards	✓			
Accepting/presenting gifts with both hands		✓		
Burning of the country's flag			✓	
Mutilation of the national currency			✓	
Casual wearing of clothings made with colors & marks of the national flag	✓			
Wearing of look-alike military (camouflage) fatigues (attire)	✓			
Sitting on the floor (on floor mats)		✓		
Discussion of religion	✓			
Discussion of politics	✓			
Discussion of sex	✓			
Patting/slapping someone on the buttocks		✓		
Patting/slapping someone on the back	✓			
Touching or patting someone's head/hair		✓		
Casual touching of any part of someone's body		✓		
Drinking directly out of a bottle/can		✓		
Placing one's leg(s) on the table or chair	✓			

ICELAND

	Is customary Is allowed Is permissible Is used. Is OK	Is not customary Is frowned upon	Is disallowed Is forbidden Is a crime	(See last page for comments on items referenced here)
Showing the sole of one's foot (feet)	✓			n/a
People standing very close when talking	✓			
Maintaining steady eye contact (direct gaze) when talking to someone	✓			
Kissing or exchange of kisses on the cheek	✓			
Counting money (change) in someone's palm	✓			n/a
Finger pointing in public (in a daring manner)	✓			
Seeking attention by winking the eyes				
Tapping the head to indicate someone is crazy	✓			
Twirling the head to indicate someone is crazy	✓			
Whistling as a way of requesting something/seeking attention		✓		
Using "thumbs-up" sign to mean OK	✓			
Forming a circle with the thumb and index finger (forefinger) to mean OK		✓		
Using the fingers to make a "V" sign for victory		✓		
Beckoning to someone with the index finger (forefinger)		✓		
The left to right waving of the hand with open palms facing outward to indicate "Good bye"	✓			
The use of a nod to show acknowledgement	✓			
Stopping/beckoning a taxi using a stretched hand with the thumb pointing upward	✓			
Using the thumb finger pointed to a direction, to request a ride or a hike	✓			
Raising one's hand/waving with an open fist to summon a taxi	✓			
Tapping one's foot/feet on the floor in a public gathering	✓			
Wiggling one's leg(s) when in a sitting position	✓			
Use of the hand (by motorists and cyclists) to signal direction of traffic	✓			

ICELAND

		(See last page for comments on items referenced here)
Foreign tourists are welcome in the country.	yes	
The use of seat belt is mandatory.	yes	
International driving license is accepted.	yes	
U.S. driver's license is accepted.	yes	
It is considered impolite to yawn in public.	yes	
Death penalty for drug trafficking is the law.	no	
Life imprisonment for drug trafficking is the law.	no	
Guilty until proven innocent in court is the law.	no	
Innocent until proven guilty in court is the law.	yes	
Pedestrians always have right of way.	yes	
Exit visas are required of visitors.	no	
Crash helmet is mandatory for motor cyclist.	yes	
Hanging is used as a form of legal punishment.	no	
Decapitation of a limb is used as a form of punishment.	no	
Caning is used as a form of legal punishment.	no	
Electric shock is used as a form of legal punishment.	no	
One is expected to stand up during the playing of the national anthem.	yes	
Crash helmet is mandatory for bicyclists.	yes	
Guests are expected to eat every thing on their plates.	yes	
Table manners are very informal.	yes	
One is expected to cover one's mouth when laughing.	yes	
A vertical nod of the head means YES (OK).	yes	
A horizontal shaking of the head means NO (Not OK).	yes	
Prostitution is allowed only in designated areas.	no	
One is expected to take off one's hat during playing of national anthem.	yes	
Separate seating arrangements (between sexes) are maintained at movies.	no	
Separate seating arrangements (between sexes) are maintained at churches.	no	
Uninvited visitors or guests may not be welcome, even among acquaintances.	yes	
Pets (e.g. cats, dog) are allowed in some hotels and restaurants.	no	
Couples invited for a meal may be separated during meals according to their sex.	yes	
Punctuality is the order of business.	yes	
Automobiles are driven with headlights always turned on.	yes	
Motorcycles are driven with headlights always turned on.	yes	
Visitors with expired visa face mandatory jail time.	no	
Visitors without exit visa face jail time.	no	
Visitors without entry visa face mandatory (automatic) jail time.	no	

ADDITIONAL COUNTRY INFORMATION

(A)	**The types of gifts to avoid:**	n/a
(B)	**Appropriate gifts for a foreigner to give:**	flowers, bottle of wine, small gifts.
(C)	**Best time to present gifts (at the beginning or at the end of a visit?):**	beginning
(D)	**Best time to present gifts (on initial or later visits?):**	n/a
(E)	**Best place to present gifts (in private or in public?):**	n/a
(F)	**Number(s) with certain connotations and/or myths attached to them:**	n/a
(G)	**Basic shape(s) with negative connotations:**	n/a
(H)	**Basic color(s) with negative connotations:**	n/a
(I)	**Traditional greeting methods include:**	n/a
(J)	**Safe topics for discussion include:**	weather, fashion, travel, art, family, religion, domestic politics, food, sports, international politics, social conditions, money and personal wealth, sex.
(K)	**Best time for conversations (before, during, after meals?):**	n/a
(L)	**Forms of legal punishment:**	jailing
(M)	**Approximately length of time one could be detained by law and order authorities before being charged in court:**	few hours
(N)	**January 15, 1999, for example, will normally be written as:**	15/1/99
(O)	**Emergency code number**:	0112
(P)	**Ambulance code Number**:	0112
(Q)	**Police code number:**	0112
(R)	**Telephone (country) code:**	354
(S)	**Telex (country) code:**	858
(T)	**Electricity requirements**:	220 v
(U)	**Legal drinking age:**	20
(V)	**Systems of weights and measures:**	metric
(W)	**Legal age of incarceration**:	16
(X)	**Driving side of the road:**	right
(Y)	**Minimum expenditure expected of foreign visitors? $**	no
(Z)	**Name of currency**:	Krona
(Za)	**Some places 0ff-limits to foreign visitors:**	no
(Zb)	**Some places, structures and items prohibited from being photographed:**	no

IRELAND	Is customary Is allowed Is permissible Is used. Is OK	Is not customary Is frowned upon	Is disallowed Is forbidden Is a crime	(See last page for comments on items referenced here)
Smoking in public	✓			
Eating in public	✓			
Not flushing public toilet		✓		
Spitting in public		✓		
Feeding animals & birds in public	✓			
Whistling in public	✓			
Drinking alcohol in public	✓			
Kissing in public	✓			
Breast feeding in public	✓			
Drunkenness (in public)		✓		
Cursing in public		✓		
Religious preaching in public		✓		
Begging (panhandling) in public		✓		
Giving money to beggars/panhandlers		✓		
Giving food/drink to beggars/panhandlers	✓			
Brushing teeth in public (other than in restrooms)	✓			
Strolling with pets in major public roads/streets		✓		
Chewing gum in public	✓			
Chewing gum in government offices	✓			
Combing hair in public (other than in toilets/restrooms)		✓		
Undressing/dressing in public		✓		
Wearing of dark glasses indoors in public places		✓		
Public display of wealth	✓			
Praying openly in public in non-designated areas	✓			
Walking bare feet in public	✓			
Chewing tobacco in public	✓			
Trimming one's finger or toe nails in public		✓		
Laughing aloud in public	✓			
Mingling of the sexes in public	✓			
Mixed bathing in public swimming pools	✓			
Distributing religious pamphlets (literature) in public/side streets	✓			

IRELAND

	Is customary Is allowed Is permissible Is used. Is OK	Is not customary Is frowned upon	Is disallowed Is forbidden Is a crime	(See last page for comments on items referenced here)
Dancing on side street	✓			
Nude bathing	✓	✓		
Littering		✓	✓	
Binge Drinking		✓		
hitchhiking	✓			
Jaywalking		✓		
Drunk driving			✓	
Speeding			✓	
Skating on side streets (side-walk)	✓			
Graffiti painting		✓		
Pilfering			✓	
Prostitution			✓	
Haggling in the market place	✓			
Consumption of alcoholic beverages in bars and restaurants	✓			
Gambling			✓	
Possession of pornographic materials		✓		
Possession of the Christian Bible	✓			
Possession of the Moslem Koran	✓			
Possession of bullet-proof vest				n/a
Possession of toy gun	✓			
Possession of fire crackers and fireworks			✓	
Possession of prescription drugs (without doctor's note)	✓			
Possession of regulated drugs (narcotics)			✓	
Possession of firearms (by foreigners)			✓	
Possession of pocket knife in public	✓			
Using walkie talkies	✓			
Using of "boom boxes"(loud sounding stereo system)		✓		
Using "walkman" (very small radio/cassettes with ear plugs) in public places	✓			
Using "walkman" (very small radio/cassettes with ear plugs) while driving or riding	✓			

IRELAND

	Is customary Is allowed Is permissible Is used Is OK	Is not customary Is frowned upon	Is disallowed Is forbidden Is a crime	(See last page for comments on items referenced here)
Use of cellular phone	✓			
Use of binoculars/periscopes other than in sports arena	✓			
Taking photographs of people (without their permission)	✓			
Taking photographs at airports, train and bus stations	✓			
Taking photographs of airports	✓			
Taking photographs of churches and synagogues	✓			
Taking photographs of religious statues	✓			
Taking photographs of public buildings	✓			
Taking photographs of bridges	✓			
Tipping (gratuity)	✓			
Tipping (when service is rendered)	✓			
Tipping (when service is not rendered)	✓			
Tipping waiters/waitresses at restaurants and hotels	✓			
Tipping taxi/cab drivers	✓			
Tipping baggage handlers, porters, door persons	✓			
Tipping of hair dressers/barbers	✓			
Overtipping	✓			
Undertipping	✓			
Spilling cigarette butt (ash) on side streets/on the floor	✓			
Men wearing lipstick		✓		
Wearing visible tattoo marks	✓			
Men painting/coloring their finger or toe nails		✓		
Cross dressing (men dressed like women & vice versa)		✓		
Walking in public without a shirt (i.e. with the upper half of the body naked)	✓			
Men wearing braided hair	✓			
Men wearing earrings	✓			
Men wearing dreadlock hair style	✓			
Homosexuality	✓			
Lesbianism	✓			

IRELAND

	Is customary Is allowed Is permissible Is used Is OK	Is not customary Is frowned upon	Is disallowed Is forbidden Is a crime	(See last page for comments on items referenced here)
Females covering their hair (wearing headgear) in public	✓			
Females exposing their full face in public	✓			
Females driving automobiles	✓			
Females riding motorcycles	✓			
Females riding bicycles	✓			
Females smoking in public	✓			
Women wearing bras (braziers) in public	✓			
Use of lipstick by women	✓			
A woman extending her hands first when introduced	✓			
Female bashing		✓		
Females wearing trousers	✓			
Females wearing minis (short dresses)	✓			
Females wearing bikinis	✓			
Females wearing shorts	✓			
Persons of opposite sex holding hands in public	✓			
Persons of same sex holding hands in public	✓			
Handshake between opposite sex	✓			
Hugging in public by same sex	✓			
Hugging in public by opposite sex	✓			
Men and women walking side by side in public	✓			
Man walking ahead (in public), with the woman following		✓		
Woman walking ahead (in public), with the man following		✓		
Men opening doors for women	✓			
Sitting with legs crossed in the presence of elders	✓			
Talking to an elderly person with one's hat/cap on		✓		
Talking to an elderly person with hands positioned on both sides of one's waist				n/a
Blowing one's nose in public	✓			
Blowing one's nose in the presence of others	✓			
Addressing people by their title	✓			

IRELAND

	Is customary Is allowed Is permissible Is used. Is OK	Is not customary Is frowned upon	Is disallowed Is forbidden Is a crime	(See last page for comments on items referenced here)
Addressing people by their family name/surname/last name/given name	✓			
Addressing people by their first name/ given name	✓			
Women going through doors first	✓			
Men helping women with their coats	✓			
Men extending their hands to women first during greetings	✓			
Taking off one's hat when entering a private home	✓			
Removing one's shoes when entering a private home		✓		
Invited guests bringing food at social gatherings	✓			
Guests bringing drinks at social gatherings	✓			
Shaking hands when leaving a small group	✓			
Shaking hands with everyone present, upon arrival at a social gathering	✓			
Eating with the right hand	✓			
Eating with the left hand	✓			
Eating with both hands	✓			
Presenting a gift or passing on an object with the left hand	✓			
Asking a man about his wife	✓			
Asking a woman about her husband	✓			
Making prior appointments before a meeting or visit	✓			
Addressing an audience with one or both hands in the pocket	✓			
Carrying on conversation during meals	✓			
Females sitting with legs crossed	✓			
People discussing their wealth	✓			
Asking someone his or her age, or how old the person is	✓			
Complementing someone on his/her physical looks	✓			
Complementing someone on his/her attire	✓			
Use of both hands in handshake	✓			
In greeting, a handshake accompanied by a slight bow		✓		

IRELAND

	Is customary Is allowed Is permissible Is used. Is OK	Is not customary Is frowned upon	Is disallowed Is forbidden Is a crime	(See last page for comments on items referenced here)
Salutations such as "Good morning", "Good afternoon", "Good evening"	✓			
The completion of a business deal with a handshake	✓			
Starting a negotiation session with a handshake	✓			
A gift for the host/hostess	✓			
Giving a business gift	✓			
A gift of money (use of money as gift)		✓		
Use of flowers as a gift	✓			
Use of business cards	✓			
Accepting/presenting gifts with both hands	✓			
Burning of the country's flag			✓	
Mutilation of the national currency			✓	
Casual wearing of clothings made with colors & marks of the national flag	✓			
Wearing of look-alike military (camouflage) fatigues (attire)	✓			
Sitting on the floor (on floor mats)	✓			
Discussion of religion	✓			
Discussion of politics	✓			
Discussion of sex	✓			
Patting/slapping someone on the buttocks		✓		
Patting/slapping someone on the back	✓			
Touching or patting someone's head/hair	✓			
Casual touching of any part of someone's body	✓			
Drinking directly out of a bottle/can	✓			
Placing one's leg(s) on the table or chair	✓			

IRELAND

	Is customary Is allowed Is permissible Is used. Is OK	Is not customary Is frowned upon	Is disallowed Is forbidden Is a crime	(See last page for comments on items referenced here)
Showing the sole of one's foot (feet)	✓			
People standing very close when talking	✓			
Maintaining steady eye contact (direct gaze) when talking to someone	✓			
Kissing or exchange of kisses on the cheek	✓			
Counting money (change) in someone's palm	✓			
Finger pointing in public (in a daring manner)		✓		
Seeking attention by winking the eyes	✓			
Tapping the head to indicate someone is crazy	✓			
Twirling the head to indicate someone is crazy	✓			
Whistling as a way of requesting something/seeking attention		✓		
Using "thumbs-up" sign to mean OK	✓			
Forming a circle with the thumb and index finger (forefinger) to mean OK	✓			
Using the fingers to make a "V" sign for victory	✓			
Beckoning to someone with the index finger (forefinger)	✓			
The left to right waving of the hand with open palms facing outward to indicate "Good bye"	✓			
The use of a nod to show acknowledgement	✓			
Stopping/beckoning a taxi using a stretched hand with the thumb pointing upward	✓			
Using the thumb finger pointed to a direction, to request a ride or a hike	✓			
Raising one's hand/waving with an open fist to summon a taxi	✓			
Tapping one's foot/feet on the floor in a public gathering	✓			
Wiggling one's leg(s) when in a sitting position	✓			
Use of the hand (by motorists and cyclists) to signal direction of traffic	✓			

IRELAND

		(See last page for comments on items referenced here)
Foreign tourists are welcome in the country.	yes	
The use of seat belt is mandatory.	yes	
International driving license is accepted.	yes	
U.S. driver's license is accepted.	yes	
It is considered impolite to yawn in public.	no	
Death penalty for drug trafficking is the law.	no	
Life imprisonment for drug trafficking is the law.	no	
Guilty until proven innocent in court is the law.	yes	
Innocent until proven guilty in court is the law.	yes	
Pedestrians always have right of way.	n/a	
Exit visas are required of visitors.	no	
Crash helmet is mandatory for motor cyclist.	yes	
Hanging is used as a form of legal punishment.	no	
Decapitation of a limb is used as a form of punishment.	no	
Caning is used as a form of legal punishment.	no	
Electric shock is used as a form of legal punishment.	no	
One is expected to stand up during the playing of the national anthem.	yes	
Crash helmet is mandatory for bicyclists.	no	
Guests are expected to eat every thing on their plates.	no	
Table manners are very informal.	yes/no	
One is expected to cover one's mouth when laughing.	no	
A vertical nod of the head means YES (OK).	yes	
A horizontal shaking of the head means NO (Not OK).	yes	
Prostitution is allowed only in designated areas.	no	
One is expected to take off one's hat during playing of national anthem.	yes	
Separate seating arrangements (between sexes) are maintained at movies.	no	
Separate seating arrangements (between sexes) are maintained at churches.	no	
Uninvited visitors or guests may not be welcome, even among acquaintances.	no	
Pets (e.g. cats, dog) are allowed in some hotels and restaurants.	yes	
Couples invited for a meal may be separated during meals according to their sex.	no	
Punctuality is the order of business.	yes/no	
Automobiles are driven with headlights always turned on.	no	
Motorcycles are driven with headlights always turned on.	no	
Visitors with expired visa face mandatory jail time.	no	
Visitors without exit visa face jail time.	no	
Visitors without entry visa face mandatory (automatic) jail time.	no	

ADDITIONAL COUNTRY INFORMATION

(A)	**The types of gifts to avoid:**	none
(B)	**Appropriate gifts for a foreigner to give:**	flowers, chocolate, wine, cheese
(C)	**Best time to present gifts (at the beginning or at the end of a visit?):**	beginning
(D)	**Best time to present gifts (on initial or later visits?):**	either
(E)	**Best place to present gifts (in private or in public?):**	either
(F)	**Number(s) with certain connotations and/or myths attached to them:**	no
(G)	**Basic shape(s) with negative connotations:**	triangular
(H)	**Basic color(s) with negative connotations:**	black
(I)	**Traditional greeting methods include:**	handshake, hug
(J)	**Safe topics for discussion include:**	weather, fashion, travel, art, family, food, sports, international politics, social conditions, money and personal
(K)	**Best time for conversations (before, during, after meals?):**	before meals, during meals, after meals
(L)	**Forms of legal punishment:**	jailing
(M)	**Approximately length of time one could be detained by law and order authorities before being charged in court:**	n/a
(N)	**January 15, 1999, for example, will normally be written as:**	15/1/99
(O)	**Emergency code number**:	999
(P)	**Ambulance code Number**:	999
(Q)	**Police code number:**	999
(R)	**Telephone (country) code:**	353
(S)	**Telex (country) code:**	8532
(T)	**Electricity requirements**:	220 volt
(U)	**Legal drinking age:**	18
(V)	**Systems of weights and measures:**	n/a
(W)	**Legal age of incarceration**:	n/a
(X)	**Driving side of the road:**	n/a
(Y)	**Minimum expenditure expected of foreign visitors? $**	n/a
(Z)	**Name of currency**:	Irish Pounds or Punts
(Za)	**Some places 0ff-limits to foreign visitors:**	n/a
(Zb)	**Some places, structures and items prohibited from being photographed:**	n/a

ITALY	Is customary Is allowed Is permissible Is used. Is OK	Is not customary Is frowned upon	Is disallowed Is forbidden Is a crime	(See last page for comments on items referenced here)
Smoking in public	✓			
Eating in public	✓			
Not flushing public toilet		✓		
Spitting in public		✓		
Feeding animals & birds in public	✓			
Whistling in public	✓			
Drinking alcohol in public	✓			
Kissing in public	✓			
Breast feeding in public		✓		
Drunkenness (in public)			✓	
Cursing in public	✓			
Religious preaching in public		✓		
Begging (panhandling) in public	✓			
Giving money to beggars/panhandlers	✓			
Giving food/drink to beggars/panhandlers	✓			
Brushing teeth in public (other than in restrooms)		✓		
Strolling with pets in major public roads/streets	✓			
Chewing gum in public	✓			
Chewing gum in government offices	✓			
Combing hair in public (other than in toilets/restrooms)	✓			
Undressing/dressing in public	✓			
Wearing of dark glasses indoors in public places	✓			
Public display of wealth	✓			
Praying openly in public in non-designated areas	✓			
Walking bare feet in public		✓		
Chewing tobacco in public		✓		
Trimming one's finger or toe nails in public		✓		
Laughing aloud in public	✓			
Mingling of the sexes in public		✓		
Mixed bathing in public swimming pools	✓			
Distributing religious pamphlets (literature) in public/side streets	✓			

ITALY

	Is customary Is allowed Is permissible Is used. Is OK	Is not customary Is frowned upon	Is disallowed Is forbidden Is a crime	(See last page for comments on items referenced here)
Dancing on side street	✓			
Nude bathing			✓	
Littering			✓	
Binge Drinking	✓			
hitchhiking	✓			
Jaywalking		✓		
Drunk driving			✓	
Speeding	✓			
Skating on side streets (side-walk)		✓		
Graffiti painting		✓		
Pilfering			✓	
Prostitution	✓			
Haggling in the market place		✓		
Consumption of alcoholic beverages in bars and restaurants	✓			
Gambling	✓			1
Possession of pornographic materials		✓		
Possession of the Christian Bible	✓			
Possession of the Moslem Koran		✓		
Possession of bullet-proof vest		✓		
Possession of toy gun	✓			
Possession of fire crackers and fireworks		✓		
Possession of prescription drugs (without doctor's note)	✓			
Possession of regulated drugs (narcotics)		✓		
Possession of firearms (by foreigners)		✓		
Possession of pocket knife in public			✓	2
Using walkie talkies		✓		
Using of "boom boxes"(loud sounding stereo system)		✓		
Using "walkman" (very small radio/cassettes with ear plugs) in public places	✓			
Using "walkman" (very small radio/cassettes with ear plugs) while driving or riding	✓			

ITALY

	Is customary Is allowed Is permissible Is used Is OK	Is not customary Is frowned upon	Is disallowed Is forbidden Is a crime	(See last page for comments on items referenced here)
Use of cellular phone	✓			
Use of binoculars/periscopes other than in sports arena		✓		
Taking photographs of people (without their permission)	✓			
Taking photographs at airports, train and bus stations	✓			
Taking photographs of airports	✓			
Taking photographs of churches and synagogues	✓			
Taking photographs of religious statues	✓			
Taking photographs of public buildings	✓			
Taking photographs of bridges	✓			
Tipping (gratuity)	✓			
Tipping (when service is rendered)	✓			
Tipping (when service is not rendered)	✓			
Tipping waiters/waitresses at restaurants and hotels	✓			
Tipping taxi/cab drivers	✓			
Tipping baggage handlers, porters, door persons	✓			
Tipping of hair dressers/barbers	✓			
Overtipping		✓		
Undertipping		✓		
Spilling cigarette butt (ash) on side streets/on the floor	✓			
Men wearing lipstick		✓		
Wearing visible tattoo marks	✓			
Men painting/coloring their finger or toe nails		✓		
Cross dressing (men dressed like women & vice versa)		✓		
Walking in public without a shirt (i.e. with the upper half of the body naked)		✓		
Men wearing braided hair		✓		
Men wearing earrings		✓		
Men wearing dreadlock hair style		✓		
Homosexuality	✓			
Lesbianism	✓			

ITALY

	Is customary Is allowed Is permissible Is used Is OK	Is not customary Is frowned upon	Is disallowed Is forbidden Is a crime	(See last page for comments on items referenced here)
Females covering their hair (wearing headgear) in public	✓			
Females exposing their full face in public	✓			
Females driving automobiles	✓			
Females riding motorcycles	✓			
Females riding bicycles	✓			
Females smoking in public	✓			
Women wearing bras (braziers) in public	✓			
Use of lipstick by women	✓			
A woman extending her hands first when introduced	✓			
Female bashing		✓		
Females wearing trousers	✓			
Females wearing minis (short dresses)	✓			
Females wearing bikinis	✓			
Females wearing shorts	✓			
Persons of opposite sex holding hands in public	✓			
Persons of same sex holding hands in public		✓		
Handshake between opposite sex	✓			
Hugging in public by same sex	✓			
Hugging in public by opposite sex	✓			
Men and women walking side by side in public	✓			
Man walking ahead (in public), with the woman following		✓		
Woman walking ahead (in public), with the man following		✓		
Men opening doors for women	✓			
Sitting with legs crossed in the presence of elders	✓			
Talking to an elderly person with one's hat/cap on	✓			
Talking to an elderly person with hands positioned on both sides of one's waist	✓			
Blowing one's nose in public	✓			
Blowing one's nose in the presence of others	✓			
Addressing people by their title	✓			3

ITALY

	Is customary Is allowed Is permissible Is used. Is OK	Is not customary Is frowned upon	Is disallowed Is forbidden Is a crime	(See last page for comments on items referenced here)
Addressing people by their family name/surname/last name/given name	✓			4
Addressing people by their first name/ given name		✓		5
Women going through doors first	✓			
Men helping women with their coats	✓			
Men extending their hands to women first during greetings	✓			
Taking off one's hat when entering a private home	✓			
Removing one's shoes when entering a private home		✓		
Invited guests bringing food at social gatherings	✓			
Guests bringing drinks at social gatherings	✓			
Shaking hands when leaving a small group	✓			
Shaking hands with everyone present, upon arrival at a social gathering	✓			
Eating with the right hand	✓			
Eating with the left hand	✓			6
Eating with both hands	✓			
Presenting a gift or passing on an object with the left hand	✓			
Asking a man about his wife	✓			
Asking a woman about her husband	✓			
Making prior appointments before a meeting or visit	✓			
Addressing an audience with one or both hands in the pocket		✓		
Carrying on conversation during meals	✓			
Females sitting with legs crossed	✓			
People discussing their wealth		✓		
Asking someone his or her age, or how old the person is		✓		
Complementing someone on his/her physical looks	✓			
Complementing someone on his/her attire	✓			
Use of both hands in handshake		✓		
In greeting, a handshake accompanied by a slight bow		✓		

ITALY

	Is customary Is allowed Is permissible Is used. Is OK	Is not customary Is frowned upon	Is disallowed Is forbidden Is a crime	(See last page for comments on items referenced here)
Salutations such as "Good morning", "Good afternoon", "Good evening"	✓			
The completion of a business deal with a handshake	✓			
Starting a negotiation session with a handshake	✓			
A gift for the host/hostess	✓			
Giving a business gift		✓		
A gift of money (use of money as gift)		✓		
Use of flowers as a gift	✓			
Use of business cards	✓			
Accepting/presenting gifts with both hands	✓			
Burning of the country's flag			✓	
Mutilation of the national currency			✓	
Casual wearing of clothings made with colors & marks of the national flag		✓		
Wearing of look-alike military (camouflage) fatigues (attire)	✓			
Sitting on the floor (on floor mats)		✓		
Discussion of religion		✓		
Discussion of politics	✓			
Discussion of sex	✓			
Patting/slapping someone on the buttocks			✓	
Patting/slapping someone on the back	✓			
Touching or patting someone's head/hair		✓		
Casual touching of any part of someone's body			✓	
Drinking directly out of a bottle/can		✓		
Placing one's leg(s) on the table or chair		✓		

ITALY

	Is customary Is allowed Is permissible Is used. Is OK	Is not customary Is frowned upon	Is disallowed Is forbidden Is a crime	(See last page for comments on items referenced here)
Showing the sole of one's foot (feet)		✓		
People standing very close when talking	✓			
Maintaining steady eye contact (direct gaze) when talking to someone	✓			
Kissing or exchange of kisses on the cheek	✓			
Counting money (change) in someone's palm		✓		
Finger pointing in public (in a daring manner)		✓		
Seeking attention by winking the eyes		✓		
Tapping the head to indicate someone is crazy	✓			
Twirling the head to indicate someone is crazy		✓		
Whistling as a way of requesting something/seeking attention		✓		
Using "thumbs-up" sign to mean OK		✓		
Forming a circle with the thumb and index finger (forefinger) to mean OK		✓		
Using the fingers to make a "V" sign for victory		✓		
Beckoning to someone with the index finger (forefinger)	✓			
The left to right waving of the hand with open palms facing outward to indicate "Good bye"	✓			
The use of a nod to show acknowledgement	✓			
Stopping/beckoning a taxi using a stretched hand with the thumb pointing upward	✓			
Using the thumb finger pointed to a direction, to request a ride or a hike	✓			
Raising one's hand/waving with an open fist to summon a taxi		✓		
Tapping one's foot/feet on the floor in a public gathering				n/a
Wiggling one's leg(s) when in a sitting position				n/a
Use of the hand (by motorists and cyclists) to signal direction of traffic	✓			

ITALY

		(See last page for comments on items referenced here)
Foreign tourists are welcome in the country.	yes	
The use of seat belt is mandatory.	yes	
International driving license is accepted.	yes	
U.S. driver's license is accepted.	yes	7
It is considered impolite to yawn in public.	yes	
Death penalty for drug trafficking is the law.	no	
Life imprisonment for drug trafficking is the law.	no	
Guilty until proven innocent in court is the law.	no	
Innocent until proven guilty in court is the law.	yes	
Pedestrians always have right of way.	yes	
Exit visas are required of visitors.	no	
Crash helmet is mandatory for motor cyclist.	yes	8
Hanging is used as a form of legal punishment.	no	
Decapitation of a limb is used as a form of punishment.	no	
Caning is used as a form of legal punishment.	no	
Electric shock is used as a form of legal punishment.	no	
One is expected to stand up during the playing of the national anthem.	yes	
Crash helmet is mandatory for bicyclists.	no	
Guests are expected to eat every thing on their plates.	yes	
Table manners are very informal.	no	
One is expected to cover one's mouth when laughing.	no	
A vertical nod of the head means YES (OK).	yes	
A horizontal shaking of the head means NO (Not OK).	yes	
Prostitution is allowed only in designated areas.	no	
One is expected to take off one's hat during playing of national anthem.	yes	
Separate seating arrangements (between sexes) are maintained at movies.	no	
Separate seating arrangements (between sexes) are maintained at churches.	no	
Uninvited visitors or guests may not be welcome, even among acquaintances.	yes	
Pets (e.g. cats, dog) are allowed in some hotels and restaurants.	yes	9
Couples invited for a meal may be separated during meals according to their sex.	no	
Punctuality is the order of business.	no	
Automobiles are driven with headlights always turned on.	no	
Motorcycles are driven with headlights always turned on.	no	
Visitors with expired visa face mandatory jail time.	no	
Visitors without exit visa face jail time.	no	
Visitors without entry visa face mandatory (automatic) jail time.	no	

ADDITIONAL COUNTRY INFORMATION

(A)	**The types of gifts to avoid:**	chrysanthemums
(B)	**Appropriate gifts for a foreigner to give:**	flowers (odd # or a dozen), wine , chocolate
(C)	**Best time to present gifts (at the beginning or at the end of a visit?):**	at the beginning
(D)	**Best time to present gifts (on initial or later visits?):**	n/a
(E)	**Best place to present gifts (in private or in public?):**	n/a
(F)	**Number(s) with certain connotations and/or myths attached to them:**	17 (negative) 13 (good)
(G)	**Basic shape(s) with negative connotations:**	no
(H)	**Basic color(s) with negative connotations:**	no
(I)	**Traditional greeting methods include:**	n/a
(J)	**Safe topics for discussion include:**	weather, fashion, travel, art, family, religion, domestic politics, food, sports, international politics, social conditions, money and personal wealth, sex, business
(K)	**Best time for conversations (before, during, after meals?):**	n/a
(L)	**Forms of legal punishment:**	fining and jailing
(M)	**Approximately length of time one could be detained by law and order authorities before being charged in court:**	depends on crimes: maximum one year can be extended by order of a judge
(N)	**January 15, 1999, for example, will normally be written as:**	15/1/99
(O)	**Emergency code number**:	113
(P)	**Ambulance code Number**:	113
(Q)	**Police code number:**	113
(R)	**Telephone (country) code:**	39
(S)	**Telex (country) code:**	843
(T)	**Electricity requirements**:	220
(U)	**Legal drinking age:**	18
(V)	**Systems of weights and measures:**	metric
(W)	**Legal age of incarceration**:	18
(X)	**Driving side of the road:**	right
(Y)	**Minimum expenditure expected of foreign visitors? $**	none
(Z)	**Name of currency**:	Italian Lira
(Za)	**Some places 0ff-limits to foreign visitors:**	none
(Zb)	**Some places, structures and items prohibited from being photographed:**	none, unless specifically indicated.

ENDNOTES

Item Number: COMMENTS/EXPLANATIONS

n/a: Not applicable/Not available/No response
(1) Except in casinos
(2) Blades over four inches are forbidden
(3) Depending on the degree of familiarity
(4) Depending on the degree of familiarity
(5) Depending on the degree of familiarity
(6) Unless left-handed
(7) Up to six months
(8) Over 50cc
(9) Check first

LIECHTENSTEIN	Is customary Is allowed Is permissible Is used. Is OK	Is not customary Is frowned upon	Is disallowed Is forbidden Is a crime	(See last page for comments on items referenced here)
Smoking in public	✓			
Eating in public	✓			
Not flushing public toilet		✓		
Spitting in public		✓		
Feeding animals & birds in public	✓			
Whistling in public	✓			
Drinking alcohol in public	✓			
Kissing in public	✓			
Breast feeding in public	✓			
Drunkenness (in public)	✓			
Cursing in public	✓			
Religious preaching in public	✓			
Begging (panhandling) in public		✓		
Giving money to beggars/panhandlers	✓			
Giving food/drink to beggars/panhandlers	✓			
Brushing teeth in public (other than in restrooms)	✓			
Strolling with pets in major public roads/streets	✓			
Chewing gum in public	✓			
Chewing gum in government offices	✓			
Combing hair in public (other than in toilets/restrooms)	✓			
Undressing/dressing in public	✓			
Wearing of dark glasses indoors in public places	✓			
Public display of wealth	✓			
Praying openly in public in non-designated areas	✓			
Walking bare feet in public	✓			
Chewing tobacco in public	✓			
Trimming one's finger or toe nails in public	✓			
Laughing aloud in public	✓			
Mingling of the sexes in public				n/a
Mixed bathing in public swimming pools				n/a
Distributing religious pamphlets (literature) in public/side streets				n/a

LIECHTENSTEIN

	Is customary Is allowed Is permissible Is used. Is OK	Is not customary Is frowned upon	Is disallowed Is forbidden Is a crime	(See last page for comments on items referenced here)
Dancing on side street	✓			
Nude bathing		✓		
Littering		✓		
Binge Drinking		✓		
hitchhiking	✓			
Jaywalking		✓		
Drunk driving			✓	
Speeding	✓			
Skating on side streets (side-walk)	✓			
Graffiti painting			✓	
Pilfering			✓	
Prostitution			✓	
Haggling in the market place				n/a
Consumption of alcoholic beverages in bars and restaurants				n/a
Gambling	✓			
Possession of pornographic materials	✓			
Possession of the Christian Bible	✓			
Possession of the Moslem Koran	✓			
Possession of bullet-proof vest	✓			
Possession of toy gun	✓			
Possession of fire crackers and fireworks	✓			
Possession of prescription drugs (without doctor's note)		✓		
Possession of regulated drugs (narcotics)			✓	
Possession of firearms (by foreigners)			✓	
Possession of pocket knife in public	✓			
Using walkie talkies	✓			
Using of "boom boxes"(loud sounding stereo system)	✓			
Using "walkman" (very small radio/cassettes with ear plugs) in public places	✓			
Using "walkman" (very small radio/cassettes with ear plugs) while driving or riding				n/a

LIECHTENSTEIN

	Is customary Is allowed Is permissible Is used Is OK	Is not customary Is frowned upon	Is disallowed Is forbidden Is a crime	(See last page for comments on items referenced here)
Use of cellular phone	✓			
Use of binoculars/periscopes other than in sports arena	✓			
Taking photographs of people (without their permission)		✓		
Taking photographs at airports, train and bus stations			✓	
Taking photographs of airports	✓			
Taking photographs of churches and synagogues	✓			
Taking photographs of religious statues	✓			
Taking photographs of public buildings				n/a
Taking photographs of bridges				n/a
Tipping (gratuity)	✓			
Tipping (when service is rendered)	✓			
Tipping (when service is not rendered)		✓		
Tipping waiters/waitresses at restaurants and hotels				n/a
Tipping taxi/cab drivers				n/a
Tipping baggage handlers, porters, door persons				n/a
Tipping of hair dressers/barbers				n/a
Overtipping	✓			
Undertipping		✓		
Spilling cigarette butt (ash) on side streets/on the floor	✓			
Men wearing lipstick		✓		
Wearing visible tattoo marks	✓			
Men painting/coloring their finger or toe nails		✓		
Cross dressing (men dressed like women & vice versa)		✓		
Walking in public without a shirt (i.e. with the upper half of the body naked)				n/a
Men wearing braided hair	✓			
Men wearing earrings	✓			
Men wearing dreadlock hair style	✓			
Homosexuality	✓			
Lesbianism	✓			

LIECHTENSTEIN

	Is customary Is allowed Is permissible Is used Is OK	Is not customary Is frowned upon	Is disallowed Is forbidden Is a crime	(See last page for comments on items referenced here)
Females covering their hair (wearing headgear) in public	✓			
Females exposing their full face in public		✓		
Females driving automobiles	✓			
Females riding motorcycles	✓			
Females riding bicycles	✓			
Females smoking in public		✓		
Women wearing bras (braziers) in public		✓		
Use of lipstick by women	✓			
A woman extending her hands first when introduced	✓			
Female bashing		✓		
Females wearing trousers	✓			
Females wearing minis (short dresses)	✓			
Females wearing bikinis	✓			
Females wearing shorts	✓			
Persons of opposite sex holding hands in public	✓			
Persons of same sex holding hands in public	✓			
Handshake between opposite sex	✓			
Hugging in public by same sex	✓			
Hugging in public by opposite sex	✓			
Men and women walking side by side in public				n/a
Man walking ahead (in public), with the woman following				n/a
Woman walking ahead (in public), with the man following				n/a
Men opening doors for women	✓			
Sitting with legs crossed in the presence of elders	✓			
Talking to an elderly person with one's hat/cap on				n/a
Talking to an elderly person with hands positioned on both sides of one's waist				n/a
Blowing one's nose in public	✓			
Blowing one's nose in the presence of others	✓			
Addressing people by their title	✓			

LIECHTENSTEIN

	Is customary Is allowed Is permissible Is used. Is OK	Is not customary Is frowned upon	Is disallowed Is forbidden Is a crime	(See last page for comments on items referenced here)
Addressing people by their family name/surname/last name/given name	✓			
Addressing people by their first name/ given name		✓		
Women going through doors first	✓			
Men helping women with their coats	✓			
Men extending their hands to women first during greetings	✓			
Taking off one's hat when entering a private home	✓			
Removing one's shoes when entering a private home				n/a
Invited guests bringing food at social gatherings		✓		
Guests bringing drinks at social gatherings		✓		
Shaking hands when leaving a small group	✓			
Shaking hands with everyone present, upon arrival at a social gathering		✓		
Eating with the right hand		✓		
Eating with the left hand	✓			
Eating with both hands				n/a
Presenting a gift or passing on an object with the left hand	✓			
Asking a man about his wife	✓			
Asking a woman about her husband	✓			
Making prior appointments before a meeting or visit	✓			
Addressing an audience with one or both hands in the pocket	✓			
Carrying on conversation during meals				n/a
Females sitting with legs crossed	✓			
People discussing their wealth		✓		
Asking someone his or her age, or how old the person is	✓			
Complementing someone on his/her physical looks	✓			
Complementing someone on his/her attire	✓			
Use of both hands in handshake	✓			
In greeting, a handshake accompanied by a slight bow	✓			

LIECHTENSTEIN

	Is customary Is allowed Is permissible Is used. Is OK	Is not customary Is frowned upon	Is disallowed Is forbidden Is a crime	(See last page for comments on items referenced here)
Salutations such as "Good morning", "Good afternoon", "Good evening"	✓			
The completion of a business deal with a handshake				n/a
Starting a negotiation session with a handshake				n/a
A gift for the host/hostess	✓			
Giving a business gift	✓			
A gift of money (use of money as gift)		✓		
Use of flowers as a gift	✓			
Use of business cards	✓			
Accepting/presenting gifts with both hands	✓			
Burning of the country's flag		✓		
Mutilation of the national currency		✓		
Casual wearing of clothings made with colors & marks of the national flag				n/a
Wearing of look-alike military (camouflage) fatigues (attire)		✓		
Sitting on the floor (on floor mats)	✓			
Discussion of religion	✓			
Discussion of politics	✓			
Discussion of sex		✓		
Patting/slapping someone on the buttocks	✓			
Patting/slapping someone on the back		✓		
Touching or patting someone's head/hair		✓		
Casual touching of any part of someone's body				n/a
Drinking directly out of a bottle/can	✓			
Placing one's leg(s) on the table or chair	✓			

LIECHTENSTEIN

	Is customary Is allowed Is permissible Is used. Is OK	Is not customary Is frowned upon	Is disallowed Is forbidden Is a crime	(See last page for comments on items referenced here)
Showing the sole of one's foot (feet)				n/a
People standing very close when talking		✓		
Maintaining steady eye contact (direct gaze) when talking to someone	✓			
Kissing or exchange of kisses on the cheek	✓			
Counting money (change) in someone's palm				n/a
Finger pointing in public (in a daring manner)		✓		
Seeking attention by winking the eyes				n/a
Tapping the head to indicate someone is crazy				n/a
Twirling the head to indicate someone is crazy				n/a
Whistling as a way of requesting something/seeking attention				n/a
Using "thumbs-up" sign to mean OK				n/a
Forming a circle with the thumb and index finger (forefinger) to mean OK				n/a
Using the fingers to make a "V" sign for victory				n/a
Beckoning to someone with the index finger (forefinger)				n/a
The left to right waving of the hand with open palms facing outward to indicate "Good bye"				n/a
The use of a nod to show acknowledgement				n/a
Stopping/beckoning a taxi using a stretched hand with the thumb pointing upward				n/a
Using the thumb finger pointed to a direction, to request a ride or a hike				n/a
Raising one's hand/waving with an open fist to summon a taxi				n/a
Tapping one's foot/feet on the floor in a public gathering				n/a
Wiggling one's leg(s) when in a sitting position				n/a
Use of the hand (by motorists and cyclists) to signal direction of traffic				n/a

LIECHTENSTEIN

		(See last page for comments on items referenced here)
Foreign tourists are welcome in the country.	yes	
The use of seat belt is mandatory.	yes	
International driving license is accepted.	yes	
U.S. driver's license is accepted.	yes	
It is considered impolite to yawn in public.	no	
Death penalty for drug trafficking is the law.	no	
Life imprisonment for drug trafficking is the law.	no	
Guilty until proven innocent in court is the law.	no	
Innocent until proven guilty in court is the law.	yes	
Pedestrians always have right of way.	yes	
Exit visas are required of visitors.	no	
Crash helmet is mandatory for motor cyclist.	yes	
Hanging is used as a form of legal punishment.	no	
Decapitation of a limb is used as a form of punishment.	no	
Caning is used as a form of legal punishment.	no	
Electric shock is used as a form of legal punishment.	no	
One is expected to stand up during the playing of the national anthem.	no	
Crash helmet is mandatory for bicyclists.	no	
Guests are expected to eat every thing on their plates.	no	
Table manners are very informal.	no	
One is expected to cover one's mouth when laughing.	no	
A vertical nod of the head means YES (OK).	no	
A horizontal shaking of the head means NO (Not OK).	yes	
Prostitution is allowed only in designated areas.	yes	
One is expected to take off one's hat during playing of national anthem.	yes	
Separate seating arrangements (between sexes) are maintained at movies.	no	
Separate seating arrangements (between sexes) are maintained at churches.	no	
Uninvited visitors or guests may not be welcome, even among acquaintances.	no	
Pets (e.g. cats, dog) are allowed in some hotels and restaurants.	yes	
Couples invited for a meal may be separated during meals according to their sex.	yes	
Punctuality is the order of business.	yes	
Automobiles are driven with headlights always turned on.		n/a
Motorcycles are driven with headlights always turned on.		n/a
Visitors with expired visa face mandatory jail time.	yes	
Visitors without exit visa face jail time.	yes	
Visitors without entry visa face mandatory (automatic) jail time.	yes	

ADDITIONAL COUNTRY INFORMATION

(A)	**The types of gifts to avoid:**	n/a
(B)	**Appropriate gifts for a foreigner to give:**	n/a
(C)	**Best time to present gifts (at the beginning or at the end of a visit?):**	n/a
(D)	**Best time to present gifts (on initial or later visits?):**	n/a
(E)	**Best place to present gifts (in private or in public?):**	n/a
(F)	**Number(s) with certain connotations and/or myths attached to them:**	n/a
(G)	**Basic shape(s) with negative connotations:**	n/a
(H)	**Basic color(s) with negative connotations:**	n/a
(I)	**Traditional greeting methods include:**	n/a
(J)	**Safe topics for discussion include:**	weather, fashion, travel, art,family, religion, domestic politics, foods, sports, international politics, social conditions, money and personal wealth, sex.
(K)	**Best time for conversations (before, during, after meals?):**	n/a
(L)	**Forms of legal punishment:**	n/a
(M)	**Approximately length of time one could be detained by law and order authorities before being charged in court:**	n/a
(N)	**January 15, 1999, for example, will normally be written as:**	Swiss Francs
(O)	**Emergency code number**:	117
(P)	**Ambulance code Number**:	144
(Q)	**Police code number:**	117
(R)	**Telephone (country) code:**	41
(S)	**Telex (country) code:**	845
(T)	**Electricity requirements**:	n/a
(U)	**Legal drinking age:**	16
(V)	**Systems of weights and measures:**	n/a
(W)	**Legal age of incarceration**:	n/a
(X)	**Driving side of the road:**	n/a
(Y)	**Minimum expenditure expected of foreign visitors? $**	no
(Z)	**Name of currency**:	Swiss Francs
(Za)	**Some places 0ff-limits to foreign visitors:**	n/a
(Zb)	**Some places, structures and items prohibited from being photographed:**	n/a

MACEDONIA	Is customary Is allowed Is permissible Is used. Is OK	Is not customary Is frowned upon	Is disallowed Is forbidden Is a crime	(See last page for comments on items referenced here)
Smoking in public			✓	
Eating in public	✓			
Not flushing public toilet		✓		
Spitting in public		✓		
Feeding animals & birds in public	✓			
Whistling in public		✓		
Drinking alcohol in public			✓	
Kissing in public		✓		
Breast feeding in public		✓		
Drunkenness (in public)			✓	
Cursing in public		✓		
Religious preaching in public			✓	
Begging (panhandling) in public		✓		
Giving money to beggars/panhandlers	✓			
Giving food/drink to beggars/panhandlers	✓			
Brushing teeth in public (other than in restrooms)		✓		
Strolling with pets in major public roads/streets	✓			
Chewing gum in public	✓			
Chewing gum in government offices		✓		
Combing hair in public (other than in toilets/restrooms)		✓		
Undressing/dressing in public		✓		
Wearing of dark glasses indoors in public places	✓			
Public display of wealth		✓		
Praying openly in public in non-designated areas		✓		
Walking bare feet in public		✓		
Chewing tobacco in public		✓		
Trimming one's finger or toe nails in public		✓		
Laughing aloud in public		✓		
Mingling of the sexes in public	✓			
Mixed bathing in public swimming pools	✓			
Distributing religious pamphlets (literature) in public/side streets			✓	

MACEDONIA

	Is customary Is allowed Is permissible Is used. Is OK	Is not customary Is frowned upon	Is disallowed Is forbidden Is a crime	(See last page for comments on items referenced here)
Dancing on side street		✓		
Nude bathing			✓	
Littering			✓	
Binge Drinking			✓	
hitchhiking	✓			
Jaywalking			✓	
Drunk driving			✓	
Speeding			✓	
Skating on side streets (side-walk)		✓		
Graffiti painting		✓		
Pilfering			✓	
Prostitution			✓	
Haggling in the market place	✓			
Consumption of alcoholic beverages in bars and restaurants	✓			
Gambling			✓	
Possession of pornographic materials		✓		
Possession of the Christian Bible	✓			
Possession of the Moslem Koran	✓			
Possession of bullet-proof vest				
Possession of toy gun	✓			
Possession of fire crackers and fireworks			✓	
Possession of prescription drugs (without doctor's note)	✓			
Possession of regulated drugs (narcotics)			✓	
Possession of firearms (by foreigners)			✓	
Possession of pocket knife in public		✓		
Using walkie talkies	✓			1
Using of "boom boxes"(loud sounding stereo system)		✓		2
Using "walkman" (very small radio/cassettes with ear plugs) in public places	✓			
Using "walkman" (very small radio/cassettes with ear plugs) while driving or riding		✓		

MACEDONIA

	Is customary Is allowed Is permissible Is used Is OK	Is not customary Is frowned upon	Is disallowed Is forbidden Is a crime	(See last page for comments on items referenced here)
Use of cellular phone	✓			
Use of binoculars/periscopes other than in sports arena	✓			
Taking photographs of people (without their permission)		✓		
Taking photographs at airports, train and bus stations		✓		
Taking photographs of airports			✓	
Taking photographs of churches and synagogues	✓			
Taking photographs of religious statues	✓			
Taking photographs of public buildings	✓			
Taking photographs of bridges				
Tipping (gratuity)	✓			
Tipping (when service is rendered)	✓			
Tipping (when service is not rendered)		✓		
Tipping waiters/waitresses at restaurants and hotels	✓			
Tipping taxi/cab drivers	✓			
Tipping baggage handlers, porters, door persons	✓			
Tipping of hair dressers/barbers	✓			
Overtipping	✓			
Undertipping	✓			
Spilling cigarette butt (ash) on side streets/on the floor		✓		
Men wearing lipstick		✓		
Wearing visible tattoo marks		✓		
Men painting/coloring their finger or toe nails		✓		
Cross dressing (men dressed like women & vice versa)		✓		
Walking in public without a shirt (i.e. with the upper half of the body naked)		✓		
Men wearing braided hair	✓			
Men wearing earrings	✓			
Men wearing dreadlock hair style	✓			
Homosexuality		✓		
Lesbianism		✓		

MACEDONIA

	Is customary Is allowed Is permissible Is used Is OK	Is not customary Is frowned upon	Is disallowed Is forbidden Is a crime	(See last page for comments on items referenced here)
Females covering their hair (wearing headgear) in public	✓			
Females exposing their full face in public	✓			
Females driving automobiles	✓			
Females riding motorcycles	✓			
Females riding bicycles	✓			
Females smoking in public			✓	
Women wearing bras (braziers) in public	✓			
Use of lipstick by women	✓			
A woman extending her hands first when introduced		✓		
Female bashing		✓		
Females wearing trousers	✓			
Females wearing minis (short dresses)	✓			
Females wearing bikinis	✓			
Females wearing shorts	✓			
Persons of opposite sex holding hands in public	✓			
Persons of same sex holding hands in public		✓		
Handshake between opposite sex	✓			
Hugging in public by same sex		✓		
Hugging in public by opposite sex	✓			
Men and women walking side by side in public	✓			
Man walking ahead (in public), with the woman following				
Woman walking ahead (in public), with the man following		✓		
Men opening doors for women	✓			
Sitting with legs crossed in the presence of elders	✓			
Talking to an elderly person with one's hat/cap on				
Talking to an elderly person with hands positioned on both sides of one's waist		✓		
Blowing one's nose in public		✓		
Blowing one's nose in the presence of others		✓		
Addressing people by their title	✓			

MACEDONIA

	Is customary Is allowed Is permissible Is used. Is OK	Is not customary Is frowned upon	Is disallowed Is forbidden Is a crime	(See last page for comments on items referenced here)
Addressing people by their family name/surname/last name/given name	✓			
Addressing people by their first name/ given name	✓			
Women going through doors first	✓			
Men helping women with their coats	✓			
Men extending their hands to women first during greetings	✓			
Taking off one's hat when entering a private home	✓			
Removing one's shoes when entering a private home	✓			
Invited guests bringing food at social gatherings		✓		
Guests bringing drinks at social gatherings		✓		
Shaking hands when leaving a small group	✓			
Shaking hands with everyone present, upon arrival at a social gathering	✓			
Eating with the right hand	✓			
Eating with the left hand	✓			
Eating with both hands		✓		
Presenting a gift or passing on an object with the left hand	✓			
Asking a man about his wife	✓			
Asking a woman about her husband	✓			
Making prior appointments before a meeting or visit	✓			
Addressing an audience with one or both hands in the pocket		✓		
Carrying on conversation during meals		✓		
Females sitting with legs crossed	✓			
People discussing their wealth		✓		
Asking someone his or her age, or how old the person is		✓		
Complementing someone on his/her physical looks	✓			
Complementing someone on his/her attire	✓			
Use of both hands in handshake	✓			
In greeting, a handshake accompanied by a slight bow	✓			

MACEDONIA

	Is customary Is allowed Is permissible Is used. Is OK	Is not customary Is frowned upon	Is disallowed Is forbidden Is a crime	(See last page for comments on items referenced here)
Salutations such as "Good morning", "Good afternoon", "Good evening"	✓			
The completion of a business deal with a handshake	✓			
Starting a negotiation session with a handshake	✓			
A gift for the host/hostess	✓			
Giving a business gift	✓			
A gift of money (use of money as gift)	✓			
Use of flowers as a gift	✓			
Use of business cards	✓			
Accepting/presenting gifts with both hands	✓			
Burning of the country's flag			✓	
Mutilation of the national currency			✓	
Casual wearing of clothings made with colors & marks of the national flag		✓		
Wearing of look-alike military (camouflage) fatigues (attire)		✓		
Sitting on the floor (on floor mats)		✓		
Discussion of religion	✓			
Discussion of politics	✓			
Discussion of sex	✓			
Patting/slapping someone on the buttocks		✓		
Patting/slapping someone on the back	✓			
Touching or patting someone's head/hair		✓		
Casual touching of any part of someone's body		✓		
Drinking directly out of a bottle/can		✓		
Placing one's leg(s) on the table or chair		✓		

MACEDONIA

	Is customary Is allowed Is permissible Is used. Is OK	Is not customary Is frowned upon	Is disallowed Is forbidden Is a crime	(See last page for comments on items referenced here)
Showing the sole of one's foot (feet)		✓		
People standing very close when talking	✓			
Maintaining steady eye contact (direct gaze) when talking to someone	✓			
Kissing or exchange of kisses on the cheek	✓			
Counting money (change) in someone's palm		✓		
Finger pointing in public (in a daring manner)		✓		
Seeking attention by winking the eyes		✓		
Tapping the head to indicate someone is crazy		✓		
Twirling the head to indicate someone is crazy		✓		
Whistling as a way of requesting something/seeking attention		✓		
Using "thumbs-up" sign to mean OK	✓			
Forming a circle with the thumb and index finger (forefinger) to mean OK	✓			
Using the fingers to make a "V" sign for victory		✓		
Beckoning to someone with the index finger (forefinger)		✓		
The left to right waving of the hand with open palms facing outward to indicate "Good bye"	✓			
The use of a nod to show acknowledgement	✓			
Stopping/beckoning a taxi using a stretched hand with the thumb pointing upward	✓			
Using the thumb finger pointed to a direction, to request a ride or a hike	✓			
Raising one's hand/waving with an open fist to summon a taxi	✓			
Tapping one's foot/feet on the floor in a public gathering		✓		
Wiggling one's leg(s) when in a sitting position	✓			
Use of the hand (by motorists and cyclists) to signal direction of traffic	✓			

MACEDONIA

		(See last page for comments on items referenced here)
Foreign tourists are welcome in the country.	yes	
The use of seat belt is mandatory.	yes	
International driving license is accepted.	yes	
U.S. driver's license is accepted.	yes	
It is considered impolite to yawn in public.	yes	
Death penalty for drug trafficking is the law.	no	
Life imprisonment for drug trafficking is the law.	no	
Guilty until proven innocent in court is the law.	no	
Innocent until proven guilty in court is the law.	yes	
Pedestrians always have right of way.	yes	
Exit visas are required of visitors.	no	
Crash helmet is mandatory for motor cyclist.	yes	
Hanging is used as a form of legal punishment.	no	
Decapitation of a limb is used as a form of punishment.	no	
Caning is used as a form of legal punishment.	no	
Electric shock is used as a form of legal punishment.	no	
One is expected to stand up during the playing of the national anthem.	yes	
Crash helmet is mandatory for bicyclists.	yes	
Guests are expected to eat every thing on their plates.	no	
Table manners are very informal.	no	
One is expected to cover one's mouth when laughing.	yes	
A vertical nod of the head means YES (OK).	yes	
A horizontal shaking of the head means NO (Not OK).	yes	
Prostitution is allowed only in designated areas.	no	
One is expected to take off one's hat during playing of national anthem.	yes	
Separate seating arrangements (between sexes) are maintained at movies.	no	
Separate seating arrangements (between sexes) are maintained at churches.	no	
Uninvited visitors or guests may not be welcome, even among acquaintances.	yes	
Pets (e.g. cats, dog) are allowed in some hotels and restaurants.	yes	
Couples invited for a meal may be separated during meals according to their sex.	yes	
Punctuality is the order of business.	yes	
Automobiles are driven with headlights always turned on.	no	
Motorcycles are driven with headlights always turned on.	no	
Visitors with expired visa face mandatory jail time.	no	
Visitors without exit visa face jail time.	no	
Visitors without entry visa face mandatory (automatic) jail time.	no	

ADDITIONAL COUNTRY INFORMATION

(A)	**The types of gifts to avoid:**	n/a
(B)	**Appropriate gifts for a foreigner to give:**	souvenirs
(C)	**Best time to present gifts (at the beginning or at the end of a visit?):**	at the beginning
(D)	**Best time to present gifts (on initial or later visits?):**	initial
(E)	**Best place to present gifts (in private or in public?):**	in private
(F)	**Number(s) with certain connotations and/or myths attached to them:**	13 (bad luck)
(G)	**Basic shape(s) with negative connotations:**	n/a
(H)	**Basic color(s) with negative connotations:**	black
(I)	**Traditional greeting methods include:**	a handshake, hug, a kiss, a nod, patting the other's back.
(J)	**Safe topics for discussion include:**	weather, fashion, travel, art, family, food, sports
(K)	**Best time for conversations (before, during, after meals?):**	after
(L)	**Forms of legal punishment:**	jailing
(M)	**Approximately length of time one could be detained by law and order authorities before being charged in court:**	from 24 hours till 90 days
(N)	**January 15, 1999, for example, will normally be written as:**	15.01.99
(O)	**Emergency code number:**	94
(P)	**Ambulance code Number:**	n/a
(Q)	**Police code number:**	92
(R)	**Telephone (country) code:**	389
(S)	**Telex (country) code:**	597
(T)	**Electricity requirements:**	220V
(U)	**Legal drinking age:**	18
(V)	**Systems of weights and measures:**	metric system
(W)	**Legal age of incarceration:**	18
(X)	**Driving side of the road:**	right
(Y)	**Minimum expenditure expected of foreign visitors? $**	n/a
(Z)	**Name of currency:**	denar
(Za)	**Some places 0ff-limits to foreign visitors:**	n/a
(Zb)	**Some places, structures and items prohibited from being photographed:**	military and selected infrastructure objects.

ENDNOTES

Item Number: COMMENTS/EXPLANATIONS

n/a: Not applicable/Not available/No response

(1) Only on allowed frequencies

(2) With permit.

MALTA	Is customary Is allowed Is permissible Is used. Is OK	Is not customary Is frowned upon	Is disallowed Is forbidden Is a crime	(See last page for comments on items referenced here)
Smoking in public	✓			
Eating in public	✓			
Not flushing public toilet		✓		
Spitting in public			✓	
Feeding animals & birds in public	✓			
Whistling in public		✓		
Drinking alcohol in public	✓			
Kissing in public		✓		
Breast feeding in public	✓			
Drunkenness (in public)			✓	
Cursing in public			✓	
Religious preaching in public	✓			
Begging (panhandling) in public			✓	
Giving money to beggars/panhandlers	✓			
Giving food/drink to beggars/panhandlers	✓			
Brushing teeth in public (other than in restrooms)		✓		
Strolling with pets in major public roads/streets	✓			
Chewing gum in public	✓			
Chewing gum in government offices		✓		
Combing hair in public (other than in toilets/restrooms)		✓		
Undressing/dressing in public			✓	
Wearing of dark glasses indoors in public places	✓			
Public display of wealth	✓			
Praying openly in public in non-designated areas	✓			
Walking bare feet in public		✓		
Chewing tobacco in public		✓		
Trimming one's finger or toe nails in public		✓		
Laughing aloud in public	✓			
Mingling of the sexes in public	✓			
Mixed bathing in public swimming pools	✓			
Distributing religious pamphlets (literature) in public/side streets	✓			

MALTA

	Is customary Is allowed Is permissible Is used. Is OK	Is not customary Is frowned upon	Is disallowed Is forbidden Is a crime	(See last page for comments on items referenced here)
Dancing on side street		✓		
Nude bathing			✓	
Littering			✓	
Binge Drinking	✓			
hitchhiking		✓		
Jaywalking				n/a
Drunk driving			✓	
Speeding			✓	
Skating on side streets (side-walk)			✓	
Graffiti painting			✓	
Pilfering			✓	
Prostitution	✓			
Haggling in the market place	✓			
Consumption of alcoholic beverages in bars and restaurants	✓			
Gambling	✓			
Possession of pornographic materials			✓	
Possession of the Christian Bible	✓			
Possession of the Moslem Koran	✓			
Possession of bullet-proof vest	✓			
Possession of toy gun	✓			
Possession of fire crackers and fireworks		✓		
Possession of prescription drugs (without doctor's note)			✓	
Possession of regulated drugs (narcotics)			✓	
Possession of firearms (by foreigners)			✓	
Possession of pocket knife in public			✓	
Using walkie talkies			✓	
Using of "boom boxes"(loud sounding stereo system)			✓	
Using "walkman" (very small radio/cassettes with ear plugs) in public places	✓			
Using "walkman" (very small radio/cassettes with ear plugs) while driving or riding			✓	

MALTA

	Is customary Is allowed Is permissible Is used Is OK	Is not customary Is frowned upon	Is disallowed Is forbidden Is a crime	(See last page for comments on items referenced here)
Use of cellular phone	✓			
Use of binoculars/periscopes other than in sports arena		✓		
Taking photographs of people (without their permission)			✓	
Taking photographs at airports, train and bus stations	✓			
Taking photographs of airports	✓			
Taking photographs of churches and synagogues	✓			
Taking photographs of religious statues	✓			
Taking photographs of public buildings	✓			
Taking photographs of bridges	✓			
Tipping (gratuity)	✓			
Tipping (when service is rendered)	✓			
Tipping (when service is not rendered)	✓			
Tipping waiters/waitresses at restaurants and hotels	✓			
Tipping taxi/cab drivers	✓			
Tipping baggage handlers, porters, door persons	✓			
Tipping of hair dressers/barbers	✓			
Overtipping	✓			
Undertipping		✓		
Spilling cigarette butt (ash) on side streets/on the floor		✓		
Men wearing lipstick		✓		
Wearing visible tattoo marks		✓		
Men painting/coloring their finger or toe nails		✓		
Cross dressing (men dressed like women & vice versa)			✓	
Walking in public without a shirt (i.e. with the upper half of the body naked)			✓	
Men wearing braided hair	✓			
Men wearing earrings	✓			
Men wearing dreadlock hair style	✓			
Homosexuality	✓			
Lesbianism	✓			

MALTA

	Is customary Is allowed Is permissible Is used Is OK	Is not customary Is frowned upon	Is disallowed Is forbidden Is a crime	(See last page for comments on items referenced here)
Females covering their hair (wearing headgear) in public	✓			
Females exposing their full face in public	✓			
Females driving automobiles	✓			
Females riding motorcycles	✓			
Females riding bicycles	✓			
Females smoking in public	✓			
Women wearing bras (braziers) in public			✓	
Use of lipstick by women	✓			
A woman extending her hands first when introduced			✓	
Female bashing		✓		
Females wearing trousers	✓			
Females wearing minis (short dresses)	✓			
Females wearing bikinis	✓			1
Females wearing shorts	✓			
Persons of opposite sex holding hands in public	✓			
Persons of same sex holding hands in public		✓		
Handshake between opposite sex	✓			
Hugging in public by same sex		✓		
Hugging in public by opposite sex		✓		
Men and women walking side by side in public	✓			
Man walking ahead (in public), with the woman following	✓			
Woman walking ahead (in public), with the man following	✓			
Men opening doors for women	✓			
Sitting with legs crossed in the presence of elders	✓			
Talking to an elderly person with one's hat/cap on		✓		
Talking to an elderly person with hands positioned on both sides of one's waist		✓		
Blowing one's nose in public	✓			
Blowing one's nose in the presence of others	✓			
Addressing people by their title	✓			

MALTA

	Is customary Is allowed Is permissible Is used. Is OK	Is not customary Is frowned upon	Is disallowed Is forbidden Is a crime	(See last page for comments on items referenced here)
Addressing people by their family name/surname/last name/given name	✓			
Addressing people by their first name/ given name	✓			
Women going through doors first	✓			
Men helping women with their coats	✓			
Men extending their hands to women first during greetings	✓			
Taking off one's hat when entering a private home	✓			
Removing one's shoes when entering a private home		✓		
Invited guests bringing food at social gatherings		✓		
Guests bringing drinks at social gatherings		✓		
Shaking hands when leaving a small group	✓			
Shaking hands with everyone present, upon arrival at a social gathering	✓			
Eating with the right hand	✓			
Eating with the left hand		✓		
Eating with both hands		✓		
Presenting a gift or passing on an object with the left hand		✓		
Asking a man about his wife		✓		
Asking a woman about her husband		✓		
Making prior appointments before a meeting or visit	✓			
Addressing an audience with one or both hands in the pocket		✓		
Carrying on conversation during meals	✓			
Females sitting with legs crossed	✓			
People discussing their wealth		✓		
Asking someone his or her age, or how old the person is		✓		
Complementing someone on his/her physical looks	✓			
Complementing someone on his/her attire	✓			
Use of both hands in handshake		✓		
In greeting, a handshake accompanied by a slight bow		✓		

MALTA

	Is customary Is allowed Is permissible Is used. Is OK	Is not customary Is frowned upon	Is disallowed Is forbidden Is a crime	(See last page for comments on items referenced here)
Salutations such as "Good morning", "Good afternoon", "Good evening"	✓			
The completion of a business deal with a handshake	✓			
Starting a negotiation session with a handshake	✓			
A gift for the host/hostess	✓			
Giving a business gift		✓		
A gift of money (use of money as gift)		✓		
Use of flowers as a gift	✓			
Use of business cards	✓			
Accepting/presenting gifts with both hands		✓		
Burning of the country's flag			✓	
Mutilation of the national currency			✓	
Casual wearing of clothings made with colors & marks of the national flag			✓	
Wearing of look-alike military (camouflage) fatigues (attire)			✓	
Sitting on the floor (on floor mats)		✓		
Discussion of religion	✓			
Discussion of politics	✓			
Discussion of sex	✓			
Patting/slapping someone on the buttocks			✓	
Patting/slapping someone on the back		✓		
Touching or patting someone's head/hair		✓		
Casual touching of any part of someone's body			✓	
Drinking directly out of a bottle/can		✓		
Placing one's leg(s) on the table or chair		✓		

MALTA

	Is customary Is allowed Is permissible Is used. Is OK	Is not customary Is frowned upon	Is disallowed Is forbidden Is a crime	(See last page for comments on items referenced here)
Showing the sole of one's foot (feet)		✓		
People standing very close when talking		✓		
Maintaining steady eye contact (direct gaze) when talking to someone		✓		
Kissing or exchange of kisses on the cheek	✓			
Counting money (change) in someone's palm	✓			
Finger pointing in public (in a daring manner)		✓		
Seeking attention by winking the eyes		✓		
Tapping the head to indicate someone is crazy		✓		
Twirling the head to indicate someone is crazy		✓		
Whistling as a way of requesting something/seeking attention		✓		
Using "thumbs-up" sign to mean OK	✓			
Forming a circle with the thumb and index finger (forefinger) to mean OK		✓		
Using the fingers to make a "V" sign for victory	✓			
Beckoning to someone with the index finger (forefinger)		✓		
The left to right waving of the hand with open palms facing outward to indicate "Good bye"	✓			
The use of a nod to show acknowledgement	✓			
Stopping/beckoning a taxi using a stretched hand with the thumb pointing upward		✓		
Using the thumb finger pointed to a direction, to request a ride or a hike	✓			
Raising one's hand/waving with an open fist to summon a taxi		✓		
Tapping one's foot/feet on the floor in a public gathering		✓		
Wiggling one's leg(s) when in a sitting position		✓		
Use of the hand (by motorists and cyclists) to signal direction of traffic	✓			

MALTA

		(See last page for comments on items referenced here)
Foreign tourists are welcome in the country.	yes	
The use of seat belt is mandatory.	yes	
International driving license is accepted.	yes	
U.S. driver's license is accepted.	no	
It is considered impolite to yawn in public.	no	
Death penalty for drug trafficking is the law.	no	
Life imprisonment for drug trafficking is the law.	no	
Guilty until proven innocent in court is the law.	yes	
Innocent until proven guilty in court is the law.	yes	
Pedestrians always have right of way.	yes	
Exit visas are required of visitors.	no	
Crash helmet is mandatory for motor cyclist.	yes	
Hanging is used as a form of legal punishment.	no	
Decapitation of a limb is used as a form of punishment.	no	
Caning is used as a form of legal punishment.	no	
Electric shock is used as a form of legal punishment.	no	
One is expected to stand up during the playing of the national anthem.	yes	
Crash helmet is mandatory for bicyclists.	no	
Guests are expected to eat every thing on their plates.	no	
Table manners are very informal.	yes	
One is expected to cover one's mouth when laughing.	no	
A vertical nod of the head means YES (OK).	yes	
A horizontal shaking of the head means NO (Not OK).	yes	
Prostitution is allowed only in designated areas.	no	
One is expected to take off one's hat during playing of national anthem.	yes	
Separate seating arrangements (between sexes) are maintained at movies.	no	
Separate seating arrangements (between sexes) are maintained at churches.	no	
Uninvited visitors or guests may not be welcome, even among acquaintances.	yes	
Pets (e.g. cats, dog) are allowed in some hotels and restaurants.	no	
Couples invited for a meal may be separated during meals according to their sex.	no	
Punctuality is the order of business.	yes	
Automobiles are driven with headlights always turned on.	no	
Motorcycles are driven with headlights always turned on.	yes	
Visitors with expired visa face mandatory jail time.	yes	
Visitors without exit visa face jail time.	no	
Visitors without entry visa face mandatory (automatic) jail time.	yes	

MALTA

(A)	**The types of gifts to avoid:**	n/a
(B)	**Appropriate gifts for a foreigner to give:**	books, silverware
(C)	**Best time to present gifts (at the beginning or at the end of a visit?):**	at the end of visit
(D)	**Best time to present gifts (on initial or later visits?):**	initial
(E)	**Best place to present gifts (in private or in public?):**	depends on the occasion
(F)	**Number(s) with certain connotations and/or myths attached to them:**	n/a
(G)	**Basic shape(s) with negative connotations:**	n/a
(H)	**Basic color(s) with negative connotations:**	n/a
(I)	**Traditional greeting methods include:**	handshake
(J)	**Safe topics for discussion include:**	weather, fashion, travel, art, family, religion, domestic politics, food, sports international politics, social conditions, money and personal wealth sex.
(K)	**Best time for conversations (before, during, after meals?):**	anytime
(L)	**Forms of legal punishment:**	jailing
(M)	**Approximately length of time one could be detained by law and order authorities before being charged in court:**	48 hours
(N)	**January 15, 1999, for example, will normally be written as:**	15/1/99
(O)	**Emergency code number**:	191
(P)	**Ambulance code Number**:	196
(Q)	**Police code number:**	191
(R)	**Telephone (country) code:**	00356
(S)	**Telex (country) code:**	00356
(T)	**Electricity requirements**:	220volts
(U)	**Legal drinking age:**	18
(V)	**Systems of weights and measures:**	kilo
(W)	**Legal age of incarceration**:	n/a
(X)	**Driving side of the road:**	left
(Y)	**Minimum expenditure expected of foreign visitors? $**	none
(Z)	**Name of currency**:	Maltese Lira
(Za)	**Some places 0ff-limits to foreign visitors:**	clearly indicated areas
(Zb)	**Some places, structures and items prohibited from being photographed:**	n/a

ENDNOTES

Item Number: COMMENTS/EXPLANATIONS

n/a: Not applicable/Not available/No response

(1) Only on beaches

MONACO	Is customary Is allowed Is permissible Is used. Is OK	Is not customary Is frowned upon	Is disallowed Is forbidden Is a crime	(See last page for comments on items referenced here)
Smoking in public	✓			
Eating in public		✓		
Not flushing public toilet		✓		
Spitting in public		✓		
Feeding animals & birds in public	✓			
Whistling in public	✓			
Drinking alcohol in public			✓	
Kissing in public	✓			
Breast feeding in public	✓			
Drunkenness (in public)			✓	
Cursing in public			✓	
Religious preaching in public	✓			
Begging (panhandling) in public		✓		
Giving money to beggars/panhandlers	✓			
Giving food/drink to beggars/panhandlers		✓		
Brushing teeth in public (other than in restrooms)		✓		
Strolling with pets in major public roads/streets	✓			
Chewing gum in public	✓			
Chewing gum in government offices	✓			
Combing hair in public (other than in toilets/restrooms)	✓			
Undressing/dressing in public	✓			
Wearing of dark glasses indoors in public places	✓			
Public display of wealth	✓			
Praying openly in public in non-designated areas		✓		
Walking bare feet in public			✓	
Chewing tobacco in public		✓		
Trimming one's finger or toe nails in public		✓		
Laughing aloud in public	✓			
Mingling of the sexes in public	✓			
Mixed bathing in public swimming pools	✓			
Distributing religious pamphlets (literature) in public/side streets				n/a

MONACO

	Is customary Is allowed Is permissible Is used. Is OK	Is not customary Is frowned upon	Is disallowed Is forbidden Is a crime	(See last page for comments on items referenced here)
Dancing on side street			✓	
Nude bathing			✓	
Littering			✓	
Binge Drinking			✓	
hitchhiking			✓	
Jaywalking			✓	
Drunk driving			✓	
Speeding	✓			
Skating on side streets (side-walk)			✓	
Graffiti painting			✓	
Pilfering			✓	
Prostitution			✓	
Haggling in the market place		✓		
Consumption of alcoholic beverages in bars and restaurants	✓			
Gambling	✓			
Possession of pornographic materials		✓		
Possession of the Christian Bible	✓			
Possession of the Moslem Koran	✓			
Possession of bullet-proof vest	✓			
Possession of toy gun	✓			
Possession of fire crackers and fireworks	✓			
Possession of prescription drugs (without doctor's note)			✓	
Possession of regulated drugs (narcotics)			✓	
Possession of firearms (by foreigners)			✓	
Possession of pocket knife in public			✓	
Using walkie talkies	✓			
Using of "boom boxes"(loud sounding stereo system)	✓			
Using "walkman" (very small radio/cassettes with ear plugs) in public places	✓			
Using "walkman" (very small radio/cassettes with ear plugs) while driving or riding	✓			

MONACO

	Is customary Is allowed Is permissible Is used Is OK	Is not customary Is frowned upon	Is disallowed Is forbidden Is a crime	(See last page for comments on items referenced here)
Use of cellular phone	✓			
Use of binoculars/periscopes other than in sports arena	✓			
Taking photographs of people (without their permission)	✓			
Taking photographs at airports, train and bus stations		✓		
Taking photographs of airports				n/a
Taking photographs of churches and synagogues	✓			
Taking photographs of religious statues	✓			
Taking photographs of public buildings	✓			
Taking photographs of bridges				n/a
Tipping (gratuity)	✓			
Tipping (when service is rendered)	✓			
Tipping (when service is not rendered)	✓			
Tipping waiters/waitresses at restaurants and hotels		✓		
Tipping taxi/cab drivers	✓			
Tipping baggage handlers, porters, door persons	✓			
Tipping of hair dressers/barbers	✓			
Overtipping		✓		
Undertipping	✓			
Spilling cigarette butt (ash) on side streets/on the floor	✓			
Men wearing lipstick	✓			
Wearing visible tattoo marks	✓			
Men painting/coloring their finger or toe nails		✓		
Cross dressing (men dressed like women & vice versa)		✓		
Walking in public without a shirt (i.e. with the upper half of the body naked)			✓	
Men wearing braided hair				n/a
Men wearing earrings		✓		
Men wearing dreadlock hair style		✓		
Homosexuality		✓		
Lesbianism		✓		

MONACO

	Is customary Is allowed Is permissible Is used Is OK	Is not customary Is frowned upon	Is disallowed Is forbidden Is a crime	(See last page for comments on items referenced here)
Females covering their hair (wearing headgear) in public		✓		
Females exposing their full face in public	✓			
Females driving automobiles	✓			
Females riding motorcycles	✓			
Females riding bicycles	✓			
Females smoking in public	✓			
Women wearing bras (braziers) in public			✓	
Use of lipstick by women	✓			
A woman extending her hands first when introduced		✓		
Female bashing	✓			
Females wearing trousers	✓			
Females wearing minis (short dresses)	✓			
Females wearing bikinis	✓			
Females wearing shorts	✓			
Persons of opposite sex holding hands in public	✓			
Persons of same sex holding hands in public		✓		
Handshake between opposite sex	✓			
Hugging in public by same sex	✓			
Hugging in public by opposite sex	✓			
Men and women walking side by side in public	✓			
Man walking ahead (in public), with the woman following		✓		
Woman walking ahead (in public), with the man following				n/a
Men opening doors for women	✓			
Sitting with legs crossed in the presence of elders	✓			
Talking to an elderly person with one's hat/cap on				n/a
Talking to an elderly person with hands positioned on both sides of one's waist				n/a
Blowing one's nose in public	✓			
Blowing one's nose in the presence of others	✓			
Addressing people by their title	✓			

MONACO

	Is customary Is allowed Is permissible Is used. Is OK	Is not customary Is frowned upon	Is disallowed Is forbidden Is a crime	(See last page for comments on items referenced here)
Addressing people by their family name/surname/last name/given name	✓			
Addressing people by their first name/ given name	✓			
Women going through doors first	✓			
Men helping women with their coats	✓			
Men extending their hands to women first during greetings	✓			
Taking off one's hat when entering a private home	✓			
Removing one's shoes when entering a private home				n/a
Invited guests bringing food at social gatherings		✓		
Guests bringing drinks at social gatherings		✓		
Shaking hands when leaving a small group	✓			
Shaking hands with everyone present, upon arrival at a social gathering	✓			
Eating with the right hand				n/a
Eating with the left hand				n/a
Eating with both hands	✓			
Presenting a gift or passing on an object with the left hand				n/a
Asking a man about his wife		✓		
Asking a woman about her husband		✓		
Making prior appointments before a meeting or visit	✓			
Addressing an audience with one or both hands in the pocket		✓		
Carrying on conversation during meals				n/a
Females sitting with legs crossed	✓			
People discussing their wealth	✓			
Asking someone his or her age, or how old the person is				n/a
Complementing someone on his/her physical looks				n/a
Complementing someone on his/her attire	✓			
Use of both hands in handshake		✓		
In greeting, a handshake accompanied by a slight bow		✓		

MONACO

	Is customary Is allowed Is permissible Is used. Is OK	Is not customary Is frowned upon	Is disallowed Is forbidden Is a crime	(See last page for comments on items referenced here)
Salutations such as "Good morning", "Good afternoon", "Good evening"	✓			
The completion of a business deal with a handshake				n/a
Starting a negotiation session with a handshake				n/a
A gift for the host/hostess	✓			
Giving a business gift	✓			
A gift of money (use of money as gift)		✓		
Use of flowers as a gift	✓			
Use of business cards	✓			
Accepting/presenting gifts with both hands		✓		
Burning of the country's flag			✓	
Mutilation of the national currency			✓	
Casual wearing of clothings made with colors & marks of the national flag				n/a
Wearing of look-alike military (camouflage) fatigues (attire)	✓			
Sitting on the floor (on floor mats)		✓		
Discussion of religion	✓			
Discussion of politics	✓			
Discussion of sex	✓			
Patting/slapping someone on the buttocks			✓	
Patting/slapping someone on the back	✓			
Touching or patting someone's head/hair	✓			
Casual touching of any part of someone's body				n/a
Drinking directly out of a bottle/can		✓		
Placing one's leg(s) on the table or chair		✓		

MONACO

	Is customary Is allowed Is permissible Is used. Is OK	Is not customary Is frowned upon	Is disallowed Is forbidden Is a crime	(See last page for comments on items referenced here)
Showing the sole of one's foot (feet)				n/a
People standing very close when talking	✓			
Maintaining steady eye contact (direct gaze) when talking to someone	✓			
Kissing or exchange of kisses on the cheek	✓			
Counting money (change) in someone's palm				n/a
Finger pointing in public (in a daring manner)		✓		
Seeking attention by winking the eyes				n/a
Tapping the head to indicate someone is crazy				n/a
Twirling the head to indicate someone is crazy				n/a
Whistling as a way of requesting something/seeking attention				n/a
Using "thumbs-up" sign to mean OK				n/a
Forming a circle with the thumb and index finger (forefinger) to mean OK				n/a
Using the fingers to make a "V" sign for victory				n/a
Beckoning to someone with the index finger (forefinger)				n/a
The left to right waving of the hand with open palms facing outward to indicate "Good bye"				n/a
The use of a nod to show acknowledgement	✓			
Stopping/beckoning a taxi using a stretched hand with the thumb pointing upward				n/a
Using the thumb finger pointed to a direction, to request a ride or a hike				n/a
Raising one's hand/waving with an open fist to summon a taxi				n/a
Tapping one's foot/feet on the floor in a public gathering				n/a
Wiggling one's leg(s) when in a sitting position				n/a
Use of the hand (by motorists and cyclists) to signal direction of traffic				n/a

MONACO

		(See last page for comments on items referenced here)
Foreign tourists are welcome in the country.	yes	
The use of seat belt is mandatory.	no	
International driving license is accepted.	yes	
U.S. driver's license is accepted.	yes	
It is considered impolite to yawn in public.	yes	
Death penalty for drug trafficking is the law.		n/a
Life imprisonment for drug trafficking is the law.		n/a
Guilty until proven innocent in court is the law.		n/a
Innocent until proven guilty in court is the law.		n/a
Pedestrians always have right of way.	yes	
Exit visas are required of visitors.	no	
Crash helmet is mandatory for motor cyclist.	yes	
Hanging is used as a form of legal punishment.	no	
Decapitation of a limb is used as a form of punishment.	no	
Caning is used as a form of legal punishment.	no	
Electric shock is used as a form of legal punishment.	no	
One is expected to stand up during the playing of the national anthem.	yes	
Crash helmet is mandatory for bicyclists.	yes	
Guests are expected to eat every thing on their plates.	no	
Table manners are very informal.	no	
One is expected to cover one's mouth when laughing.	no	
A vertical nod of the head means YES (OK).	yes	
A horizontal shaking of the head means NO (Not OK).	yes	
Prostitution is allowed only in designated areas.	no	
One is expected to take off one's hat during playing of national anthem.	yes	
Separate seating arrangements (between sexes) are maintained at movies.	no	
Separate seating arrangements (between sexes) are maintained at churches.	no	
Uninvited visitors or guests may not be welcome, even among acquaintances.	no	
Pets (e.g. cats, dog) are allowed in some hotels and restaurants.	yes	
Couples invited for a meal may be separated during meals according to their sex.	no	
Punctuality is the order of business.	yes	
Automobiles are driven with headlights always turned on.		n/a
Motorcycles are driven with headlights always turned on.		n/a
Visitors with expired visa face mandatory jail time.	no	
Visitors without exit visa face jail time.	no	
Visitors without entry visa face mandatory (automatic) jail time	no	

MONACO

(A)	**The types of gifts to avoid:**	n/a
(B)	**Appropriate gifts for a foreigner to give:**	n/a
(C)	**Best time to present gifts (at the beginning or at the end of a visit?):**	n/a
(D)	**Best time to present gifts (on initial or later visits?):**	n/a
(E)	**Best place to present gifts (in private or in public?)**:	n/a
(F)	**Number(s) with certain connotations and/or myths attached to them:**	n/a
(G)	**Basic shape(s) with negative connotations:**	n/a
(H)	**Basic color(s) with negative connotations:**	n/a
(I)	**Traditional greeting methods include:**	n/a
(J)	**Safe topics for discussion include:**	n/a
(K)	**Best time for conversations (before, during, after meals?):**	n/a
(L)	**Forms of legal punishment:**	n/a
(M)	**Approximately length of time one could be detained by law and order authorities before being charged in court:**	n/a
(N)	**January 15, 1999, for example, will normally be written as:**	15/1/99
(O)	**Emergency code number**:	n/a
(P)	**Ambulance code Number**:	93.30.04.85 or 93.30.19.45 or 18
(Q)	**Police code number:**	17
(R)	**Telephone (country) code:**	33
(S)	**Telex (country) code:**	n/a
(T)	**Electricity requirements**:	220/ volts
(U)	**Legal drinking age:**	n/a
(V)	**Systems of weights and measures:**	metric
(W)	**Legal age of incarceration**:	n/a
(X)	**Driving side of the road:**	right
(Y)	**Minimum expenditure expected of foreign visitors? $**	n/a
(Z)	**Name of currency**:	French Franc
(Za)	**Some places 0ff-limits to foreign visitors:**	n/a
(Zb)	**Some places, structures and items prohibited from being photographed:**	n/a

THE NETHERLANDS	Is customary Is allowed Is permissible Is used. Is OK	Is not customary Is frowned upon	Is disallowed Is forbidden Is a crime	(See last page for comments on items referenced here)
Smoking in public	✓			
Eating in public	✓			
Not flushing public toilet		✓		
Spitting in public		✓		
Feeding animals & birds in public	✓			
Whistling in public	✓			
Drinking alcohol in public	✓			
Kissing in public	✓			
Breast feeding in public	✓			
Drunkenness (in public)		✓		
Cursing in public		✓		
Religious preaching in public	✓			
Begging (panhandling) in public		✓		
Giving money to beggars/panhandlers	✓			
Giving food/drink to beggars/panhandlers	✓			
Brushing teeth in public (other than in restrooms)	✓			
Strolling with pets in major public roads/streets	✓			
Chewing gum in public	✓			
Chewing gum in government offices	✓			
Combing hair in public (other than in toilets/restrooms)	✓			
Undressing/dressing in public		✓		
Wearing of dark glasses indoors in public places	✓	✓		
Public display of wealth	✓			
Praying openly in public in non-designated areas		✓	✓	
Walking bare feet in public	✓			
Chewing tobacco in public	✓			
Trimming one's finger or toe nails in public		✓		
Laughing aloud in public	✓			
Mingling of the sexes in public	✓			
Mixed bathing in public swimming pools	✓			
Distributing religious pamphlets (literature) in public/side streets	✓			

THE NETHERLANDS

	Is customary Is allowed Is permissible Is used. Is OK	Is not customary Is frowned upon	Is disallowed Is forbidden Is a crime	(See last page for comments on items referenced here)
Dancing on side street	✓			
Nude bathing	✓			
Littering			✓	
Binge Drinking		✓		
hitchhiking	✓			
Jaywalking			✓	
Drunk driving			✓	
Speeding			✓	
Skating on side streets (side-walk)		✓		
Graffiti painting			✓	
Pilfering			✓	
Prostitution	✓			
Haggling in the market place	✓			
Consumption of alcoholic beverages in bars and restaurants	✓			
Gambling	✓			
Possession of pornographic materials			✓	
Possession of the Christian Bible	✓			
Possession of the Moslem Koran	✓			
Possession of bullet-proof vest	✓			
Possession of toy gun	✓			
Possession of fire crackers and fireworks		✓		
Possession of prescription drugs (without doctor's note)			✓	
Possession of regulated drugs (narcotics)			✓	
Possession of firearms (by foreigners)			✓	
Possession of pocket knife in public	✓			
Using walkie talkies	✓			
Using of "boom boxes"(loud sounding stereo system)		✓		
Using "walkman" (very small radio/cassettes with ear plugs) in public places	✓			
Using "walkman" (very small radio/cassettes with ear plugs) while driving or riding			✓	

THE NETHERLANDS

	Is customary Is allowed Is permissible Is used Is OK	Is not customary Is frowned upon	Is disallowed Is forbidden Is a crime	(See last page for comments on items referenced here)
Use of cellular phone	✓			
Use of binoculars/periscopes other than in sports arena	✓			
Taking photographs of people (without their permission)	✓			
Taking photographs at airports, train and bus stations	✓			
Taking photographs of airports	✓			
Taking photographs of churches and synagogues	✓			
Taking photographs of religious statues	✓			
Taking photographs of public buildings	✓			
Taking photographs of bridges	✓			
Tipping (gratuity)	✓			
Tipping (when service is rendered)	✓			
Tipping (when service is not rendered)	✓			
Tipping waiters/waitresses at restaurants and hotels	✓			
Tipping taxi/cab drivers	✓			
Tipping baggage handlers, porters, door persons	✓			
Tipping of hair dressers/barbers	✓			
Overtipping	✓			
Undertipping	✓			
Spilling cigarette butt (ash) on side streets/on the floor		✓		
Men wearing lipstick		✓		
Wearing visible tattoo marks		✓		
Men painting/coloring their finger or toe nails		✓		
Cross dressing (men dressed like women & vice versa)			✓	
Walking in public without a shirt (i.e. with the upper half of the body naked)		✓		
Men wearing braided hair	✓			
Men wearing earrings	✓			
Men wearing dreadlock hair style	✓			
Homosexuality	✓			
Lesbianism	✓			

THE NETHERLANDS

	Is customary Is allowed Is permissible Is used Is OK	Is not customary Is frowned upon	Is disallowed Is forbidden Is a crime	(See last page for comments on items referenced here)
Females covering their hair (wearing headgear) in public	✓			
Females exposing their full face in public	✓			
Females driving automobiles	✓			
Females riding motorcycles	✓			
Females riding bicycles	✓			
Females smoking in public	✓			
Women wearing bras (braziers) in public	✓			
Use of lipstick by women	✓			
A woman extending her hands first when introduced	✓			
Female bashing			✓	
Females wearing trousers	✓			
Females wearing minis (short dresses)	✓			
Females wearing bikinis	✓			
Females wearing shorts	✓			
Persons of opposite sex holding hands in public	✓			
Persons of same sex holding hands in public	✓			
Handshake between opposite sex	✓			
Hugging in public by same sex	✓			
Hugging in public by opposite sex	✓			
Men and women walking side by side in public	✓			
Man walking ahead (in public), with the woman following		✓		
Woman walking ahead (in public), with the man following				n/a
Men opening doors for women	✓			
Sitting with legs crossed in the presence of elders	✓			
Talking to an elderly person with one's hat/cap on	✓			
Talking to an elderly person with hands positioned on both sides of one's waist	✓			
Blowing one's nose in public	✓			
Blowing one's nose in the presence of others	✓			
Addressing people by their title		✓		

THE NETHERLANDS

	Is customary Is allowed Is permissible Is used. Is OK	Is not customary Is frowned upon	Is disallowed Is forbidden Is a crime	(See last page for comments on items referenced here)
Addressing people by their family name/surname/last name/given name	✓			
Addressing people by their first name/ given name	✓			
Women going through doors first	✓			
Men helping women with their coats	✓			
Men extending their hands to women first during greetings	✓			
Taking off one's hat when entering a private home	✓			
Removing one's shoes when entering a private home		✓		
Invited guests bringing food at social gatherings		✓		
Guests bringing drinks at social gatherings	✓			
Shaking hands when leaving a small group	✓			
Shaking hands with everyone present, upon arrival at a social gathering	✓			
Eating with the right hand	✓			
`Eating with the left hand	✓			
Eating with both hands		✓		
Presenting a gift or passing on an object with the left hand	✓			
Asking a man about his wife	✓			
Asking a woman about her husband	✓			
Making prior appointments before a meeting or visit	✓			
Addressing an audience with one or both hands in the pocket		✓		
Carrying on conversation during meals	✓			
Females sitting with legs crossed	✓			
People discussing their wealth	✓			
Asking someone his or her age, or how old the person is		✓		
Complementing someone on his/her physical looks	✓			
Complementing someone on his/her attire	✓			
Use of both hands in handshake	✓			
In greeting, a handshake accompanied by a slight bow	✓			

THE NETHERLANDS

	Is customary Is allowed Is permissible Is used. Is OK	Is not customary Is frowned upon	Is disallowed Is forbidden Is a crime	(See last page for comments on items referenced here)
Salutations such as "Good morning", "Good afternoon", "Good evening"	✓			
The completion of a business deal with a handshake	✓			
Starting a negotiation session with a handshake	✓			
A gift for the host/hostess	✓			
Giving a business gift	✓			
A gift of money (use of money as gift)			✓	
Use of flowers as a gift	✓			
Use of business cards	✓			
Accepting/presenting gifts with both hands	✓			
Burning of the country's flag			✓	
Mutilation of the national currency			✓	
Casual wearing of clothings made with colors & marks of the national flag	✓			
Wearing of look-alike military (camouflage) fatigues (attire)	✓			
Sitting on the floor (on floor mats)		✓		
Discussion of religion	✓			
Discussion of politics	✓			
Discussion of sex	✓			
Patting/slapping someone on the buttocks		✓		
Patting/slapping someone on the back	✓			
Touching or patting someone's head/hair	✓			
Casual touching of any part of someone's body		✓		
Drinking directly out of a bottle/can	✓			
Placing one's leg(s) on the table or chair		✓		

THE NETHERLANDS

	Is customary Is allowed Is permissible Is used. Is OK	Is not customary Is frowned upon	Is disallowed Is forbidden Is a crime	(See last page for comments on items referenced here)
Showing the sole of one's foot (feet)		✓		
People standing very close when talking		✓		
Maintaining steady eye contact (direct gaze) when talking to someone	✓			
Kissing or exchange of kisses on the cheek	✓			
Counting money (change) in someone's palm		✓		
Finger pointing in public (in a daring manner)		✓		
Seeking attention by winking the eyes		✓		
Tapping the head to indicate someone is crazy		✓		
Twirling the head to indicate someone is crazy		✓		
Whistling as a way of requesting something/seeking attention		✓		
Using "thumbs-up" sign to mean OK	✓			
Forming a circle with the thumb and index finger (forefinger) to mean OK	✓			
Using the fingers to make a "V" sign for victory	✓			
Beckoning to someone with the index finger (forefinger)	✓			
The left to right waving of the hand with open palms facing outward to indicate "Good bye"	✓			
The use of a nod to show acknowledgement	✓			
Stopping/beckoning a taxi using a stretched hand with the thumb pointing upward		✓		
Using the thumb finger pointed to a direction, to request a ride or a hike	✓			
Raising one's hand/waving with an open fist to summon a taxi	✓			
Tapping one's foot/feet on the floor in a public gathering		✓		
Wiggling one's leg(s) when in a sitting position		✓		
Use of the hand (by motorists and cyclists) to signal direction of traffic	✓			

THE NETHERLANDS

		(See last page for comments on items referenced here)
Foreign tourists are welcome in the country.	yes	
The use of seat belt is mandatory.	yes	
International driving license is accepted.	yes	
U.S. driver's license is accepted.	yes	
It is considered impolite to yawn in public.	yes	
Death penalty for drug trafficking is the law.	no	
Life imprisonment for drug trafficking is the law.	no	
Guilty until proven innocent in court is the law.	no	
Innocent until proven guilty in court is the law.	yes	
Pedestrians always have right of way.	no	
Exit visas are required of visitors.	no	
Crash helmet is mandatory for motor cyclist.	yes	
Hanging is used as a form of legal punishment.	no	
Decapitation of a limb is used as a form of punishment.	no	
Caning is used as a form of legal punishment.	no	
Electric shock is used as a form of legal punishment.	no	
One is expected to stand up during the playing of the national anthem.	yes	
Crash helmet is mandatory for bicyclists.	no	
Guests are expected to eat every thing on their plates.	no	
Table manners are very informal.	no	
One is expected to cover one's mouth when laughing.	yes	
A vertical nod of the head means YES (OK).	yes	
A horizontal shaking of the head means NO (Not OK).	yes	
Prostitution is allowed only in designated areas.	yes	
One is expected to take off one's hat during playing of national anthem.	yes	
Separate seating arrangements (between sexes) are maintained at movies.	no	
Separate seating arrangements (between sexes) are maintained at churches.	no	
Uninvited visitors or guests may not be welcome, even among acquaintances.	no	
Pets (e.g. cats, dog) are allowed in some hotels and restaurants.	yes	
Couples invited for a meal may be separated during meals according to their sex.	no	
Punctuality is the order of business.	yes	
Automobiles are driven with headlights always turned on.	no	
Motorcycles are driven with headlights always turned on.	no	
`Visitors with expired visa face mandatory jail time.	no	1
Visitors without exit visa face jail time.	no	2
Visitors without entry visa face mandatory (automatic) jail time.	no	

ADDITIONAL COUNTRY INFORMATION

(A)	**The types of gifts to avoid:**	gun of any sort, food.
(B)	**Appropriate gifts for a foreigner to give:**	chocolate, flowers and gifts typical of country of origin
(C)	**Best time to present gifts (at the beginning or at the end of a visit?):**	at the beginning
(D)	**Best time to present gifts (on initial or later later visits?):**	n/a
(E)	**Best place to present gifts (in private or in public?):**	n/a
(F)	**Number(s) with certain connotations and/or myths attached to them:**	13= unlucky
(G)	**Basic shape(s) with negative connotations:**	no
(H)	**Basic color(s) with negative connotations:**	no
(I)	**Traditional greeting methods include:**	handshake
(J)	**Safe topics for discussion include:**	weather, fashion, travel, art, family, religion, domestic politics, food, sports, international politics, social conditions, money and personal wealth, sex.
(K)	**Best time for conversations (before, during, after meals?):**	n/a
(L)	**Forms of legal punishment:**	jailing, fining, social work
(M)	**Approximately length of time one could be detained by law and order authorities before being charged in court:**	n/a
(N)	**January 15, 1999, for example, will normally be written as:**	15/01/99
(O)	**Emergency code number:**	06.11
(P)	**Ambulance code Number:**	06.11
(Q)	**Police code number:**	06.11
(R)	**Telephone (country) code:**	31
(S)	**Telex (country) code:**	844
(T)	**Electricity requirements:**	220/50
(U)	**Legal drinking age:**	216
(V)	**Systems of weights and measures:**	n/a
(W)	**Legal age of incarceration:**	18
(X)	**Driving side of the road:**	right
(Y)	**Minimum expenditure expected of foreign visitors? $**	n/a
(Z)	**Name of currency:**	Netherlands Guilder
(Za)	**Some places 0ff-limits to foreign visitors:**	none
(Zb)	**Some places, structures and items prohibited from being photographed:**	none

ENDNOTES

Item Number: COMMENTS/EXPLANATIONS

n/a: Not applicable/Not available/No response

(1) Visas are not required for U.S. Citizens

(2) Exit visas are not required for U.S. Citizens

NORWAY	Is customary Is allowed Is permissible Is used. Is OK	Is not customary Is frowned upon	Is disallowed Is forbidden Is a crime	(See last page for comments on items referenced here)
Smoking in public	✓			1
Eating in public	✓			
Not flushing public toilet		✓		
Spitting in public		✓		
Feeding animals & birds in public	✓			
Whistling in public		✓		
Drinking alcohol in public	✓			2
Kissing in public	✓			
Breast feeding in public	✓			
Drunkenness (in public)			✓	3
Cursing in public	✓			
Religious preaching in public	✓			
Begging (panhandling) in public			✓	
Giving money to beggars/panhandlers	✓			
Giving food/drink to beggars/panhandlers	✓			
Brushing teeth in public (other than in restrooms)		✓		
Strolling with pets in major public roads/streets	✓			
Chewing gum in public	✓			
Chewing gum in government offices		✓		
Combing hair in public (other than in toilets/restrooms)	✓			
Undressing/dressing in public		✓		
Wearing of dark glasses indoors in public places		✓		
Public display of wealth		✓		4
Praying openly in public in non-designated areas	✓			
Walking bare feet in public	✓			
Chewing tobacco in public	✓			
Trimming one's finger or toe nails in public		✓		
Laughing aloud in public	✓			
Mingling of the sexes in public	✓			n/a
Mixed bathing in public swimming pools	✓			n/a
Distributing religious pamphlets (literature) in public/side streets	✓			n/a

NORWAY

	Is customary Is allowed Is permissible Is used. Is OK	Is not customary Is frowned upon	Is disallowed Is forbidden Is a crime	(See last page for comments on items referenced here)
Dancing on side street	✓			5
Nude bathing	✓			6
Littering			✓	
Binge Drinking		✓		7
hitchhiking	✓			
Jaywalking		✓		
Drunk driving			✓	
Speeding			✓	
Skating on side streets (side-walk)		✓		
Graffiti painting			✓	
Pilfering			✓	
Prostitution			✓	
Haggling in the market place		✓		
Consumption of alcoholic beverages in bars and restaurants	✓			
Gambling		✓		
Possession of pornographic materials	✓			8
Possession of the Christian Bible	✓			
Possession of the Moslem Koran	✓			
Possession of bullet-proof vest		✓		
Possession of toy gun	✓			
Possession of fire crackers and fireworks	✓			9
Possession of prescription drugs (without doctor's note)		✓		
Possession of regulated drugs (narcotics)			✓	
Possession of firearms (by foreigners)			✓	
Possession of pocket knife in public			✓	
Using walkie talkies	✓			
Using of "boom boxes"(loud sounding stereo system)		✓		
Using "walkman" (very small radio/cassettes with ear plugs) in public places	✓			
Using "walkman" (very small radio/cassettes with ear plugs) while driving or riding		✓		

NORWAY

	Is customary Is allowed Is permissible Is used Is OK	Is not customary Is frowned upon	Is disallowed Is forbidden Is a crime	(See last page for comments on items referenced here)
Use of cellular phone	✓			
Use of binoculars/periscopes other than in sports arena	✓			
Taking photographs of people (without their permission)	✓			
Taking photographs at airports, train and bus stations	✓			
Taking photographs of airports	✓			
Taking photographs of churches and synagogues	✓			
Taking photographs of religious statues	✓			
Taking photographs of public buildings	✓			
Taking photographs of bridges	✓			
Tipping (gratuity)	✓			
Tipping (when service is rendered)	✓			
Tipping (when service is not rendered)		✓		
Tipping waiters/waitresses at restaurants and hotels	✓			
Tipping taxi/cab drivers	✓			
Tipping baggage handlers, porters, door persons	✓			
Tipping of hair dressers/barbers		✓		
Overtipping	✓			
Undertipping	✓			
Spilling cigarette butt (ash) on side streets/on the floor		✓		10
Men wearing lipstick		✓		
Wearing visible tattoo marks	✓			
Men painting/coloring their finger or toe nails		✓		
Cross dressing (men dressed like women & vice versa)		✓		
Walking in public without a shirt (i.e. with the upper half of the body naked)		✓		
Men wearing braided hair	✓			
Men wearing earrings	✓			
Men wearing dreadlock hair style	✓			
Homosexuality	✓			
Lesbianism	✓			

NORWAY

	Is customary Is allowed Is permissible Is used Is OK	Is not customary Is frowned upon	Is disallowed Is forbidden Is a crime	(See last page for comments on items referenced here)
Females covering their hair (wearing headgear) in public		✓		11
Females exposing their full face in public	✓			
Females driving automobiles	✓			
Females riding motorcycles	✓			
Females riding bicycles	✓			
Females smoking in public	✓			
Women wearing bras (braziers) in public		✓		
Use of lipstick by women	✓			
A woman extending her hands first when introduced	✓			
Female bashing			✓	
Females wearing trousers	✓			
Females wearing minis (short dresses)	✓			
Females wearing bikinis	✓			
Females wearing shorts	✓			
Persons of opposite sex holding hands in public	✓			
Persons of same sex holding hands in public		✓		
Handshake between opposite sex	✓			
Hugging in public by same sex	✓			
Hugging in public by opposite sex	✓			
Men and women walking side by side in public	✓			
Man walking ahead (in public), with the woman following		✓		
Woman walking ahead (in public), with the man following		✓		
Men opening doors for women		✓		
Sitting with legs crossed in the presence of elders	✓			
Talking to an elderly person with one's hat/cap on	✓			
Talking to an elderly person with hands positioned on both sides of one's waist	✓			
Blowing one's nose in public	✓			
Blowing one's nose in the presence of others	✓			
Addressing people by their title	✓			12

NORWAY

	Is customary Is allowed Is permissible Is used. Is OK	Is not customary Is frowned upon	Is disallowed Is forbidden Is a crime	(See last page for comments on items referenced here)
Addressing people by their family name/surname/last name/given name	✓			
Addressing people by their first name/ given name	✓			
Women going through doors first	✓			
Men helping women with their coats	✓			
Men extending their hands to women first during greetings	✓			
Taking off one's hat when entering a private home	✓			
Removing one's shoes when entering a private home	✓			
Invited guests bringing food at social gatherings		✓		13
Guests bringing drinks at social gatherings	✓			14
Shaking hands when leaving a small group	✓			
Shaking hands with everyone present, upon arrival at a social gathering	✓			
Eating with the right hand	✓			
Eating with the left hand	✓			
Eating with both hands		✓		15
Presenting a gift or passing on an object with the left hand		✓		16
Asking a man about his wife		✓		17
Asking a woman about her husband		✓		18
Making prior appointments before a meeting or visit		✓		
Addressing an audience with one or both hands in the pocket		✓		
Carrying on conversation during meals	✓			
Females sitting with legs crossed	✓			
People discussing their wealth		✓		
Asking someone his or her age, or how old the person is		✓		
Complementing someone on his/her physical looks	✓			
Complementing someone on his/her attire	✓			
Use of both hands in handshake		✓		
In greeting, a handshake accompanied by a slight bow	✓			

NORWAY

	Is customary Is allowed Is permissible Is used. Is OK	Is not customary Is frowned upon	Is disallowed Is forbidden Is a crime	(See last page for comments on items referenced here)
Salutations such as "Good morning", "Good afternoon", "Good evening"	✓			
The completion of a business deal with a handshake	✓			
Starting a negotiation session with a handshake	✓			
A gift for the host/hostess	✓			
Giving a business gift		✓		
A gift of money (use of money as gift)		✓		19
Use of flowers as a gift	✓			
Use of business cards	✓			
Accepting/presenting gifts with both hands		✓		
Burning of the country's flag			✓	
Mutilation of the national currency	✓			
Casual wearing of clothings made with colors & marks of the national flag		✓		
Wearing of look-alike military (camouflage) fatigues (attire)		✓		
Sitting on the floor (on floor mats)		✓		
Discussion of religion	✓			
Discussion of politics	✓			
Discussion of sex	✓			
Patting/slapping someone on the buttocks		✓		
Patting/slapping someone on the back	✓			
Touching or patting someone's head/hair	✓			
Casual touching of any part of someone's body		✓		
Drinking directly out of a bottle/can	✓			
Placing one's leg(s) on the table or chair	✓			

NORWAY

	Is customary Is allowed Is permissible Is used. Is OK	Is not customary Is frowned upon	Is disallowed Is forbidden Is a crime	(See last page for comments on items referenced here)
Showing the sole of one's foot (feet)		✓		
People standing very close when talking	✓			
Maintaining steady eye contact (direct gaze) when talking to someone	✓			
Kissing or exchange of kisses on the cheek	✓			
Counting money (change) in someone's palm		✓		
Finger pointing in public (in a daring manner)		✓		
Seeking attention by winking the eyes	✓			
Tapping the head to indicate someone is crazy	✓			
Twirling the head to indicate someone is crazy		✓		
Whistling as a way of requesting something/seeking attention		✓		
Using "thumbs-up" sign to mean OK	✓			
Forming a circle with the thumb and index finger (forefinger) to mean OK	✓			
Using the fingers to make a "V" sign for victory	✓			
Beckoning to someone with the index finger (forefinger)		✓		
The left to right waving of the hand with open palms facing outward to indicate "Good bye"		✓		
The use of a nod to show acknowledgement	✓			
Stopping/beckoning a taxi using a stretched hand with the thumb pointing upward		✓		
Using the thumb finger pointed to a direction, to request a ride or a hike	✓			
Raising one's hand/waving with an open fist to summon a taxi	✓			
Tapping one's foot/feet on the floor in a public gathering		✓		
Wiggling one's leg(s) when in a sitting position		✓		
Use of the hand (by motorists and cyclists) to signal direction of traffic	✓			

NORWAY

		(See last page for comments on items referenced here)
Foreign tourists are welcome in the country.	yes	
The use of seat belt is mandatory.	yes	
International driving license is accepted.	yes	
U.S. driver's license is accepted.	yes	
It is considered impolite to yawn in public.	yes	
Death penalty for drug trafficking is the law.	yes	
Life imprisonment for drug trafficking is the law.	no	20
Guilty until proven innocent in court is the law.	no	
Innocent until proven guilty in court is the law.	yes	
Pedestrians always have right of way.	yes	
Exit visas are required of visitors.	no	
Crash helmet is mandatory for motor cyclist.	yes	
Hanging is used as a form of legal punishment.	no	
Decapitation of a limb is used as a form of punishment.	no	
Caning is used as a form of legal punishment.	no	
Electric shock is used as a form of legal punishment.	no	
One is expected to stand up during the playing of the national anthem.	yes	
Crash helmet is mandatory for bicyclists.	yes	
Guests are expected to eat every thing on their plates.	no	
Table manners are very informal.	no	
One is expected to cover one's mouth when laughing.	no	
A vertical nod of the head means YES (OK).	yes	
A horizontal shaking of the head means NO (Not OK).	yes	
Prostitution is allowed only in designated areas.	no	
One is expected to take off one's hat during playing of national anthem.	yes	
Separate seating arrangements (between sexes) are maintained at movies.	no	
Separate seating arrangements (between sexes) are maintained at churches.	no	
Uninvited visitors or guests may not be welcome, even among acquaintances.	no	21
Pets (e.g. cats, dog) are allowed in some hotels and restaurants.	yes	
Couples invited for a meal may be separated during meals according to their sex.	no	
Punctuality is the order of business.	yes	
Automobiles are driven with headlights always turned on.	yes	
Motorcycles are driven with headlights always turned on.	yes	
Visitors with expired visa face mandatory jail time.	no	
Visitors without exit visa face jail time.	no	
Visitors without entry visa face mandatory (automatic) jail time.	no	22

ADDITIONAL COUNTRY INFORMATION

(A)	**The types of gifts to avoid:**	weapons, white flowers only, religious scriptures
(B)	**Appropriate gifts for a foreigner to give:**	books, music (CD's records,tapes), flowers, chocolate, something ethnic
(C)	**Best time to present gifts (at the beginning or at the end of a visit?):**	flowers, right away more personal gifts, upon leaving
(D)	**Best time to present gifts (on initial or later visits?):**	upon arriving
(E)	**Best place to present gifts (in private or in public?):**	in a home, meeting, on stage
(F)	**Number(s) with certain connotations and/or myths attached to them:**	666
(G)	**Basic shape(s) with negative connotations:**	nazi symbols
(H)	**Basic color(s) with negative connotations:**	black = death, funeral, mourning, white = weeding hand
(I)	**Traditional greeting methods include:**	handshaking
(J)	**Safe topics for discussion include:**	weather, fashion, travel, art, family, religion, domestic politics, food, sports, international politics, social conditions, sex, hobbies.
(K)	**Best time for conversations (before, during, after meals?):**	n/a
(L)	**Forms of legal punishment:**	no
(M)	**Approximately length of time one could be detained by law and order authorities before being charged in court:**	they can detain you for approximately 48 hours before the case goes to the magistrate's court
(N)	**January 15, 1999, for example, will normally be written as:**	15/1/99
(O)	**Emergency code number**:	O D
(P)	**Ambulance code Number**:	P E
(Q)	**Police code number:**	Q K
(R)	**Telephone (country) code:**	47
(S)	**Telex (country) code:**	856
(T)	**Electricity requirements**:	220 v
(U)	**Legal drinking age:**	18
(V)	**Systems of weights and measures:**	metric
(W)	**Legal age of incarceration**:	15
(X)	**Driving side of the road:**	right
(Y)	**Minimum expenditure expected of foreign visitors? $**	none
(Z)	**Name of currency**:	Krone
(Za)	**Some places 0ff-limits to foreign visitors:**	none
(Zb)	**Some places, structures and items prohibited from being photographed:**	airports

ENDNOTES

Item Number: COMMENTS/EXPLANATIONS

n/a: Not applicable/Not available/No response

(1) Smoking in open places/the outdoors is okay inside public building and gathering spots it is prohibited if not otherwise stated.

(2) Only drunkenness in public is not acceptable, and may cause a fine or jail time.

(3) Only drunkenness in public is not acceptable, and may cause a fine or jail time.

(4) One can display anything in the world all over the world if one is with light minded friends. Bragging is generally frowned upon in Norway especially with regards to wealth.

(5) Dancing on the side street is okay if the occasion calls for it e.g. when a band plays up.

(6) Nude bathing is okay at designated nude beaches. Topless sunbathing is common at public beaches.

(7) Only drunkenness in public is not acceptable, and may cause a fine or jail time.

(8) Possession and distribution of child pornography and materials promoting the mutilation of women are strictly forbidden.

(9) Not by minors, and preferably the possession should coincide (for all) with e.g. New Year.

(10) Dropping a cigarette butt on the street may be okay, but certainly not on a floor (public or private).

(11) Females who want to cover their hair in public may do so.

(12) As a show of respect it is ok, norms are relaxed.

(13) As gifts, yes.

(14) If the occasion calls for it, yes.

(15) As in knife and fork, yes.

(16) Yes, if the person is left handed.

(17) depends on how intimate the question is.

(18) Depends on how intimate the question is.

(19) Depends on the occasion.

(20) "Life" as in long sentences.

(21) Depends on the level of familiarity.

(22) But if visa is needed and then lacking, deportation.

POLAND	Is customary Is allowed Is permissible Is used. Is OK	Is not customary Is frowned upon	Is disallowed Is forbidden Is a crime	(See last page for comments on items referenced here)
Smoking in public	✓			
Eating in public	✓			
Not flushing public toilet		✓		
Spitting in public		✓		
Feeding animals & birds in public	✓			
Whistling in public		✓		
Drinking alcohol in public			✓	
Kissing in public	✓			
Breast feeding in public		✓		
Drunkenness (in public)		✓		
Cursing in public	✓			
Religious preaching in public	✓			
Begging (panhandling) in public		✓		
Giving money to beggars/panhandlers	✓			
Giving food/drink to beggars/panhandlers	✓			
Brushing teeth in public (other than in restrooms)		✓		
Strolling with pets in major public roads/streets	✓			
Chewing gum in public	✓			
Chewing gum in government offices		✓		
Combing hair in public (other than in toilets/restrooms)	✓			
Undressing/dressing in public		✓		
Wearing of dark glasses indoors in public places	✓			
Public display of wealth	✓			
Praying openly in public in non-designated areas		✓		
Walking bare feet in public		✓		
Chewing tobacco in public		✓		
Trimming one's finger or toe nails in public		✓		
Laughing aloud in public	✓			
Mingling of the sexes in public		✓		
Mixed bathing in public swimming pools		✓		
Distributing religious pamphlets (literature) in public/side streets	✓			

POLAND

	Is customary Is allowed Is permissible Is used. Is OK	Is not customary Is frowned upon	Is disallowed Is forbidden Is a crime	(See last page for comments on items referenced here)
Dancing on side street		✓		
Nude bathing		✓		
Littering	✓			
Binge Drinking			✓	
hitchhiking	✓			
Jaywalking			✓	
Drunk driving			✓	
Speeding			✓	
Skating on side streets (side-walk)	✓			
Graffiti painting	✓			
Pilfering	✓			
Prostitution			✓	
Haggling in the market place			✓	
Consumption of alcoholic beverages in bars and restaurants	✓			
Gambling	✓			
Possession of pornographic materials	✓			
Possession of the Christian Bible	✓			
Possession of the Moslem Koran		✓		
Possession of bullet-proof vest	✓			
Possession of toy gun	✓			
Possession of fire crackers and fireworks	✓			
Possession of prescription drugs (without doctor's note)	✓			
Possession of regulated drugs (narcotics)			✓	
Possession of firearms (by foreigners)			✓	
Possession of pocket knife in public		✓		
Using walkie talkies		✓		
Using of "boom boxes"(loud sounding stereo system)	✓			
Using "walkman" (very small radio/cassettes with ear plugs) in public places	✓			
Using "walkman" (very small radio/cassettes with ear plugs) while driving or riding		✓		

POLAND

	Is customary Is allowed Is permissible Is used Is OK	Is not customary Is frowned upon	Is disallowed Is forbidden Is a crime	(See last page for comments on items referenced here)
Use of cellular phone	✓			
Use of binoculars/periscopes other than in sports arena	✓			
Taking photographs of people (without their permission)	✓			
Taking photographs at airports, train and bus stations	✓			
Taking photographs of airports		✓		
Taking photographs of churches and synagogues	✓			
Taking photographs of religious statues	✓			
Taking photographs of public buildings	✓			
Taking photographs of bridges	✓			
Tipping (gratuity)	✓			
Tipping (when service is rendered)	✓			
Tipping (when service is not rendered)		✓		
Tipping waiters/waitresses at restaurants and hotels	✓			
Tipping taxi/cab drivers	✓			
Tipping baggage handlers, porters, door persons	✓			
Tipping of hair dressers/barbers	✓			
Overtipping		✓		
Undertipping	✓			
Spilling cigarette butt (ash) on side streets/on the floor		✓		
Men wearing lipstick		✓		
Wearing visible tattoo marks		✓		
Men painting/coloring their finger or toe nails		✓		
Cross dressing (men dressed like women & vice versa)		✓		
Walking in public without a shirt (i.e. with the upper half of the body naked)		✓		
Men wearing braided hair		✓		
Men wearing earrings	✓			
Men wearing dreadlock hair style	✓			
Homosexuality		✓		
Lesbianism		✓		

POLAND

	Is customary Is allowed Is permissible Is used Is OK	Is not customary Is frowned upon	Is disallowed Is forbidden Is a crime	(See last page for comments on items referenced here)
Females covering their hair (wearing headgear) in public	✓			
Females exposing their full face in public	✓			
Females driving automobiles	✓			
Females riding motorcycles	✓			
Females riding bicycles	✓			
Females smoking in public	✓			
Women wearing bras (braziers) in public		✓		
Use of lipstick by women	✓			
A woman extending her hands first when introduced	✓			
Female bashing	✓			
Females wearing trousers	✓			
Females wearing minis (short dresses)	✓			
Females wearing bikinis	✓			
Females wearing shorts	✓			
Persons of opposite sex holding hands in public	✓			
Persons of same sex holding hands in public	✓			
Handshake between opposite sex	✓			
Hugging in public by same sex	✓			
Hugging in public by opposite sex	✓			
Men and women walking side by side in public	✓			
Man walking ahead (in public), with the woman following		✓		
Woman walking ahead (in public), with the man following		✓		
Men opening doors for women	✓			
Sitting with legs crossed in the presence of elders	✓			
Talking to an elderly person with one's hat/cap on		✓		
Talking to an elderly person with hands positioned on both sides of one's waist	✓			
Blowing one's nose in public	✓			
Blowing one's nose in the presence of others	✓			
Addressing people by their title	✓			

POLAND

	Is customary Is allowed Is permissible Is used. Is OK	Is not customary Is frowned upon	Is disallowed Is forbidden Is a crime	(See last page for comments on items referenced here)
Addressing people by their family name/surname/last name/given name	✓			
Addressing people by their first name/ given name		✓		
Women going through doors first	✓			
Men helping women with their coats	✓			
Men extending their hands to women first during greetings		✓		
Taking off one's hat when entering a private home	✓			
Removing one's shoes when entering a private home		✓		
Invited guests bringing food at social gatherings		✓		
Guests bringing drinks at social gatherings	✓			
Shaking hands when leaving a small group	✓			
Shaking hands with everyone present, upon arrival at a social gathering	✓			
Eating with the right hand	✓			
Eating with the left hand		✓		
Eating with both hands		✓		
Presenting a gift or passing on an object with the left hand		✓		
Asking a man about his wife	✓			
Asking a woman about her husband	✓			
Making prior appointments before a meeting or visit	✓			
Addressing an audience with one or both hands in the pocket		✓		
Carrying on conversation during meals	✓			
Females sitting with legs crossed	✓			
People discussing their wealth	✓			
Asking someone his or her age, or how old the person is	✓			
Complementing someone on his/her physical looks	✓			
Complementing someone on his/her attire	✓			
Use of both hands in handshake		✓		
In greeting, a handshake accompanied by a slight bow	✓			

POLAND

	Is customary Is allowed Is permissible Is used. Is OK	Is not customary Is frowned upon	Is disallowed Is forbidden Is a crime	(See last page for comments on items referenced here)
Salutations such as "Good morning", "Good afternoon", "Good evening"	✓			
The completion of a business deal with a handshake	✓			
Starting a negotiation session with a handshake	✓			
A gift for the host/hostess	✓			
Giving a business gift	✓			
A gift of money (use of money as gift)		✓		
Use of flowers as a gift	✓			
Use of business cards	✓			
Accepting/presenting gifts with both hands	✓			
Burning of the country's flag			✓	
Mutilation of the national currency		✓		
Casual wearing of clothings made with colors & marks of the national flag	✓			
Wearing of look-alike military (camouflage) fatigues (attire)	✓			
Sitting on the floor (on floor mats)	✓			
Discussion of religion	✓			
Discussion of politics	✓			
Discussion of sex	✓			
Patting/slapping someone on the buttocks		✓		
Patting/slapping someone on the back	✓			
Touching or patting someone's head/hair	✓			
Casual touching of any part of someone's body		✓		
Drinking directly out of a bottle/can	✓			
Placing one's leg(s) on the table or chair		✓		

POLAND

	Is customary Is allowed Is permissible Is used. Is OK	Is not customary Is frowned upon	Is disallowed Is forbidden Is a crime	(See last page for comments on items referenced here)
Showing the sole of one's foot (feet)		✓		
People standing very close when talking	✓			
Maintaining steady eye contact (direct gaze) when talking to someone	✓			
Kissing or exchange of kisses on the cheek	✓			
Counting money (change) in someone's palm		✓		
Finger pointing in public (in a daring manner)		✓		
Seeking attention by winking the eyes		✓		
Tapping the head to indicate someone is crazy	✓			
Twirling the head to indicate someone is crazy	✓			
Whistling as a way of requesting something/seeking attention		✓		
Using "thumbs-up" sign to mean OK		✓		
Forming a circle with the thumb and index finger (forefinger) to mean OK		✓		
Using the fingers to make a "V" sign for victory	✓			
Beckoning to someone with the index finger (forefinger)		✓		
The left to right waving of the hand with open palms facing outward to indicate "Good bye"		✓		
The use of a nod to show acknowledgement		✓		
Stopping/beckoning a taxi using a stretched hand with the thumb pointing upward		✓		
Using the thumb finger pointed to a direction, to request a ride or a hike	✓			
Raising one's hand/waving with an open fist to summon a taxi	✓			
Tapping one's foot/feet on the floor in a public gathering		✓		
Wiggling one's leg(s) when in a sitting position		✓		
Use of the hand (by motorists and cyclists) to signal direction of traffic	✓			

POLAND

		(See last page for comments on items referenced here)
Foreign tourists are welcome in the country.	yes	
The use of seat belt is mandatory.	yes	
International driving license is accepted.	yes	
U.S. driver's license is accepted.	yes	
It is considered impolite to yawn in public.	yes	
Death penalty for drug trafficking is the law.	yes	
Life imprisonment for drug trafficking is the law.	yes	
Guilty until proven innocent in court is the law.	yes	
Innocent until proven guilty in court is the law.	yes	
Pedestrians always have right of way.	yes	
Exit visas are required of visitors.	yes	
Crash helmet is mandatory for motor cyclist.	yes	
Hanging is used as a form of legal punishment.	yes	
Decapitation of a limb is used as a form of punishment.	yes	
Caning is used as a form of legal punishment.	yes	
Electric shock is used as a form of legal punishment.	yes	
One is expected to stand up during the playing of the national anthem.	yes	
Crash helmet is mandatory for bicyclists.	yes	
Guests are expected to eat every thing on their plates.	yes	
Table manners are very informal.	yes	
One is expected to cover one's mouth when laughing.	yes	
A vertical nod of the head means YES (OK).	yes	
A horizontal shaking of the head means NO (Not OK).	yes	
Prostitution is allowed only in designated areas.	yes	
One is expected to take off one's hat during playing of national anthem.	yes	
Separate seating arrangements (between sexes) are maintained at movies.	yes	
Separate seating arrangements (between sexes) are maintained at churches.	yes	
Uninvited visitors or guests may not be welcome, even among acquaintances.	yes	
Pets (e.g. cats, dog) are allowed in some hotels and restaurants.	yes	
Couples invited for a meal may be separated during meals according to their sex.	yes	
Punctuality is the order of business.	yes	
Automobiles are driven with headlights always turned on.	yes	
Motorcycles are driven with headlights always turned on.	yes	
Visitors with expired visa face mandatory jail time.	yes	
Visitors without exit visa face jail time.	yes	
Visitors without entry visa face mandatory (automatic) jail time.	no	

ADDITIONAL COUNTRY INFORMATION

(A)	**The types of gifts to avoid:**	none
(B)	**Appropriate gifts for a foreigner to give:**	flowers (odd #), chocolates, vodka, cigars
(C)	**Best time to present gifts (at the beginning or at the end of a visit?):**	at beginning
(D)	**Best time to present gifts (on initial or later visits?):**	n/a
(E)	**Best place to present gifts (in private or in public?):**	home
(F)	**Number(s) with certain connotations and/or myths attached to them:**	n/a
(G)	**Basic shape(s) with negative connotations:**	n/a
(H)	**Basic color(s) with negative connotations:**	n/a
(I)	**Traditional greeting methods include:**	n/a
(J)	**Safe topics for discussion include:**	weather, fashion, travel, art, family, religion, domestic politics, food, sports, international politics, social conditions, money and personal wealth, sex.
(K)	**Best time for conversations (before, during, after meals?):**	n/a
(L)	**Forms of legal punishment:**	jailing
(M)	**Approximately length of time one could be detained by law and order authorities before being charged in court:**	n/a
(N)	**January 15, 1999, for example, will normally be written as:**	15/1/99
(O)	**Emergency code number**:	998
(P)	**Ambulance code Number**:	999
(Q)	**Police code number:**	997
(R)	**Telephone (country) code:**	48
(S)	**Telex (country) code:**	867
(T)	**Electricity requirements**:	220 v/50Hz
(U)	**Legal drinking age:**	18
(V)	**Systems of weights and measures:**	metric
(W)	**Legal age of incarceration**:	18
(X)	**Driving side of the road:**	right
(Y)	**Minimum expenditure expected of foreign visitors?** $	n/a
(Z)	**Name of currency**:	Zloty
(Za)	**Some places 0ff-limits to foreign visitors:**	n/a
(Zb)	**Some places, structures and items prohibited from being photographed:**	n/a

PORTUGAL	Is customary Is allowed Is permissible Is used. Is OK	Is not customary Is frowned upon	Is disallowed Is forbidden Is a crime	(See last page for comments on items referenced here)
Smoking in public	✓			
Eating in public	✓			
Not flushing public toilet		✓		
Spitting in public				n/a
Feeding animals & birds in public	✓			
Whistling in public	✓			
Drinking alcohol in public	✓			
Kissing in public	✓			
Breast feeding in public	✓			
Drunkenness (in public)		✓		
Cursing in public		✓		
Religious preaching in public	✓			
Begging (panhandling) in public	✓			
Giving money to beggars/panhandlers	✓			
Giving food/drink to beggars/panhandlers	✓			
Brushing teeth in public (other than in restrooms)		✓		
Strolling with pets in major public roads/streets	✓			
Chewing gum in public	✓			
Chewing gum in government offices	✓			
Combing hair in public (other than in toilets/restrooms)		✓		
Undressing/dressing in public			✓	
Wearing of dark glasses indoors in public places	✓			
Public display of wealth	✓			
Praying openly in public in non-designated areas		✓		
Walking bare feet in public			✓	
Chewing tobacco in public		✓		
Trimming one's finger or toe nails in public		✓		
Laughing aloud in public	✓			
Mingling of the sexes in public				n/a
Mixed bathing in public swimming pools	✓			
Distributing religious pamphlets (literature) in public/side streets	✓			

PORTUGAL

	Is customary Is allowed Is permissible Is used. Is OK	Is not customary Is frowned upon	Is disallowed Is forbidden Is a crime	(See last page for comments on items referenced here)
Dancing on side street	✓			
Nude bathing	✓			1
Littering			✓	
Binge Drinking	✓			
hitchhiking	✓			
Jaywalking			✓	
Drunk driving			✓	
Speeding			✓	
Skating on side streets (side-walk)	✓			
Graffiti painting			✓	
Pilfering			✓	
Prostitution			✓	
Haggling in the market place	✓			
Consumption of alcoholic beverages in bars and restaurants	✓			
Gambling	✓			2
Possession of pornographic materials	✓			
Possession of the Christian Bible	✓			
Possession of the Moslem Koran	✓			
Possession of bullet-proof vest	✓			
Possession of toy gun	✓			
Possession of fire crackers and fireworks	✓			
Possession of prescription drugs (without doctor's note)	✓			
Possession of regulated drugs (narcotics)	✓			
Possession of firearms (by foreigners)	✓			
Possession of pocket knife in public	✓			
Using walkie talkies	✓			
Using of "boom boxes"(loud sounding stereo system)	✓			
Using "walkman" (very small radio/cassettes with ear plugs) in public places	✓			
Using "walkman" (very small radio/cassettes with ear plugs) while driving or riding			✓	

PORTUGAL

	Is customary Is allowed Is permissible Is used Is OK	Is not customary Is frowned upon	Is disallowed Is forbidden Is a crime	(See last page for comments on items referenced here)
Use of cellular phone	✓			
Use of binoculars/periscopes other than in sports arena	✓			
Taking photographs of people (without their permission)		✓		
Taking photographs at airports, train and bus stations	✓			
Taking photographs of airports	✓			
Taking photographs of churches and synagogues	✓			
Taking photographs of religious statues	✓			
Taking photographs of public buildings	✓			
Taking photographs of bridges	✓			
Tipping (gratuity)	✓			
Tipping (when service is rendered)	✓			
Tipping (when service is not rendered)		✓		
Tipping waiters/waitresses at restaurants and hotels	✓			
Tipping taxi/cab drivers	✓			
Tipping baggage handlers, porters, door persons	✓			
Tipping of hair dressers/barbers	✓			
Overtipping	✓			
Undertipping	✓			
Spilling cigarette butt (ash) on side streets/on the floor	✓			
Men wearing lipstick		✓		
Wearing visible tattoo marks	✓			
Men painting/coloring their finger or toe nails		✓		
Cross dressing (men dressed like women & vice versa)		✓		
Walking in public without a shirt (i.e. with the upper half of the body naked)	✓			
Men wearing braided hair		✓		
Men wearing earrings		✓		
Men wearing dreadlock hair style	✓			
Homosexuality	✓			
Lesbianism	✓			

PORTUGAL

	Is customary Is allowed Is permissible Is used Is OK	Is not customary Is frowned upon	Is disallowed Is forbidden Is a crime	(See last page for comments on items referenced here)
Females covering their hair (wearing headgear) in public		✓		
Females exposing their full face in public		✓		
Females driving automobiles	✓			
Females riding motorcycles	✓			
Females riding bicycles	✓			
Females smoking in public	✓			
Women wearing bras (braziers) in public			✓	
Use of lipstick by women	✓			
A woman extending her hands first when introduced	✓			
Female bashing	✓			
Females wearing trousers	✓			
Females wearing minis (short dresses)	✓			
Females wearing bikinis	✓			
Females wearing shorts	✓			
Persons of opposite sex holding hands in public	✓			
Persons of same sex holding hands in public		✓		
Handshake between opposite sex	✓			
Hugging in public by same sex	✓			
Hugging in public by opposite sex	✓			
Men and women walking side by side in public	✓			
Man walking ahead (in public), with the woman following		✓		
Woman walking ahead (in public), with the man following		✓		
Men opening doors for women	✓			
Sitting with legs crossed in the presence of elders	✓			
Talking to an elderly person with one's hat/cap on	✓			
Talking to an elderly person with hands positioned on both sides of one's waist	✓			
Blowing one's nose in public	✓			
Blowing one's nose in the presence of others	✓			
Addressing people by their title	✓			3

PORTUGAL

	Is customary Is allowed Is permissible Is used. Is OK	Is not customary Is frowned upon	Is disallowed Is forbidden Is a crime	(See last page for comments on items referenced here)
Addressing people by their family name/surname/last name/given name	✓			3
Addressing people by their first name/ given name	✓			3
Women going through doors first	✓			
Men helping women with their coats	✓			
Men extending their hands to women first during greetings	✓			
Taking off one's hat when entering a private home	✓			
Removing one's shoes when entering a private home	✓			
Invited guests bringing food at social gatherings	✓			
Guests bringing drinks at social gatherings	✓			3
Shaking hands when leaving a small group	✓			
Shaking hands with everyone present, upon arrival at a social gathering	✓			
Eating with the right hand	✓			
Eating with the left hand	✓			
Eating with both hands	✓			
Presenting a gift or passing on an object with the left hand	✓			
Asking a man about his wife	✓			
Asking a woman about her husband	✓			
Making prior appointments before a meeting or visit	✓			
Addressing an audience with one or both hands in the pocket	✓			
Carrying on conversation during meals	✓			
Females sitting with legs crossed	✓			
People discussing their wealth				3
Asking someone his or her age, or how old the person is	✓			
Complementing someone on his/her physical looks	✓			
Complementing someone on his/her attire	✓			
Use of both hands in handshake	✓			
In greeting, a handshake accompanied by a slight bow		✓		

PORTUGAL

	Is customary Is allowed Is permissible Is used. Is OK	Is not customary Is frowned upon	Is disallowed Is forbidden Is a crime	(See last page for comments on items referenced here)
Salutations such as "Good morning", "Good afternoon", "Good evening"	✓			
The completion of a business deal with a handshake	✓			
Starting a negotiation session with a handshake	✓			
A gift for the host/hostess	✓			
Giving a business gift	✓			
A gift of money (use of money as gift)	✓			3
Use of flowers as a gift	✓			
Use of business cards	✓			
Accepting/presenting gifts with both hands	✓			
Burning of the country's flag			✓	
Mutilation of the national currency			✓	
Casual wearing of clothings made with colors & marks of the national flag	✓			
Wearing of look-alike military (camouflage) fatigues (attire)	✓			
Sitting on the floor (on floor mats)	✓			
Discussion of religion	✓			
Discussion of politics	✓			
Discussion of sex	✓			
Patting/slapping someone on the buttocks		✓		
Patting/slapping someone on the back	✓			
Touching or patting someone's head/hair		✓		
Casual touching of any part of someone's body		✓		
Drinking directly out of a bottle/can	✓			
Placing one's leg(s) on the table or chair	✓			

PORTUGAL

	Is customary Is allowed Is permissible Is used. Is OK	Is not customary Is frowned upon	Is disallowed Is forbidden Is a crime	(See last page for comments on items referenced here)
Showing the sole of one's foot (feet)		✓		
People standing very close when talking	✓			
Maintaining steady eye contact (direct gaze) when talking to someone	✓			
Kissing or exchange of kisses on the cheek	✓			
Counting money (change) in someone's palm	✓			
Finger pointing in public (in a daring manner)		✓		
Seeking attention by winking the eyes	✓			
Tapping the head to indicate someone is crazy	✓			
Twirling the head to indicate someone is crazy				n/a
Whistling as a way of requesting something/seeking attention	✓			
Using "thumbs-up" sign to mean OK	✓			
Forming a circle with the thumb and index finger (forefinger) to mean OK	✓			
Using the fingers to make a "V" sign for victory	✓			
Beckoning to someone with the index finger (forefinger)			✓	
The left to right waving of the hand with open palms facing outward to indicate "Good bye"	✓			
The use of a nod to show acknowledgement	✓			
Stopping/beckoning a taxi using a stretched hand with the thumb pointing upward		✓		
Using the thumb finger pointed to a direction, to request a ride or a hike	✓			
Raising one's hand/waving with an open fist to summon a taxi	✓			
Tapping one's foot/feet on the floor in a public gathering	✓			
Wiggling one's leg(s) when in a sitting position	✓			
Use of the hand (by motorists and cyclists) to signal direction of traffic	✓			

PORTUGAL

		(See last page for comments on items referenced here)
Foreign tourists are welcome in the country.	yes	
The use of seat belt is mandatory.	yes	
International driving license is accepted.	yes	
U.S. driver's license is accepted.	yes	
It is considered impolite to yawn in public.	yes	
Death penalty for drug trafficking is the law.	no	
Life imprisonment for drug trafficking is the law.	no	
Guilty until proven innocent in court is the law.	no	
Innocent until proven guilty in court is the law.	yes	
Pedestrians always have right of way.	no	
Exit visas are required of visitors.	no	
Crash helmet is mandatory for motor cyclist.	yes	
Hanging is used as a form of legal punishment.	no	
Decapitation of a limb is used as a form of punishment.	no	
Caning is used as a form of legal punishment.	no	
Electric shock is used as a form of legal punishment.	no	
One is expected to stand up during the playing of the national anthem.	yes	
Crash helmet is mandatory for bicyclists.	yes	
Guests are expected to eat every thing on their plates.	yes	
Table manners are very informal.	no	
One is expected to cover one's mouth when laughing.	yes	
A vertical nod of the head means YES (OK).	yes	
A horizontal shaking of the head means NO (Not OK).	yes	
Prostitution is allowed only in designated areas.	no	
One is expected to take off one's hat during playing of national anthem.	yes	
Separate seating arrangements (between sexes) are maintained at movies.	no	
Separate seating arrangements (between sexes) are maintained at churches.	no	
Uninvited visitors or guests may not be welcome, even among acquaintances.		3
Pets (e.g. cats, dog) are allowed in some hotels and restaurants.	yes/no	
Couples invited for a meal may be separated during meals according to their sex.	yes	
Punctuality is the order of business.	yes	
Automobiles are driven with headlights always turned on.	no	
Motorcycles are driven with headlights always turned on.	no	
Visitors with expired visa face mandatory jail time.	no	
Visitors without exit visa face jail time.	no	
Visitors without entry visa face mandatory (automatic) jail time.	no	

ADDITIONAL COUNTRY INFORMATION

(A)	**The types of gifts to avoid:**	n/a
(B)	**Appropriate gifts for a foreigner to give:**	n/a
(C)	**Best time to present gifts (at the beginning or at the end of a visit?):**	beginning
(D)	**Best time to present gifts (on initial or later visits?):**	n/a
(E)	**Best place to present gifts (in private or in public?):**	n/a
(F)	**Number(s) with certain connotations and/or myths attached to them:**	n/a
(G)	**Basic shape(s) with negative connotations:**	n/a
(H)	**Basic color(s) with negative connotations:**	n/a
(I)	**Traditional greeting methods include:**	n/a
(J)	**Safe topics for discussion include:**	weather, fashion, travel, art, family, domestic politics, food, sports, international politics, social conditions, money.
(K)	**Best time for conversations (before, during, after meals?):**	n/a
(L)	**Forms of legal punishment:**	jailing
(M)	**Approximately length of time one could be detained by law and order authorities before being charged in court:**	n/a
(N)	**January 15, 1999, for example, will normally be written as:**	15 Dec Janeiro, 1999
(O)	**Emergency code number**:	115
(P)	**Ambulance code Number**:	115
(Q)	**Police code number:**	3466141
(R)	**Telephone (country) code:**	351
(S)	**Telex (country) code:**	832
(T)	**Electricity requirements**:	210-220/50
(U)	**Legal drinking age:**	18
(V)	**Systems of weights and measures:**	metric
(W)	**Legal age of incarceration**:	n/a
(X)	**Driving side of the road:**	right
(Y)	**Minimum expenditure expected of foreign visitors? $**	no
(Z)	**Name of currency**:	Escudo
(Za)	**Some places 0ff-limits to foreign visitors:**	n/a
(Zb)	**Some places, structures and items prohibited from being photographed:**	museum (sour) inside

ENDNOTES

Item Number: COMMENTS/EXPLANATIONS

n/a: Not applicable/Not available/No response

(1) In some beaches.

(2) In casinos.

(3) It depends.

ROMANIA	Is customary Is allowed Is permissible Is used. Is OK	Is not customary Is frowned upon	Is disallowed Is forbidden Is a crime	(See last page for comments on items referenced here)
Smoking in public	✓			
Eating in public		✓		
Not flushing public toilet		✓		
Spitting in public		✓		
Feeding animals & birds in public	✓			
Whistling in public		✓		
Drinking alcohol in public		✓		
Kissing in public		✓		
Breast feeding in public		✓		
Drunkenness (in public)			✓	
Cursing in public			✓	
Religious preaching in public	✓			
Begging (panhandling) in public		✓		
Giving money to beggars/panhandlers	✓			
Giving food/drink to beggars/panhandlers	✓			
Brushing teeth in public (other than in restrooms)		✓		
Strolling with pets in major public roads/streets	✓			
Chewing gum in public		✓		
Chewing gum in government offices		✓		
Combing hair in public (other than in toilets/restrooms)		✓		
Undressing/dressing in public		✓		
Wearing of dark glasses indoors in public places		✓		
Public display of wealth		✓		
Praying openly in public in non-designated areas		✓		
Walking bare feet in public		✓		
Chewing tobacco in public		✓		
Trimming one's finger or toe nails in public		✓		
Laughing aloud in public	✓			
Mingling of the sexes in public			✓	
Mixed bathing in public swimming pools			✓	
Distributing religious pamphlets (literature) in public/side streets	✓			

ROMANIA

	Is customary Is allowed Is permissible Is used. Is OK	Is not customary Is frowned upon	Is disallowed Is forbidden Is a crime	(See last page for comments on items referenced here)
Dancing on side street		✓		
Nude bathing		✓		
Littering			✓	
Binge Drinking		✓		
hitchhiking		✓		
Jaywalking			✓	
Drunk driving			✓	
Speeding			✓	
Skating on side streets (side-walk)	✓			
Graffiti painting			✓	
Pilfering			✓	
Prostitution			✓	
Haggling in the market place		✓		
Consumption of alcoholic beverages in bars and restaurants	✓			
Gambling			✓	
Possession of pornographic materials			✓	
Possession of the Christian Bible	✓			
Possession of the Moslem Koran	✓			
Possession of bullet-proof vest		✓		
Possession of toy gun	✓			
Possession of fire crackers and fireworks			✓	
Possession of prescription drugs (without doctor's note)		✓		
Possession of regulated drugs (narcotics)			✓	
Possession of firearms (by foreigners)			✓	
Possession of pocket knife in public			✓	
Using walkie talkies		✓		
Using of "boom boxes"(loud sounding stereo system)		✓		
Using "walkman" (very small radio/cassettes with ear plugs) in public places	✓			
Using "walkman" (very small radio/cassettes with ear plugs) while driving or riding		✓		

ROMANIA

	Is customary Is allowed Is permissible Is used Is OK	Is not customary Is frowned upon	Is disallowed Is forbidden Is a crime	(See last page for comments on items referenced here)
Use of cellular phone		✓		
Use of binoculars/periscopes other than in sports arena		✓		
Taking photographs of people (without their permission)	✓			
Taking photographs at airports, train and bus stations				1
Taking photographs of airports			✓	
Taking photographs of churches and synagogues	✓			
Taking photographs of religious statues	✓			
Taking photographs of public buildings	✓			
Taking photographs of bridges	✓			
Tipping (gratuity)	✓			
Tipping (when service is rendered)	✓			
Tipping (when service is not rendered)		✓		
Tipping waiters/waitresses at restaurants and hotels		✓		
Tipping taxi/cab drivers		✓		
Tipping baggage handlers, porters, door persons		✓		
Tipping of hair dressers/barbers		✓		
Overtipping		✓		
Undertipping		✓		
Spilling cigarette butt (ash) on side streets/on the floor		✓		
Men wearing lipstick		✓		
Wearing visible tattoo marks		✓		
Men painting/coloring their finger or toe nails		✓		
Cross dressing (men dressed like women & vice versa)		✓		
Walking in public without a shirt (i.e. with the upper half of the body naked)		✓		
Men wearing braided hair		✓		
Men wearing earrings		✓		
Men wearing dreadlock hair style		✓		
Homosexuality			✓	2
Lesbianism			✓	2

ROMANIA

	Is customary Is allowed Is permissible Is used Is OK	Is not customary Is frowned upon	Is disallowed Is forbidden Is a crime	(See last page for comments on items referenced here)
Females covering their hair (wearing headgear) in public		✓		
Females exposing their full face in public				
Females driving automobiles	✓			
Females riding motorcycles	✓			
Females riding bicycles	✓			
Females smoking in public		✓		
Women wearing bras (braziers) in public		✓		
Use of lipstick by women	✓			
A woman extending her hands first when introduced	✓			
Female bashing			✓	
Females wearing trousers	✓			
Females wearing minis (short dresses)	✓			
Females wearing bikinis	✓			
Females wearing shorts	✓			
Persons of opposite sex holding hands in public	✓			
Persons of same sex holding hands in public		✓		
Handshake between opposite sex		✓		
Hugging in public by same sex	✓			
Hugging in public by opposite sex		✓		
Men and women walking side by side in public	✓			
Man walking ahead (in public), with the woman following		✓		
Woman walking ahead (in public), with the man following		✓		
Men opening doors for women	✓			
Sitting with legs crossed in the presence of elders	✓			
Talking to an elderly person with one's hat/cap on		✓		
Talking to an elderly person with hands positioned on both sides of one's waist	✓			
Blowing one's nose in public		✓		
Blowing one's nose in the presence of others		✓		
Addressing people by their title	✓			

ROMANIA

	Is customary Is allowed Is permissible Is used. Is OK	**Is not customary Is frowned upon**	**Is disallowed Is forbidden Is a crime**	**(See last page for comments on items referenced here)**
Addressing people by their family name/surname/last name/given name	✓			
Addressing people by their first name/ given name		✓		
Women going through doors first	✓			
Men helping women with their coats	✓			
Men extending their hands to women first during greetings	✓			
Taking off one's hat when entering a private home	✓			
Removing one's shoes when entering a private home		✓		
Invited guests bringing food at social gatherings		✓		
Guests bringing drinks at social gatherings		✓		
Shaking hands when leaving a small group	✓			
Shaking hands with everyone present, upon arrival at a social gathering	✓			
Eating with the right hand	✓			
Eating with the left hand	✓			
Eating with both hands	✓			
Presenting a gift or passing on an object with the left hand		✓		
Asking a man about his wife		✓		
Asking a woman about her husband		✓		
Making prior appointments before a meeting or visit	✓			
Addressing an audience with one or both hands in the pocket		✓		
Carrying on conversation during meals		✓		
Females sitting with legs crossed	✓			
People discussing their wealth		✓		
Asking someone his or her age, or how old the person is		✓		
Complementing someone on his/her physical looks	✓			
Complementing someone on his/her attire	✓			
Use of both hands in handshake		✓		
In greeting, a handshake accompanied by a slight bow	✓			

ROMANIA

	Is customary Is allowed Is permissible Is used. Is OK	Is not customary Is frowned upon	Is disallowed Is forbidden Is a crime	(See last page for comments on items referenced here)
Salutations such as "Good morning", "Good afternoon", "Good evening"	✓			
The completion of a business deal with a handshake	✓			
Starting a negotiation session with a handshake	✓			
A gift for the host/hostess	✓			
Giving a business gift		✓		
A gift of money (use of money as gift)		✓		
Use of flowers as a gift	✓			
Use of business cards	✓			
Accepting/presenting gifts with both hands	✓			
Burning of the country's flag			✓	
Mutilation of the national currency			✓	
Casual wearing of clothings made with colors & marks of the national flag	✓			
Wearing of look-alike military (camouflage) fatigues (attire)		✓		
Sitting on the floor (on floor mats)		✓		
Discussion of religion	✓			
Discussion of politics	✓			
Discussion of sex		✓		
Patting/slapping someone on the buttocks		✓		
Patting/slapping someone on the back	✓			
Touching or patting someone's head/hair		✓		
Casual touching of any part of someone's body		✓		
Drinking directly out of a bottle/can	✓			
Placing one's leg(s) on the table or chair		✓		

ROMANIA

	Is customary Is allowed Is permissible Is used. Is OK	Is not customary Is frowned upon	Is disallowed Is forbidden Is a crime	(See last page for comments on items referenced here)
Showing the sole of one's foot (feet)	✓			
People standing very close when talking		✓		
Maintaining steady eye contact (direct gaze) when talking to someone		✓		
Kissing or exchange of kisses on the cheek	✓			
Counting money (change) in someone's palm		✓		
Finger pointing in public (in a daring manner)		✓		
Seeking attention by winking the eyes		✓		
Tapping the head to indicate someone is crazy		✓		
Twirling the head to indicate someone is crazy		✓		
Whistling as a way of requesting something/seeking attention		✓		
Using "thumbs-up" sign to mean OK		✓		
Forming a circle with the thumb and index finger (forefinger) to mean OK		✓		
Using the fingers to make a "V" sign for victory	✓			
Beckoning to someone with the index finger (forefinger)		✓		
The left to right waving of the hand with open palms facing outward to indicate "Good bye"	✓			
The use of a nod to show acknowledgement				n/a
Stopping/beckoning a taxi using a stretched hand with the thumb pointing upward	✓			
Using the thumb finger pointed to a direction, to request a ride or a hike	✓			
Raising one's hand/waving with an open fist to summon a taxi	✓			
Tapping one's foot/feet on the floor in a public gathering		✓		
Wiggling one's leg(s) when in a sitting position		✓		
Use of the hand (by motorists and cyclists) to signal direction of traffic	✓			

ROMANIA

		(See last page for comments on items referenced here)
Foreign tourists are welcome in the country.	yes	
The use of seat belt is mandatory.	yes	
International driving license is accepted.	yes	
U.S. driver's license is accepted.	yes	
It is considered impolite to yawn in public.	yes	
Death penalty for drug trafficking is the law.	no	
Life imprisonment for drug trafficking is the law.	no	
Guilty until proven innocent in court is the law.	no	
Innocent until proven guilty in court is the law.	yes	
Pedestrians always have right of way.	no	
Exit visas are required of visitors.	no	
Crash helmet is mandatory for motor cyclist.	yes	
Hanging is used as a form of legal punishment.	no	
Decapitation of a limb is used as a form of punishment.	no	
Caning is used as a form of legal punishment.	no	
Electric shock is used as a form of legal punishment.	no	
One is expected to stand up during the playing of the national anthem.	yes	
Crash helmet is mandatory for bicyclists.	no	
Guests are expected to eat every thing on their plates.	yes	
Table manners are very informal.	yes	
One is expected to cover one's mouth when laughing.	yes	
A vertical nod of the head means YES (OK).	yes	
A horizontal shaking of the head means NO (Not OK).	yes	
Prostitution is allowed only in designated areas.	no	
One is expected to take off one's hat during playing of national anthem.	yes	
Separate seating arrangements (between sexes) are maintained at movies.	no	
Separate seating arrangements (between sexes) are maintained at churches.	no	
Uninvited visitors or guests may not be welcome, even among acquaintances.	no	
Pets (e.g. cats, dog) are allowed in some hotels and restaurants.	no	
Couples invited for a meal may be separated during meals according to their sex.	no	
Punctuality is the order of business.	no	
Automobiles are driven with headlights always turned on.	no	
Motorcycles are driven with headlights always turned on.	no	
Visitors with expired visa face mandatory jail time.	no	
Visitors without exit visa face jail time.	no	
Visitors without entry visa face mandatory (automatic) jail time.	no	

ADDITIONAL COUNTRY INFORMATION

(A)	**The types of gifts to avoid:**	certain types of flowers, handkerchiefs, soaps
(B)	**Appropriate gifts for a foreigner to give:**	flowers (except red roses), Good books or something specific to visitors country, perfume, coffee, cosmetics
(C)	**Best time to present gifts (at the beginning or at the end of a visit?):**	at beginning
(D)	**Best time to present gifts (on initial or later visits?):**	n/a
(E)	**Best place to present gifts (in private or in public?)**:	n/a
(F)	**Number(s) with certain connotations and/or myths attached to them:**	n/a
(G)	**Basic shape(s) with negative connotations:**	n/a
(H)	**Basic color(s) with negative connotations:**	n/a
(I)	**Traditional greeting methods include:**	n/a
(J)	**Safe topics for discussion include:**	weather, fashion, travel, art, family, religion, domestic politics, food, sports, international politics, social conditions, music, books
(K)	**Best time for conversations (before, during, after meals?):**	n/a
(L)	**Forms of legal punishment:**	jailing
(M)	**Approximately length of time one could be detained by law and order authorities before being charged in court:**	detention may not exceed 24 hrs.
(N)	**January 15, 1999, for example, will normally be written as:**	15.01.1999
(O)	**Emergency code number**:	bucharest: 051
(P)	**Ambulance code Number**:	bucharest: 961
(Q)	**Police code number:**	bucharest: 955
(R)	**Telephone (country) code:**	011
(S)	**Telex (country) code:**	864
(T)	**Electricity requirements**:	220v
(U)	**Legal drinking age:**	n/a
(V)	**Systems of weights and measures:**	European
(W)	**Legal age of incarceration**:	18 years
(X)	**Driving side of the road:**	right
(Y)	**Minimum expenditure expected of foreign visitors? $**	no
(Z)	**Name of currency**:	Led (lei)
(Za)	**Some places 0ff-limits to foreign visitors:**	n/a
(Zb)	**Some places, structures and items prohibited from being photographed:**	Military objective

ENDNOTES

Item Number: COMMENTS/EXPLANATIONS

n/a: Not applicable/Not available/No response

(1) Taking photographs at airports is forbidden.

(2) Homosexuality & lesbianism are punishable by law if committed in public places.

SLOVAK REPUBLIC	Is customary Is allowed Is permissible Is used. Is OK	Is not customary Is frowned upon	Is disallowed Is forbidden Is a crime	(See last page for comments on items referenced here)
Smoking in public	✓			
Eating in public	✓			
Not flushing public toilet		✓		
Spitting in public		✓		
Feeding animals & birds in public	✓			
Whistling in public		✓		
Drinking alcohol in public	✓			
Kissing in public		✓		
Breast feeding in public		✓		
Drunkenness (in public)		✓		
Cursing in public		✓		
Religious preaching in public	✓			
Begging (panhandling) in public	✓			
Giving money to beggars/panhandlers	✓			
Giving food/drink to beggars/panhandlers	✓			
Brushing teeth in public (other than in restrooms)		✓		
Strolling with pets in major public roads/streets	✓			
Chewing gum in public	✓			
Chewing gum in government offices		✓		
Combing hair in public (other than in toilets/restrooms)	✓			
Undressing/dressing in public		✓		
Wearing of dark glasses indoors in public places		✓		
Public display of wealth				n/a
Praying openly in public in non-designated areas	✓			
Walking bare feet in public	✓			
Chewing tobacco in public		✓		
Trimming one's finger or toe nails in public		✓		
Laughing aloud in public		✓		
Mingling of the sexes in public		✓		
Mixed bathing in public swimming pools	✓			
Distributing religious pamphlets (literature) in public/side streets	✓			

SLOVAK REPUBLIC

	Is customary Is allowed Is permissible Is used. Is OK	Is not customary Is frowned upon	Is disallowed Is forbidden Is a crime	(See last page for comments on items referenced here)
Dancing on side street	✓			
Nude bathing		✓		
Littering		✓		
Binge Drinking	✓			
hitchhiking	✓			
Jaywalking	✓			
Drunk driving	.		✓	
Speeding	✓			
Skating on side streets (side-walk)	✓			
Graffiti painting			✓	
Pilfering			✓	
Prostitution			✓	
Haggling in the market place	✓			
Consumption of alcoholic beverages in bars and restaurants	✓			
Gambling	✓			
Possession of pornographic materials	✓			
Possession of the Christian Bible	✓			
Possession of the Moslem Koran	✓			
Possession of bullet-proof vest	✓			
Possession of toy gun	✓			
Possession of fire crackers and fireworks	✓			
Possession of prescription drugs (without doctor's note)			✓	
Possession of regulated drugs (narcotics)			✓	
Possession of firearms (by foreigners)			✓	
Possession of pocket knife in public	✓			
Using walkie talkies				n/a
Using of "boom boxes"(loud sounding stereo system)		✓		
Using "walkman" (very small radio/cassettes with ear plugs) in public places	✓			
Using "walkman" (very small radio/cassettes with ear plugs) while driving or riding	✓			

SLOVAK REPUBLIC

	Is customary Is allowed Is permissible Is used Is OK	Is not customary Is frowned upon	Is disallowed Is forbidden Is a crime	(See last page for comments on items referenced here)
Use of cellular phone	✓			
Use of binoculars/periscopes other than in sports arena	✓			
Taking photographs of people (without their permission)		✓		
Taking photographs at airports, train and bus stations				n/a
Taking photographs of airports	✓			
Taking photographs of churches and synagogues	✓			
Taking photographs of religious statues	✓			
Taking photographs of public buildings	✓			
Taking photographs of bridges	✓			
Tipping (gratuity)	✓			
Tipping (when service is rendered)	✓			
Tipping (when service is not rendered)	✓			
Tipping waiters/waitresses at restaurants and hotels	✓			
Tipping taxi/cab drivers	✓			
Tipping baggage handlers, porters, door persons	✓			
Tipping of hair dressers/barbers	✓			
Overtipping				n/a
Undertipping				n/a
Spilling cigarette butt (ash) on side streets/on the floor		✓		
Men wearing lipstick		✓		
Wearing visible tattoo marks	✓			
Men painting/coloring their finger or toe nails		✓		
Cross dressing (men dressed like women & vice versa)		✓		
Walking in public without a shirt (i.e. with the upper half of the body naked)		✓		
Men wearing braided hair	✓			
Men wearing earrings	✓			
Men wearing dreadlock hair style		✓		
Homosexuality		✓		
Lesbianism		✓		

SLOVAK REPUBLIC

	Is customary **Is allowed** **Is permissible** **Is used** **Is OK**	**Is not customary** **Is frowned upon**	**Is disallowed** **Is forbidden** **Is a crime**	**(See last page for comments on items referenced here)**
Females covering their hair (wearing headgear) in public	✓			
Females exposing their full face in public	✓			
Females driving automobiles	✓			
Females riding motorcycles	✓			
Females riding bicycles	✓			
Females smoking in public	✓			
Women wearing bras (braziers) in public	✓			
Use of lipstick by women	✓			
A woman extending her hands first when introduced	✓			
Female bashing			✓	
Females wearing trousers	✓			
Females wearing minis (short dresses)	✓			
Females wearing bikinis	✓			
Females wearing shorts	✓			
Persons of opposite sex holding hands in public	✓			
Persons of same sex holding hands in public		✓		
Handshake between opposite sex	✓			
Hugging in public by same sex	✓			
Hugging in public by opposite sex		✓		
Men and women walking side by side in public	✓			
Man walking ahead (in public), with the woman following		✓		
Woman walking ahead (in public), with the man following		✓		
Men opening doors for women	✓			
Sitting with legs crossed in the presence of elders	✓			
Talking to an elderly person with one's hat/cap on	✓			
Talking to an elderly person with hands positioned on both sides of one's waist	✓			
Blowing one's nose in public		✓		
Blowing one's nose in the presence of others		✓		
Addressing people by their title	✓			

SLOVAK REPUBLIC

	Is customary Is allowed Is permissible Is used. Is OK	Is not customary Is frowned upon	Is disallowed Is forbidden Is a crime	(See last page for comments on items referenced here)
Addressing people by their family name/surname/last name/given name	✓			
Addressing people by their first name/ given name	✓			
Women going through doors first	✓			
Men helping women with their coats	✓			
Men extending their hands to women first during greetings		✓		
Taking off one's hat when entering a private home	✓			
Removing one's shoes when entering a private home	✓			
Invited guests bringing food at social gatherings		✓		
Guests bringing drinks at social gatherings	✓			
Shaking hands when leaving a small group	✓			
Shaking hands with everyone present, upon arrival at a social gathering		✓		
Eating with the right hand	✓			
Eating with the left hand	✓			
Eating with both hands	✓			
Presenting a gift or passing on an object with the left hand	✓			
Asking a man about his wife	✓			
Asking a woman about her husband	✓			
Making prior appointments before a meeting or visit	✓			
Addressing an audience with one or both hands in the pocket		✓		
Carrying on conversation during meals		✓		
Females sitting with legs crossed	✓			
People discussing their wealth	✓			
Asking someone his or her age, or how old the person is		✓		
Complementing someone on his/her physical looks		✓		
Complementing someone on his/her attire		✓		
Use of both hands in handshake	✓			
In greeting, a handshake accompanied by a slight bow	✓			

SLOVAK REPUBLIC

	Is customary Is allowed Is permissible Is used. Is OK	Is not customary Is frowned upon	Is disallowed Is forbidden Is a crime	(See last page for comments on items referenced here)
Salutations such as "Good morning", "Good afternoon", "Good evening"	✓			
The completion of a business deal with a handshake	✓			
Starting a negotiation session with a handshake		✓		
A gift for the host/hostess	✓			
Giving a business gift		✓		
A gift of money (use of money as gift)	✓			
Use of flowers as a gift	✓			
Use of business cards	✓			
Accepting/presenting gifts with both hands		✓		
Burning of the country's flag			✓	
Mutilation of the national currency			✓	
Casual wearing of clothings made with colors & marks of the national flag	✓			
Wearing of look-alike military (camouflage) fatigues (attire)	✓			
Sitting on the floor (on floor mats)				n/a
Discussion of religion	✓			
Discussion of politics	✓			
Discussion of sex	✓			
Patting/slapping someone on the buttocks		✓		
Patting/slapping someone on the back	✓			
Touching or patting someone's head/hair	✓			
Casual touching of any part of someone's body		✓		
Drinking directly out of a bottle/can	✓			
Placing one's leg(s) on the table or chair		✓		

SLOVAK REPUBLIC

	Is customary **Is allowed** **Is permissible** **Is used.** **Is OK**	**Is not customary** **Is frowned upon**	**Is disallowed** **Is forbidden** **Is a crime**	**(See last page for comments on items referenced here)**
Showing the sole of one's foot (feet)	✓			
People standing very close when talking	✓			
Maintaining steady eye contact (direct gaze) when talking to someone	✓			
Kissing or exchange of kisses on the cheek	✓			
Counting money (change) in someone's palm				n/a
Finger pointing in public (in a daring manner)		✓		
Seeking attention by winking the eyes	✓			
Tapping the head to indicate someone is crazy		✓		
Twirling the head to indicate someone is crazy		✓		
Whistling as a way of requesting something/seeking attention	✓			
Using "thumbs-up" sign to mean OK	✓			
Forming a circle with the thumb and index finger (forefinger) to mean OK		✓		
Using the fingers to make a "V" sign for victory		✓		
Beckoning to someone with the index finger (forefinger)		✓		
The left to right waving of the hand with open palms facing outward to indicate "Good bye"	✓			
The use of a nod to show acknowledgement	✓			
Stopping/beckoning a taxi using a stretched hand with the thumb pointing upward	✓			
Using the thumb finger pointed to a direction, to request a ride or a hike	✓			
Raising one's hand/waving with an open fist to summon a taxi	✓			
Tapping one's foot/feet on the floor in a public gathering		✓		
Wiggling one's leg(s) when in a sitting position		✓		
Use of the hand (by motorists and cyclists) to signal direction of traffic	✓			

SLOVAK REPUBLIC

		(See last page for comments on items referenced here)
Foreign tourists are welcome in the country.	yes	
The use of seat belt is mandatory.	yes	
International driving license is accepted.	yes	
U.S. driver's license is accepted.	yes	
It is considered impolite to yawn in public.	no	
Death penalty for drug trafficking is the law.	no	
Life imprisonment for drug trafficking is the law.	no	
Guilty until proven innocent in court is the law.	yes	
Innocent until proven guilty in court is the law.	no	
Pedestrians always have right of way.	yes & no	
Exit visas are required of visitors.	yes	
Crash helmet is mandatory for motor cyclist.	no	
Hanging is used as a form of legal punishment.	no	
Decapitation of a limb is used as a form of punishment.	no	
Caning is used as a form of legal punishment.	no	
Electric shock is used as a form of legal punishment.	no	
One is expected to stand up during the playing of the national anthem.	yes	
Crash helmet is mandatory for bicyclists.	no	
Guests are expected to eat every thing on their plates.	yes	
Table manners are very informal.	no	
One is expected to cover one's mouth when laughing.	no	
A vertical nod of the head means YES (OK).	yes	
A horizontal shaking of the head means NO (Not OK).	yes	
Prostitution is allowed only in designated areas.	no	
One is expected to take off one's hat during playing of national anthem.	yes	
Separate seating arrangements (between sexes) are maintained at movies.	no	
Separate seating arrangements (between sexes) are maintained at churches.	no	
Uninvited visitors or guests may not be welcome, even among acquaintances.	yes	
Pets (e.g. cats, dog) are allowed in some hotels and restaurants.	yes	
Couples invited for a meal may be separated during meals according to their sex.	no	
Punctuality is the order of business.	yes	
Automobiles are driven with headlights always turned on.	yes	
Motorcycles are driven with headlights always turned on.	yes	
Visitors with expired visa face mandatory jail time.	no	
Visitors without exit visa face jail time.	no	
Visitors without entry visa face mandatory (automatic) jail time.	no	

ADDITIONAL COUNTRY INFORMATION

(A)	**The types of gifts to avoid:**	n/a
(B)	**Appropriate gifts for a foreigner to give:**	n/a
(C)	**Best time to present gifts (at the beginning or at the end of a visit?):**	the end
(D)	**Best time to present gifts (on initial or later visits?):**	afterwards
(E)	**Best place to present gifts (in private or in public?):**	n/a
(F)	**Number(s) with certain connotations and/or myths attached to them:**	7- good luck, 13 bad luck
(G)	**Basic shape(s) with negative connotations:**	n/a
(H)	**Basic color(s) with negative connotations:**	n/a
(I)	**Traditional greeting methods include:**	handshake, kiss
(J)	**Safe topics for discussion include:**	fashion, travel, art,
(K)	**Best time for conversations (before, during, after meals?):**	after meals
(L)	**Forms of legal punishment:**	jailing
(M)	**Approximately length of time one could be detained by law and order authorities before being charged in court:**	48 hours
(N)	**January 15, 1999, for example, will normally be written as:**	15/1/99
(O)	**Emergency code number:**	150
(P)	**Ambulance code Number:**	155
(Q)	**Police code number:**	158
(R)	**Telephone (country) code:**	0042
(S)	**Telex (country) code:**	n/a
(T)	**Electricity requirements:**	n/a
(U)	**Legal drinking age:**	18
(V)	**Systems of weights and measures:**	n/a
(W)	**Legal age of incarceration:**	n/a
(X)	**Driving side of the road:**	right
(Y)	**Minimum expenditure expected of foreign visitors? $**	n/a
(Z)	**Name of currency:**	Slovak crown
(Za)	**Some places 0ff-limits to foreign visitors:**	no limits
(Zb)	**Some places, structures and items prohibited from being photographed:**	military

SPAIN	Is customary Is allowed Is permissible Is used. Is OK	Is not customary Is frowned upon	Is disallowed Is forbidden Is a crime	(See last page for comments on items referenced here)
Smoking in public	✓			
Eating in public		✓		
Not flushing public toilet		✓		
Spitting in public		✓		
Feeding animals & birds in public	✓			
Whistling in public	✓			
Drinking alcohol in public	✓			
Kissing in public	✓			
Breast feeding in public		✓		
Drunkenness (in public)		✓		
Cursing in public	✓			
Religious preaching in public		✓		
Begging (panhandling) in public		✓		
Giving money to beggars/panhandlers	✓			
Giving food/drink to beggars/panhandlers	✓			
Brushing teeth in public (other than in restrooms)		✓		
Strolling with pets in major public roads/streets	✓			
Chewing gum in public	✓			
Chewing gum in government offices		✓		
Combing hair in public (other than in toilets/restrooms)		✓		
Undressing/dressing in public		✓		
Wearing of dark glasses indoors in public places		✓		
Public display of wealth	✓			
Praying openly in public in non-designated areas		✓		
Walking bare feet in public		✓		
Chewing tobacco in public		✓		
Trimming one's finger or toe nails in public		✓		
Laughing aloud in public	✓			
Mingling of the sexes in public	✓			
Mixed bathing in public swimming pools	✓			
Distributing religious pamphlets (literature) in public/side streets	✓			

SPAIN

	Is customary Is allowed Is permissible Is used. Is OK	Is not customary Is frowned upon	Is disallowed Is forbidden Is a crime	(See last page for comments on items referenced here)
Dancing on side street	✓			
Nude bathing		✓		
Littering	✓			
Binge Drinking			✓	
hitchhiking	✓			
Jaywalking	✓			
Drunk driving			✓	
Speeding			✓	
Skating on side streets (side-walk)		✓		
Graffiti painting			✓	
Pilfering			✓	
Prostitution	✓			
Haggling in the market place	✓			
Consumption of alcoholic beverages in bars and restaurants	✓			
Gambling	✓			
Possession of pornographic materials	✓			
Possession of the Christian Bible	✓			
Possession of the Moslem Koran	✓			
Possession of bullet-proof vest	✓			
Possession of toy gun	✓			
Possession of fire crackers and fireworks	✓			
Possession of prescription drugs (without doctor's note)			✓	
Possession of regulated drugs (narcotics)			✓	
Possession of firearms (by foreigners)			✓	
Possession of pocket knife in public			✓	
Using walkie talkies	✓			
Using of "boom boxes"(loud sounding stereo system)	✓			
Using "walkman" (very small radio/cassettes with ear plugs) in public places	✓			
Using "walkman" (very small radio/cassettes with ear plugs) while driving or riding			✓	

SPAIN

	Is customary Is allowed Is permissible Is used Is OK	Is not customary Is frowned upon	Is disallowed Is forbidden Is a crime	(See last page for comments on items referenced here)
Use of cellular phone	✓			
Use of binoculars/periscopes other than in sports arena	✓			
Taking photographs of people (without their permission)	✓			
Taking photographs at airports, train and bus stations	✓			
Taking photographs of airports	✓			
Taking photographs of churches and synagogues	✓			
Taking photographs of religious statues	✓			
Taking photographs of public buildings	✓			
Taking photographs of bridges	✓			
Tipping (gratuity)	✓			
Tipping (when service is rendered)	✓			
Tipping (when service is not rendered)		✓		
Tipping waiters/waitresses at restaurants and hotels	✓			
Tipping taxi/cab drivers	✓			
Tipping baggage handlers, porters, door persons	✓			
Tipping of hair dressers/barbers	✓			
Overtipping	✓			
Undertipping	✓			
Spilling cigarette butt (ash) on side streets/on the floor	✓			
Men wearing lipstick		✓		
Wearing visible tattoo marks	✓			
Men painting/coloring their finger or toe nails		✓		
Cross dressing (men dressed like women & vice versa)		✓		
Walking in public without a shirt (i.e. with the upper half of the body naked)		✓		
Men wearing braided hair	✓	✓		
Men wearing earrings	✓			
Men wearing dreadlock hair style	✓			
Homosexuality	✓			
Lesbianism	✓			

SPAIN

	Is customary Is allowed Is permissible Is used Is OK	Is not customary Is frowned upon	Is disallowed Is forbidden Is a crime	(See last page for comments on items referenced here)
Females covering their hair (wearing headgear) in public	✓			
Females exposing their full face in public				n/a
Females driving automobiles	✓			
Females riding motorcycles	✓			
Females riding bicycles	✓			
Females smoking in public	✓			
Women wearing bras (braziers) in public		✓		
Use of lipstick by women	✓			
A woman extending her hands first when introduced	✓			
Female bashing		✓		
Females wearing trousers	✓			
Females wearing minis (short dresses)	✓			
Females wearing bikinis	✓			
Females wearing shorts	✓			
Persons of opposite sex holding hands in public	✓			
Persons of same sex holding hands in public	✓			
Handshake between opposite sex	✓			
Hugging in public by same sex	✓			
Hugging in public by opposite sex	✓			
Men and women walking side by side in public	✓			
Man walking ahead (in public), with the woman following				n/a
Woman walking ahead (in public), with the man following				n/a
Men opening doors for women	✓			
Sitting with legs crossed in the presence of elders				n/a
Talking to an elderly person with one's hat/cap on				n/a
Talking to an elderly person with hands positioned on both sides of one's waist				n/a
Blowing one's nose in public	✓			
Blowing one's nose in the presence of others	✓			
Addressing people by their title	✓			

SPAIN

	Is customary Is allowed Is permissible Is used. Is OK	Is not customary Is frowned upon	Is disallowed Is forbidden Is a crime	(See last page for comments on items referenced here)
Addressing people by their family name/surname/last name/given name	✓			
Addressing people by their first name/ given name	✓			
Women going through doors first	✓			
Men helping women with their coats	✓			
Men extending their hands to women first during greetings	✓			
Taking off one's hat when entering a private home				n/a
Removing one's shoes when entering a private home				n/a
Invited guests bringing food at social gatherings	✓			
Guests bringing drinks at social gatherings	✓			
Shaking hands when leaving a small group	✓			
Shaking hands with everyone present, upon arrival at a social gathering	✓			
Eating with the right hand	✓			
Eating with the left hand	✓			
Eating with both hands		✓		
Presenting a gift or passing on an object with the left hand				n/a
Asking a man about his wife				n/a
Asking a woman about her husband				n/a
Making prior appointments before a meeting or visit	✓			
Addressing an audience with one or both hands in the pocket				n/a
Carrying on conversation during meals	✓			
Females sitting with legs crossed	✓			
People discussing their wealth		✓		
Asking someone his or her age, or how old the person is		✓		
Complementing someone on his/her physical looks	✓			
Complementing someone on his/her attire	✓			
Use of both hands in handshake	✓			
In greeting, a handshake accompanied by a slight bow		✓		

SPAIN

	Is customary Is allowed Is permissible Is used. Is OK	Is not customary Is frowned upon	Is disallowed Is forbidden Is a crime	(See last page for comments on items referenced here)
Salutations such as "Good morning", "Good afternoon", "Good evening"	✓			
The completion of a business deal with a handshake	✓			
Starting a negotiation session with a handshake	✓			
A gift for the host/hostess	✓			
Giving a business gift	✓			
A gift of money (use of money as gift)	✓			
Use of flowers as a gift	✓			
Use of business cards	✓			
Accepting/presenting gifts with both hands	✓			
Burning of the country's flag			✓	
Mutilation of the national currency			✓	
Casual wearing of clothings made with colors & marks of the national flag		✓		
Wearing of look-alike military (camouflage) fatigues (attire)		✓		
Sitting on the floor (on floor mats)		✓		
Discussion of religion	✓			
Discussion of politics	✓			
Discussion of sex	✓			
Patting/slapping someone on the buttocks		✓		
Patting/slapping someone on the back	✓			
Touching or patting someone's head/hair		✓		
Casual touching of any part of someone's body	✓			
Drinking directly out of a bottle/can	✓			
Placing one's leg(s) on the table or chair		✓		

SPAIN

	Is customary Is allowed Is permissible Is used. Is OK	Is not customary Is frowned upon	Is disallowed Is forbidden Is a crime	(See last page for comments on items referenced here)
Showing the sole of one's foot (feet)	✓			
People standing very close when talking	✓			
Maintaining steady eye contact (direct gaze) when talking to someone	✓			
Kissing or exchange of kisses on the cheek	✓			
Counting money (change) in someone's palm	✓			
Finger pointing in public (in a daring manner)		✓		
Seeking attention by winking the eyes		✓		
Tapping the head to indicate someone is crazy		✓		
Twirling the head to indicate someone is crazy	✓			
Whistling as a way of requesting something/seeking attention		✓		
Using "thumbs-up" sign to mean OK	✓			
Forming a circle with the thumb and index finger (forefinger) to mean OK	✓			
Using the fingers to make a "V" sign for victory	✓			
Beckoning to someone with the index finger (forefinger)	✓			
The left to right waving of the hand with open palms facing outward to indicate "Good bye"	✓			
The use of a nod to show acknowledgement	✓			
Stopping/beckoning a taxi using a stretched hand with the thumb pointing upward	✓			
Using the thumb finger pointed to a direction, to request a ride or a hike	✓			
Raising one's hand/waving with an open fist to summon a taxi	✓			
Tapping one's foot/feet on the floor in a public gathering		✓		
Wiggling one's leg(s) when in a sitting position	✓			
Use of the hand (by motorists and cyclists) to signal direction of traffic	✓			

SPAIN

		(See last page for comments on items referenced here)
Foreign tourists are welcome in the country.	yes	
The use of seat belt is mandatory.	yes	
International driving license is accepted.	yes	
U.S. driver's license is accepted.	no	
It is considered impolite to yawn in public.	yes	
Death penalty for drug trafficking is the law.	no	
Life imprisonment for drug trafficking is the law.	no	
Guilty until proven innocent in court is the law.	no	
Innocent until proven guilty in court is the law.	yes	
Pedestrians always have right of way.	no	
Exit visas are required of visitors.	no	
Crash helmet is mandatory for motor cyclist.	no	
Hanging is used as a form of legal punishment.	no	
Decapitation of a limb is used as a form of punishment.	no	
Caning is used as a form of legal punishment.	no	
Electric shock is used as a form of legal punishment.	no	
One is expected to stand up during the playing of the national anthem.	yes	
Crash helmet is mandatory for bicyclists.	yes	
Guests are expected to eat every thing on their plates.	no	
Table manners are very informal.	no	
One is expected to cover one's mouth when laughing.	no	
A vertical nod of the head means YES (OK).	yes	
A horizontal shaking of the head means NO (Not OK).	yes	
Prostitution is allowed only in designated areas.	yes	
One is expected to take off one's hat during playing of national anthem.	yes	
Separate seating arrangements (between sexes) are maintained at movies.	no	
Separate seating arrangements (between sexes) are maintained at churches.	no	
Uninvited visitors or guests may not be welcome, even among acquaintances.	yes	
Pets (e.g. cats, dog) are allowed in some hotels and restaurants.	no	
Couples invited for a meal may be separated during meals according to their sex.	yes	
Punctuality is the order of business.	yes	
Automobiles are driven with headlights always turned on.	no	
Motorcycles are driven with headlights always turned on.	yes	
Visitors with expired visa face mandatory jail time.	no	
Visitors without exit visa face jail time.	no	
Visitors without entry visa face mandatory (automatic) jail time.	no	

ADDITIONAL COUNTRY INFORMATION

(A)	**The types of gifts to avoid:**	dahlias and chrystanthemums
(B)	**Appropriate gifts for a foreigner to give:**	flowers, pasteries, cakes, chocolate, items typical souvenir from visitor country
(C)	**Best time to present gifts (at the beginning or at the end of a visit?):**	n/a
(D)	**Best time to present gifts (on initial or later visits?):**	n/a
(E)	**Best place to present gifts (in private or in public?):**	n/a
(F)	**Number(s) with certain connotations and/or myths attached to them:**	13
(G)	**Basic shape(s) with negative connotations:**	n/a
(H)	**Basic color(s) with negative connotations:**	n/a
(I)	**Traditional greeting methods include:**	n/a
(J)	**Safe topics for discussion include:**	weather, fashion, travel, art, family, religion, domestic politics, food, sports, international politics, social conditions,
(K)	**Best time for conversations (before, during, after meals?):**	n/a
(L)	**Forms of legal punishment:**	no physical violence
(M)	**Approximately length of time one could be detained by law and order authorities before being charged in court:**	72 hrs
(N)	**January 15, 1999, for example, will normally be written as:**	1-15-99
(O)	**Emergency code number:**	091
(P)	**Ambulance code Number:**	091
(Q)	**Police code number:**	091
(R)	**Telephone (country) code:**	34
(S)	**Telex (country) code:**	831
(T)	**Electricity requirements:**	220-240v
(U)	**Legal drinking age:**	18
(V)	**Systems of weights and measures:**	metric
(W)	**Legal age of incarceration:**	16
(X)	**Driving side of the road:**	right
(Y)	**Minimum expenditure expected of foreign visitors? $**	yes, $50
(Z)	**Name of currency:**	Peseta
(Za)	**Some places 0ff-limits to foreign visitors:**	n/a
(Zb)	**Some places, structures and items prohibited from being photographed:**	n/a

SWEDEN	Is customary Is allowed Is permissible Is used. Is OK	Is not customary Is frowned upon	Is disallowed Is forbidden Is a crime	(See last page for comments on items referenced here)
Smoking in public	✓			
Eating in public	✓			
Not flushing public toilet	✓			
Spitting in public	✓			
Feeding animals & birds in public	✓			
Whistling in public	✓			
Drinking alcohol in public		✓		
Kissing in public	✓			
Breast feeding in public	✓			
Drunkenness (in public)	✓			
Cursing in public	✓			
Religious preaching in public				
Begging (panhandling) in public		✓		
Giving money to beggars/panhandlers	✓			
Giving food/drink to beggars/panhandlers	✓			
Brushing teeth in public (other than in restrooms)		✓		
Strolling with pets in major public roads/streets	✓			
Chewing gum in public	✓			
Chewing gum in government offices	✓			
Combing hair in public (other than in toilets/restrooms)		✓		
Undressing/dressing in public		✓		
Wearing of dark glasses indoors in public places	✓			
Public display of wealth	✓			
Praying openly in public in non-designated areas		✓		
Walking bare feet in public	✓			
Chewing tobacco in public	✓			
Trimming one's finger or toe nails in public		✓		
Laughing aloud in public		✓		
Mingling of the sexes in public	✓			
Mixed bathing in public swimming pools	✓			
Distributing religious pamphlets (literature) in public/side streets	✓			

DO'S AND DON'TS AROUND THE WORLD: A COUNTRY GUIDE TO CULTURAL AND SOCIAL TABOOS AND ETIQUETTE

SWEDEN

	Is customary Is allowed Is permissible Is used. Is OK	Is not customary Is frowned upon	Is disallowed Is forbidden Is a crime	(See last page for comments on items referenced here)
Dancing on side street		✓		
Nude bathing		✓		
Littering		✓		
Binge Drinking		✓		
hitchhiking	✓			
Jaywalking	✓			
Drunk driving			✓	
Speeding			✓	
Skating on side streets (side-walk)		✓		
Graffiti painting	✓			
Pilfering	✓			
Prostitution		✓		
Haggling in the market place		✓		
Consumption of alcoholic beverages in bars and restaurants	✓			
Gambling		✓		
Possession of pornographic materials		✓		
Possession of the Christian Bible	✓			
Possession of the Moslem Koran	✓			
Possession of bullet-proof vest		✓		
Possession of toy gun			✓	
Possession of fire crackers and fireworks			✓	
Possession of prescription drugs (without doctor's note)				
Possession of regulated drugs (narcotics)			✓	
Possession of firearms (by foreigners)			✓	
Possession of pocket knife in public		✓		
Using walkie talkies		✓		
Using of "boom boxes"(loud sounding stereo system)	✓			
Using "walkman" (very small radio/cassettes with ear plugs) in public places	✓			
Using "walkman" (very small radio/cassettes with ear plugs) while driving or riding	✓			

SWEDEN

	Is customary Is allowed Is permissible Is used Is OK	Is not customary Is frowned upon	Is disallowed Is forbidden Is a crime	(See last page for comments on items referenced here)
Use of cellular phone	✓			
Use of binoculars/periscopes other than in sports arena	✓			
Taking photographs of people (without their permission)	✓			
Taking photographs at airports, train and bus stations	✓			
Taking photographs of airports	✓			
Taking photographs of churches and synagogues	✓			
Taking photographs of religious statues	✓			
Taking photographs of public buildings	✓			
Taking photographs of bridges	✓			
Tipping (gratuity)	✓			
Tipping (when service is rendered)	✓			
Tipping (when service is not rendered)		✓		
Tipping waiters/waitresses at restaurants and hotels	✓			
Tipping taxi/cab drivers	✓			
Tipping baggage handlers, porters, door persons	✓			
Tipping of hair dressers/barbers	✓			
Overtipping	✓			
Undertipping	✓			
Spilling cigarette butt (ash) on side streets/on the floor		✓		
Men wearing lipstick		✓		
Wearing visible tattoo marks				
Men painting/coloring their finger or toe nails		✓		
Cross dressing (men dressed like women & vice versa)		✓		
Walking in public without a shirt (i.e. with the upper half of the body naked)		✓		
Men wearing braided hair		✓		
Men wearing earrings		✓		
Men wearing dreadlock hair style		✓		
Homosexuality	✓			
Lesbianism	✓			

SWEDEN

	Is customary Is allowed Is permissible Is used Is OK	Is not customary Is frowned upon	Is disallowed Is forbidden Is a crime	(See last page for comments on items referenced here)
Females covering their hair (wearing headgear) in public	✓			
Females exposing their full face in public	✓			
Females driving automobiles	✓			
Females riding motorcycles	✓			
Females riding bicycles	✓			
Females smoking in public	✓			
Women wearing bras (braziers) in public		✓		
Use of lipstick by women	✓			
A woman extending her hands first when introduced	✓			
Female bashing		✓		
Females wearing trousers	✓			
Females wearing minis (short dresses)	✓			
Females wearing bikinis	✓			
Females wearing shorts	✓			
Persons of opposite sex holding hands in public	✓			
Persons of same sex holding hands in public	✓			
Handshake between opposite sex	✓			
Hugging in public by same sex	✓			
Hugging in public by opposite sex	✓			
Men and women walking side by side in public	✓			
Man walking ahead (in public), with the woman following		✓		
Woman walking ahead (in public), with the man following		✓		
Men opening doors for women	✓			
Sitting with legs crossed in the presence of elders	✓			
Talking to an elderly person with one's hat/cap on	✓			
Talking to an elderly person with hands positioned on both sides of one's waist	✓			
Blowing one's nose in public	✓			
Blowing one's nose in the presence of others	✓			
Addressing people by their title	✓			

SWEDEN

	Is customary Is allowed Is permissible Is used. Is OK	Is not customary Is frowned upon	Is disallowed Is forbidden Is a crime	(See last page for comments on items referenced here)
Addressing people by their family name/surname/last name/given name	✓			
Addressing people by their first name/ given name		✓		
Women going through doors first	✓			
Men helping women with their coats	✓			
Men extending their hands to women first during greetings	✓			
Taking off one's hat when entering a private home	✓			
Removing one's shoes when entering a private home	✓			
Invited guests bringing food at social gatherings		✓		
Guests bringing drinks at social gatherings		✓		
Shaking hands when leaving a small group	✓			
Shaking hands with everyone present, upon arrival at a social gathering	✓			
Eating with the right hand	✓			
Eating with the left hand	✓			
Eating with both hands	✓			
Presenting a gift or passing on an object with the left hand		✓		
Asking a man about his wife		✓		
Asking a woman about her husband		✓		
Making prior appointments before a meeting or visit	✓			
Addressing an audience with one or both hands in the pocket		✓		
Carrying on conversation during meals				
Females sitting with legs crossed	✓			
People discussing their wealth	✓			
Asking someone his or her age, or how old the person is	✓			
Complementing someone on his/her physical looks	✓			
Complementing someone on his/her attire	✓			
Use of both hands in handshake		✓		
In greeting, a handshake accompanied by a slight bow	✓			

SWEDEN

	Is customary Is allowed Is permissible Is used. Is OK	Is not customary Is frowned upon	Is disallowed Is forbidden Is a crime	(See last page for comments on items referenced here)
Salutations such as "Good morning", "Good afternoon", "Good evening"	✓			
The completion of a business deal with a handshake	✓			
Starting a negotiation session with a handshake	✓			
A gift for the host/hostess	✓			
Giving a business gift		✓		
A gift of money (use of money as gift)	✓			
Use of flowers as a gift	✓			
Use of business cards	✓			
Accepting/presenting gifts with both hands	✓			
Burning of the country's flag			✓	
Mutilation of the national currency			✓	
Casual wearing of clothings made with colors & marks of the national flag	✓			
Wearing of look-alike military (camouflage) fatigues (attire)		✓		
Sitting on the floor (on floor mats)	✓			
Discussion of religion	✓			
Discussion of politics	✓			
Discussion of sex	✓			
Patting/slapping someone on the buttocks		✓		
Patting/slapping someone on the back		✓		
Touching or patting someone's head/hair	✓			
Casual touching of any part of someone's body	✓			
Drinking directly out of a bottle/can		✓		
Placing one's leg(s) on the table or chair	✓			

SWEDEN

	Is customary Is allowed Is permissible Is used. Is OK	Is not customary Is frowned upon	Is disallowed Is forbidden Is a crime	(See last page for comments on items referenced here)
Showing the sole of one's foot (feet)				n/a
People standing very close when talking		✓		
Maintaining steady eye contact (direct gaze) when talking to someone	✓			
Kissing or exchange of kisses on the cheek	✓			
Counting money (change) in someone's palm		✓		
Finger pointing in public (in a daring manner)		✓		
Seeking attention by winking the eyes	✓			
Tapping the head to indicate someone is crazy		✓		
Twirling the head to indicate someone is crazy		✓		
Whistling as a way of requesting something/seeking attention		✓		
Using "thumbs-up" sign to mean OK	✓			
Forming a circle with the thumb and index finger (forefinger) to mean OK	✓			
Using the fingers to make a "V" sign for victory	✓			
Beckoning to someone with the index finger (forefinger)	✓			
The left to right waving of the hand with open palms facing outward to indicate "Good bye"	✓			
The use of a nod to show acknowledgement	✓			
Stopping/beckoning a taxi using a stretched hand with the thumb pointing upward	✓			
Using the thumb finger pointed to a direction, to request a ride or a hike	✓			
Raising one's hand/waving with an open fist to summon a taxi	✓			
Tapping one's foot/feet on the floor in a public gathering	✓			
Wiggling one's leg(s) when in a sitting position	✓			
Use of the hand (by motorists and cyclists) to signal direction of traffic	✓			

SWEDEN

		(See last page for comments on items referenced here)
Foreign tourists are welcome in the country.	yes	
The use of seat belt is mandatory.	yes	
International driving license is accepted.	yes	
U.S. driver's license is accepted.	yes	
It is considered impolite to yawn in public.	yes	
Death penalty for drug trafficking is the law.	no	
Life imprisonment for drug trafficking is the law.	no	
Guilty until proven innocent in court is the law.	no	
Innocent until proven guilty in court is the law.	yes	
Pedestrians always have right of way.	yes	
Exit visas are required of visitors.	yes	
Crash helmet is mandatory for motor cyclist.	no	
Hanging is used as a form of legal punishment.	yes	
Decapitation of a limb is used as a form of punishment.	no	
Caning is used as a form of legal punishment.	no	
Electric shock is used as a form of legal punishment.	no	
One is expected to stand up during the playing of the national anthem.	no	
Crash helmet is mandatory for bicyclists.	yes	
Guests are expected to eat every thing on their plates.	no	
Table manners are very informal.	yes	
One is expected to cover one's mouth when laughing.	no	
A vertical nod of the head means YES (OK).	no	
A horizontal shaking of the head means NO (Not OK).	yes	
Prostitution is allowed only in designated areas.	no	
One is expected to take off one's hat during playing of national anthem.	yes	
Separate seating arrangements (between sexes) are maintained at movies.	no	
Separate seating arrangements (between sexes) are maintained at churches.	no	
Uninvited visitors or guests may not be welcome, even among acquaintances.	no	
Pets (e.g. cats, dog) are allowed in some hotels and restaurants.	ues	
Couples invited for a meal may be separated during meals according to their sex.	yes	
Punctuality is the order of business.	yes	
Automobiles are driven with headlights always turned on.	yes	
Motorcycles are driven with headlights always turned on.	yes	
Visitors with expired visa face mandatory jail time.	no	
Visitors without exit visa face jail time.	no	
Visitors without entry visa face mandatory (automatic) jail time.	no	

ADDITIONAL COUNTRY INFORMATION

(A)	**The types of gifts to avoid:**	personal
(B)	**Appropriate gifts for a foreigner to give:**	flowers
(C)	**Best time to present gifts (at the beginning or at the end of a visit?):**	at the beginning
(D)	**Best time to present gifts (on initial or later visits?):**	n/a
(E)	**Best place to present gifts (in private or in public?):**	n/a
(F)	**Number(s) with certain connotations and/or myths attached to them:**	n/a
(G)	**Basic shape(s) with negative connotations:**	n/a
(H)	**Basic color(s) with negative connotations:**	n/a
(I)	**Traditional greeting methods include:**	n/a
(J)	**Safe topics for discussion include:**	weather, fashion, travel, art, family, religion, domestic politics, food, sports, international politics, social conditions
(K)	**Best time for conversations (before, during, after meals?):**	n/a
(L)	**Forms of legal punishment:**	n/a
(M)	**Approximately length of time one could be detained by law and order authorities before being charged in court:**	2
(N)	**January 15, 1999, for example, will normally be written as:**	1999-01-15
(O)	**Emergency code number:**	90 000
(P)	**Ambulance code Number:**	90 000
(Q)	**Police code number:**	90 000
(R)	**Telephone (country) code:**	46
(S)	**Telex (country) code:**	46
(T)	**Electricity requirements:**	220 v
(U)	**Legal drinking age:**	18
(V)	**Systems of weights and measures:**	metric
(W)	**Legal age of incarceration:**	18
(X)	**Driving side of the road:**	right
(Y)	**Minimum expenditure expected of foreign visitors? $**	no
(Z)	**Name of currency:**	Krona
(Za)	**Some places 0ff-limits to foreign visitors:**	military
(Zb)	**Some places, structures and items prohibited from being photographed:**	military

SWITZERLAND	Is customary Is allowed Is permissible Is used. Is OK	Is not customary Is frowned upon	Is disallowed Is forbidden Is a crime	(See last page for comments on items referenced here)
Smoking in public	✓			
Eating in public	✓			
Not flushing public toilet		✓		
Spitting in public		✓		
Feeding animals & birds in public	✓			
Whistling in public	✓			
Drinking alcohol in public	✓			
Kissing in public	✓			
Breast feeding in public	✓			
Drunkenness (in public)		✓		
Cursing in public		✓		
Religious preaching in public	✓			
Begging (panhandling) in public		✓		
Giving money to beggars/panhandlers	✓			
Giving food/drink to beggars/panhandlers	✓			
Brushing teeth in public (other than in restrooms)		✓		
Strolling with pets in major public roads/streets	✓			
Chewing gum in public	✓			
Chewing gum in government offices	✓			
Combing hair in public (other than in toilets/restrooms)	✓			
Undressing/dressing in public		✓		
Wearing of dark glasses indoors in public places	✓			
Public display of wealth	✓			
Praying openly in public in non-designated areas		✓		
Walking bare feet in public		✓		
Chewing tobacco in public	✓			
Trimming one's finger or toe nails in public		✓		
Laughing aloud in public	✓			
Mingling of the sexes in public	✓			
Mixed bathing in public swimming pools	✓			
Distributing religious pamphlets (literature) in public/side streets	✓			

SWITZERLAND

	Is customary Is allowed Is permissible Is used. Is OK	Is not customary Is frowned upon	Is disallowed Is forbidden Is a crime	(See last page for comments on items referenced here)
Dancing on side street		✓		
Nude bathing		✓		
Littering		✓		
Binge Drinking		✓		
hitchhiking	✓			
Jaywalking		✓		
Drunk driving			✓	
Speeding		✓		
Skating on side streets (side-walk)	✓			
Graffiti painting			✓	
Pilfering			✓	
Prostitution			✓	
Haggling in the market place		✓		
Consumption of alcoholic beverages in bars and restaurants	✓			
Gambling	✓			
Possession of pornographic materials	✓			
Possession of the Christian Bible	✓			
Possession of the Moslem Koran	✓			
Possession of bullet-proof vest	✓			
Possession of toy gun	✓			
Possession of fire crackers and fireworks	✓			
Possession of prescription drugs (without doctor's note)		✓		
Possession of regulated drugs (narcotics)			✓	
Possession of firearms (by foreigners)			✓	
Possession of pocket knife in public	✓			
Using walkie talkies	✓			
Using of "boom boxes"(loud sounding stereo system)	✓			
Using "walkman" (very small radio/cassettes with ear plugs) in public places	✓			
Using "walkman" (very small radio/cassettes with ear plugs) while driving or riding			✓	

SWITZERLAND

	Is customary Is allowed Is permissible Is used Is OK	Is not customary Is frowned upon	Is disallowed Is forbidden Is a crime	(See last page for comments on items referenced here)
Use of cellular phone	✓			
Use of binoculars/periscopes other than in sports arena	✓			
Taking photographs of people (without their permission)		✓		
Taking photographs at airports, train and bus stations			✓	
Taking photographs of airports	✓			
Taking photographs of churches and synagogues	✓			
Taking photographs of religious statues	✓			
Taking photographs of public buildings	✓			n/a
Taking photographs of bridges	✓			n/a
Tipping (gratuity)	✓			
Tipping (when service is rendered)	✓			
Tipping (when service is not rendered)		✓		
Tipping waiters/waitresses at restaurants and hotels	✓			
Tipping taxi/cab drivers		✓		
Tipping baggage handlers, porters, door persons	✓			
Tipping of hair dressers/barbers		✓		
Overtipping	✓			
Undertipping		✓		
Spilling cigarette butt (ash) on side streets/on the floor		✓		
Men wearing lipstick		✓		
Wearing visible tattoo marks	✓			
Men painting/coloring their finger or toe nails		✓		
Cross dressing (men dressed like women & vice versa)		✓		
Walking in public without a shirt (i.e. with the upper half of the body naked)		✓		
Men wearing braided hair	✓			
Men wearing earrings	✓			
Men wearing dreadlock hair style	✓			
Homosexuality	✓			
Lesbianism	✓			

SWITZERLAND

	Is customary Is allowed Is permissible Is used Is OK	**Is not customary Is frowned upon**	**Is disallowed Is forbidden Is a crime**	**(See last page for comments on items referenced here)**
Females covering their hair (wearing headgear) in public	✓			
Females exposing their full face in public	✓			
Females driving automobiles	✓			
Females riding motorcycles	✓			
Females riding bicycles	✓			
Females smoking in public	✓			
Women wearing bras (braziers) in public	✓			
Use of lipstick by women	✓			
A woman extending her hands first when introduced	✓			
Female bashing		✓		
Females wearing trousers	✓			
Females wearing minis (short dresses)	✓			
Females wearing bikinis	✓			
Females wearing shorts	✓			
Persons of opposite sex holding hands in public	✓			
Persons of same sex holding hands in public	✓			
Handshake between opposite sex	✓			
Hugging in public by same sex	✓			
Hugging in public by opposite sex	✓			
Men and women walking side by side in public	✓			
Man walking ahead (in public), with the woman following		✓		
Woman walking ahead (in public), with the man following		✓		
Men opening doors for women	✓			
Sitting with legs crossed in the presence of elders	✓			
Talking to an elderly person with one's hat/cap on	✓			
Talking to an elderly person with hands positioned on both sides of one's waist	✓			
Blowing one's nose in public	✓			
Blowing one's nose in the presence of others	✓			
Addressing people by their title	✓			

SWITZERLAND

	Is customary Is allowed Is permissible Is used. Is OK	Is not customary Is frowned upon	Is disallowed Is forbidden Is a crime	(See last page for comments on items referenced here)
Addressing people by their family name/surname/last name/given name	✓			
Addressing people by their first name/ given name		✓		
Women going through doors first	✓			
Men helping women with their coats	✓			
Men extending their hands to women first during greetings	✓			
Taking off one's hat when entering a private home	✓			
Removing one's shoes when entering a private home				
Invited guests bringing food at social gatherings	✓			
Guests bringing drinks at social gatherings	✓			
Shaking hands when leaving a small group	✓			
Shaking hands with everyone present, upon arrival at a social gathering		✓		
Eating with the right hand		✓		
Eating with the left hand	✓			
Eating with both hands	✓			
Presenting a gift or passing on an object with the left hand	✓			
Asking a man about his wife	✓			
Asking a woman about her husband	✓			
Making prior appointments before a meeting or visit	✓			
Addressing an audience with one or both hands in the pocket		✓		
Carrying on conversation during meals				
Females sitting with legs crossed	✓			
People discussing their wealth		✓		
Asking someone his or her age, or how old the person is	✓			
Complementing someone on his/her physical looks	✓			
Complementing someone on his/her attire	✓			
Use of both hands in handshake	✓			
In greeting, a handshake accompanied by a slight bow		✓		

SWITZERLAND

	Is customary **Is allowed** **Is permissible** **Is used.** **Is OK**	**Is not customary** **Is frowned upon**	**Is disallowed** **Is forbidden** **Is a crime**	**(See last page for comments on items referenced here)**
Salutations such as "Good morning", "Good afternoon", "Good evening"	✓			
The completion of a business deal with a handshake		✓		
Starting a negotiation session with a handshake		✓		
A gift for the host/hostess	✓			
Giving a business gift	✓			
A gift of money (use of money as gift)		✓		
Use of flowers as a gift	✓			
Use of business cards	✓			
Accepting/presenting gifts with both hands	✓			
Burning of the country's flag		✓		
Mutilation of the national currency		✓		
Casual wearing of clothings made with colors & marks of the national flag	✓			
Wearing of look-alike military (camouflage) fatigues (attire)		✓		
Sitting on the floor (on floor mats)	✓			
Discussion of religion	✓			
Discussion of politics	✓			
Discussion of sex		✓		
Patting/slapping someone on the buttocks		✓		
Patting/slapping someone on the back		✓		
Touching or patting someone's head/hair		✓		
Casual touching of any part of someone's body				n/a
Drinking directly out of a bottle/can	✓			
Placing one's leg(s) on the table or chair		✓		

SWITZERLAND

	Is customary Is allowed Is permissible Is used. Is OK	Is not customary Is frowned upon	Is disallowed Is forbidden Is a crime	(See last page for comments on items referenced here)
Showing the sole of one's foot (feet)	✓			
People standing very close when talking		✓		
Maintaining steady eye contact (direct gaze) when talking to someone	✓			
Kissing or exchange of kisses on the cheek	✓			
Counting money (change) in someone's palm		✓		
Finger pointing in public (in a daring manner)		✓		
Seeking attention by winking the eyes	✓			
Tapping the head to indicate someone is crazy		✓		
Twirling the head to indicate someone is crazy		✓		
Whistling as a way of requesting something/seeking attention		✓		
Using "thumbs-up" sign to mean OK	✓			
Forming a circle with the thumb and index finger (forefinger) to mean OK	✓			
Using the fingers to make a "V" sign for victory	✓			
Beckoning to someone with the index finger (forefinger)		✓		
The left to right waving of the hand with open palms facing outward to indicate "Good bye"	✓			
The use of a nod to show acknowledgement	✓			
Stopping/beckoning a taxi using a stretched hand with the thumb pointing upward		✓		
Using the thumb finger pointed to a direction, to request a ride or a hike	✓			
Raising one's hand/waving with an open fist to summon a taxi	✓			
Tapping one's foot/feet on the floor in a public gathering		✓		
Wiggling one's leg(s) when in a sitting position	✓			
Use of the hand (by motorists and cyclists) to signal direction of traffic	✓			

SWITZERLAND

		(See last page for comments on items referenced here)
Foreign tourists are welcome in the country.	yes	
The use of seat belt is mandatory.	yes	
International driving license is accepted.	yes	
U.S. driver's license is accepted.	yes	
It is considered impolite to yawn in public.	no	
Death penalty for drug trafficking is the law.	no	
Life imprisonment for drug trafficking is the law.	no	
Guilty until proven innocent in court is the law.	no	
Innocent until proven guilty in court is the law.	yes	
Pedestrians always have right of way.	yes	
Exit visas are required of visitors.	no	
Crash helmet is mandatory for motor cyclist.	yes	
Hanging is used as a form of legal punishment.	no	
Decapitation of a limb is used as a form of punishment.	no	
Caning is used as a form of legal punishment.	no	
Electric shock is used as a form of legal punishment.	no	
One is expected to stand up during the playing of the national anthem.	no	
Crash helmet is mandatory for bicyclists.	no	
Guests are expected to eat every thing on their plates.	no	
Table manners are very informal.	no	
One is expected to cover one's mouth when laughing.	no	
A vertical nod of the head means YES (OK).	no	
A horizontal shaking of the head means NO (Not OK).	yes	
Prostitution is allowed only in designated areas.	yes	
One is expected to take off one's hat during playing of national anthem.	yes	
Separate seating arrangements (between sexes) are maintained at movies.	no	
Separate seating arrangements (between sexes) are maintained at churches.	no	
Uninvited visitors or guests may not be welcome, even among acquaintances.	no	
Pets (e.g. cats, dog) are allowed in some hotels and restaurants.	yes	
Couples invited for a meal may be separated during meals according to their sex.	yes	
Punctuality is the order of business.	yes	
Automobiles are driven with headlights always turned on.	no	
Motorcycles are driven with headlights always turned on.	yes	
Visitors with expired visa face mandatory jail time.	yes	
Visitors without exit visa face jail time.	yes	
Visitors without entry visa face mandatory (automatic) jail time.	yes	

ADDITIONAL COUNTRY INFORMATION

(A)	**The types of gifts to avoid:**	n/a
(B)	**Appropriate gifts for a foreigner to give:**	flowers, candy
(C)	**Best time to present gifts (at the beginning or at the end of a visit?):**	n/a
(D)	**Best time to present gifts (on initial or later visits?):**	n/a
(E)	**Best place to present gifts (in private or in public?)**:	n/a
(F)	**Number(s) with certain connotations and/or myths attached to them:**	n/a
(G)	**Basic shape(s) with negative connotations:**	n/a
(H)	**Basic color(s) with negative connotations:**	n/a
(I)	**Traditional greeting methods include:**	n/a
(J)	**Safe topics for discussion include:**	weather, fashion, travel, art,family, religion, domestic politics, foods, sports, international politics, social conditions, money and personal wealth, sex.
(K)	**Best time for conversations (before, during, after meals?):**	n/a
(L)	**Forms of legal punishment:**	imprisonment
(M)	**Approximately length of time one could be detained by law and order authorities before being charged in court:**	n/a
(N)	**January 15, 1999, for example, will normally be written as:**	15. January 1999
(O)	**Emergency code number**:	117
(P)	**Ambulance code Number**:	144
(Q)	**Police code number:**	117
(R)	**Telephone (country) code:**	41
(S)	**Telex (country) code:**	845
(T)	**Electricity requirements**:	220 v
(U)	**Legal drinking age:**	16
(V)	**Systems of weights and measures:**	kg/metric
(W)	**Legal age of incarceration**:	n/a
(X)	**Driving side of the road:**	right
(Y)	**Minimum expenditure expected of foreign visitors?** $	none
(Z)	**Name of currency**:	Swiss Franc
(Za)	**Some places 0ff-limits to foreign visitors:**	n/a
(Zb)	**Some places, structures and items prohibited from being photographed:**	n/a

TURKEY	Is customary Is allowed Is permissible Is used. Is OK	Is not customary Is frowned upon	Is disallowed Is forbidden Is a crime	(See last page for comments on items referenced here)
Smoking in public	✓			
Eating in public	✓			
Not flushing public toilet		✓		
Spitting in public		✓		
Feeding animals & birds in public	✓			
Whistling in public		✓		
Drinking alcohol in public		✓		
Kissing in public	✓			
Breast feeding in public		✓		
Drunkenness (in public)		✓		
Cursing in public		✓		
Religious preaching in public		✓		
Begging (panhandling) in public		✓		
Giving money to beggars/panhandlers	✓			
Giving food/drink to beggars/panhandlers	✓			
Brushing teeth in public (other than in restrooms)		✓		
Strolling with pets in major public roads/streets	✓			
Chewing gum in public	✓			
Chewing gum in government offices		✓		
Combing hair in public (other than in toilets/restrooms)	✓			
Undressing/dressing in public		✓		
Wearing of dark glasses indoors in public places		✓		
Public display of wealth		✓		
Praying openly in public in non-designated areas		✓		
Walking bare feet in public		✓		
Chewing tobacco in public		✓		
Trimming one's finger or toe nails in public		✓		
Laughing aloud in public	✓			
Mingling of the sexes in public	✓			
Mixed bathing in public swimming pools	✓			
Distributing religious pamphlets (literature) in public/side streets		✓		

TURKEY

	Is customary Is allowed Is permissible Is used. Is OK	Is not customary Is frowned upon	Is disallowed Is forbidden Is a crime	(See last page for comments on items referenced here)
Dancing on side street	✓			
Nude bathing		✓		
Littering		✓		
Binge Drinking		✓		
hitchhiking		✓		
Jaywalking		✓		
Drunk driving			✓	
Speeding			✓	
Skating on side streets (side-walk)	✓			
Graffiti painting			✓	
Pilfering			✓	
Prostitution			✓	
Haggling in the market place	✓			
Consumption of alcoholic beverages in bars and restaurants	✓			
Gambling		✓		
Possession of pornographic materials		✓		
Possession of the Christian Bible	✓			
Possession of the Moslem Koran	✓			
Possession of bullet-proof vest	✓			
Possession of toy gun	✓			
Possession of fire crackers and fireworks		✓		
Possession of prescription drugs (without doctor's note)		✓		
Possession of regulated drugs (narcotics)			✓	
Possession of firearms (by foreigners)			✓	
Possession of pocket knife in public	✓			
Using walkie talkies	✓			
Using of "boom boxes"(loud sounding stereo system)		✓		
Using "walkman" (very small radio/cassettes with ear plugs) in public places	✓			
Using "walkman" (very small radio/cassettes with ear plugs) while driving or riding		✓		

TURKEY

	Is customary Is allowed Is permissible Is used Is OK	Is not customary Is frowned upon	Is disallowed Is forbidden Is a crime	(See last page for comments on items referenced here)
Use of cellular phone	✓			
Use of binoculars/periscopes other than in sports arena	✓			
Taking photographs of people (without their permission)		✓		
Taking photographs at airports, train and bus stations	✓			
Taking photographs of airports	✓			
Taking photographs of churches and synagogues	✓			
Taking photographs of religious statues	✓			
Taking photographs of public buildings	✓			
Taking photographs of bridges	✓			
Tipping (gratuity)	✓			
Tipping (when service is rendered)	✓			
Tipping (when service is not rendered)		✓		
Tipping waiters/waitresses at restaurants and hotels	✓			
Tipping taxi/cab drivers	✓			
Tipping baggage handlers, porters, door persons	✓			
Tipping of hair dressers/barbers	✓			
Overtipping	✓			
Undertipping		✓		
Spilling cigarette butt (ash) on side streets/on the floor		✓		
Men wearing lipstick		✓		
Wearing visible tattoo marks		✓		
Men painting/coloring their finger or toe nails		✓		
Cross dressing (men dressed like women & vice versa)		✓		
Walking in public without a shirt (i.e. with the upper half of the body naked)		✓		
Men wearing braided hair		✓		
Men wearing earrings		✓		
Men wearing dreadlock hair style	✓			
Homosexuality		✓		
Lesbianism		✓		

TURKEY

	Is customary Is allowed Is permissible Is used Is OK	Is not customary Is frowned upon	Is disallowed Is forbidden Is a crime	(See last page for comments on items referenced here)
Females covering their hair (wearing headgear) in public	✓			
Females exposing their full face in public	✓			
Females driving automobiles	✓			
Females riding motorcycles	✓			
Females riding bicycles	✓			
Females smoking in public	✓			
Women wearing bras (braziers) in public	✓			
Use of lipstick by women	✓			
A woman extending her hands first when introduced	✓			
Female bashing	✓			
Females wearing trousers	✓			
Females wearing minis (short dresses)	✓			
Females wearing bikinis	✓			
Females wearing shorts	✓			
Persons of opposite sex holding hands in public	✓			
Persons of same sex holding hands in public	✓			
Handshake between opposite sex	✓			
Hugging in public by same sex	✓			
Hugging in public by opposite sex	✓			
Men and women walking side by side in public	✓			
Man walking ahead (in public), with the woman following		✓		
Woman walking ahead (in public), with the man following		✓		
Men opening doors for women	✓			
Sitting with legs crossed in the presence of elders		✓		
Talking to an elderly person with one's hat/cap on	✓			
Talking to an elderly person with hands positioned on both sides of one's waist		✓		
Blowing one's nose in public		✓		
Blowing one's nose in the presence of others		✓		
Addressing people by their title	✓			

TURKEY

	Is customary Is allowed Is permissible Is used. Is OK	Is not customary Is frowned upon	Is disallowed Is forbidden Is a crime	(See last page for comments on items referenced here)
Addressing people by their family name/surname/last name/given name	✓			
Addressing people by their first name/ given name	✓			
Women going through doors first	✓			
Men helping women with their coats	✓			
Men extending their hands to women first during greetings	✓			
Taking off one's hat when entering a private home	✓			
Removing one's shoes when entering a private home				n/a
Invited guests bringing food at social gatherings	✓			
Guests bringing drinks at social gatherings	✓			
Shaking hands when leaving a small group	✓			
Shaking hands with everyone present, upon arrival at a social gathering	✓			
Eating with the right hand	✓			
Eating with the left hand		✓		
Eating with both hands		✓		
Presenting a gift or passing on an object with the left hand	✓			
Asking a man about his wife	✓			
Asking a woman about her husband	✓			
Making prior appointments before a meeting or visit	✓			
Addressing an audience with one or both hands in the pocket		✓		
Carrying on conversation during meals	✓			
Females sitting with legs crossed	✓			
People discussing their wealth	✓			
Asking someone his or her age, or how old the person is	✓			
Complementing someone on his/her physical looks	✓			
Complementing someone on his/her attire	✓			
Use of both hands in handshake	✓			
In greeting, a handshake accompanied by a slight bow	✓			

TURKEY

	Is customary Is allowed Is permissible Is used. Is OK	Is not customary Is frowned upon	Is disallowed Is forbidden Is a crime	(See last page for comments on items referenced here)
Salutations such as "Good morning", "Good afternoon", "Good evening"	✓			
The completion of a business deal with a handshake	✓			
Starting a negotiation session with a handshake	✓			
A gift for the host/hostess	✓			
Giving a business gift	✓			
A gift of money (use of money as gift)		✓		
Use of flowers as a gift	✓			
Use of business cards	✓			
Accepting/presenting gifts with both hands	✓			
Burning of the country's flag			✓	
Mutilation of the national currency		✓		
Casual wearing of clothings made with colors & marks of the national flag		✓		
Wearing of look-alike military (camouflage) fatigues (attire)		✓		
Sitting on the floor (on floor mats)		✓		
Discussion of religion	✓			
Discussion of politics	✓			
Discussion of sex		✓		
Patting/slapping someone on the buttocks		✓		
Patting/slapping someone on the back	✓			
Touching or patting someone's head/hair	✓			
Casual touching of any part of someone's body		✓		
Drinking directly out of a bottle/can	✓			
Placing one's leg(s) on the table or chair		✓		

TURKEY

	Is customary Is allowed Is permissible Is used. Is OK	Is not customary Is frowned upon	Is disallowed Is forbidden Is a crime	(See last page for comments on items referenced here)
Showing the sole of one's foot (feet)		✓		
People standing very close when talking		✓		
Maintaining steady eye contact (direct gaze) when talking to someone	✓			
Kissing or exchange of kisses on the cheek	✓			
Counting money (change) in someone's palm		✓		
Finger pointing in public (in a daring manner)		✓		
Seeking attention by winking the eyes		✓		
Tapping the head to indicate someone is crazy		✓		
Twirling the head to indicate someone is crazy		✓		
Whistling as a way of requesting something/seeking attention		✓		
Using "thumbs-up" sign to mean OK		✓		
Forming a circle with the thumb and index finger (forefinger) to mean OK	✓			
Using the fingers to make a "V" sign for victory		✓		
Beckoning to someone with the index finger (forefinger)		✓		
The left to right waving of the hand with open palms facing outward to indicate "Good bye"	✓			
The use of a nod to show acknowledgement	✓			
Stopping/beckoning a taxi using a stretched hand with the thumb pointing upward	✓			
Using the thumb finger pointed to a direction, to request a ride or a hike	✓			
Raising one's hand/waving with an open fist to summon a taxi	✓			
Tapping one's foot/feet on the floor in a public gathering		✓		
Wiggling one's leg(s) when in a sitting position		✓		
Use of the hand (by motorists and cyclists) to signal direction of traffic		✓		

TURKEY

		(See last page for comments on items referenced here)
Foreign tourists are welcome in the country.	yes	
The use of seat belt is mandatory.	yes	
International driving license is accepted.	yes	
U.S. driver's license is accepted.	yes	
It is considered impolite to yawn in public.	yes	
Death penalty for drug trafficking is the law.	no	
Life imprisonment for drug trafficking is the law.	yes	
Guilty until proven innocent in court is the law.	no	
Innocent until proven guilty in court is the law.	yes	
Pedestrians always have right of way.	yes	
Exit visas are required of visitors.	no	
Crash helmet is mandatory for motor cyclist.	yes	
Hanging is used as a form of legal punishment.	yes	
Decapitation of a limb is used as a form of punishment.	no	
Caning is used as a form of legal punishment.	no	
Electric shock is used as a form of legal punishment.	no	
One is expected to stand up during the playing of the national anthem.	yes	
Crash helmet is mandatory for bicyclists.	no	
Guests are expected to eat every thing on their plates.	no	
Table manners are very informal.	yes	
One is expected to cover one's mouth when laughing.	yes	
A vertical nod of the head means YES (OK).	yes	
A horizontal shaking of the head means NO (Not OK).	yes	
Prostitution is allowed only in designated areas.	yes	
One is expected to take off one's hat during playing of national anthem.	yes	
Separate seating arrangements (between sexes) are maintained at movies.	no	
Separate seating arrangements (between sexes) are maintained at churches.	n/a	
Uninvited visitors or guests may not be welcome, even among acquaintances.	no	
Pets (e.g. cats, dog) are allowed in some hotels and restaurants.	yes	
Couples invited for a meal may be separated during meals according to their sex.	no	
Punctuality is the order of business.	yes	
Automobiles are driven with headlights always turned on.	no	
Motorcycles are driven with headlights always turned on.	no	
Visitors with expired visa face mandatory jail time.	no	
Visitors without exit visa face jail time.	no	
Visitors without entry visa face mandatory (automatic) jail time.	no	

ADDITIONAL COUNTRY INFORMATION

(A)	**The types of gifts to avoid:**	money
(B)	**Appropriate gifts for a foreigner to give:**	flowers, candy, pasteries, anything memorable of the visitor/s country
(C)	**Best time to present gifts (at the beginning or at the end of a visit?):**	beginning
(D)	**Best time to present gifts (on initial or later visits?):**	initial visit
(E)	**Best place to present gifts (in private or in public?)**:	in private
(F)	**Number(s) with certain connotations and/or myths attached to them:**	none
(G)	**Basic shape(s) with negative connotations:**	none
(H)	**Basic color(s) with negative connotations:**	none
(I)	**Traditional greeting methods include:**	handshake, hug, kiss
(J)	**Safe topics for discussion include:**	weather, fashion, travel, art, family, domestic politics, food, sports, international politics, social conditions, money, personal wealth, hobbies, profession.
(K)	**Best time for conversations (before, during, after meals?):**	before and during meals
(L)	**Forms of legal punishment:**	imprisonment, hanging (for death penalty)
(M)	**Approximately length of time one could be detained by law and order authorities before being charged in court:**	48 hours
(N)	**January 15, 1999, for example, will normally be written as:**	15-01-1999
(O)	**Emergency code number**:	110
(P)	**Ambulance code Number**:	112
(Q)	**Police code number:**	155
(R)	**Telephone (country) code:**	90
(S)	**Telex (country) code:**	821
(T)	**Electricity requirements**:	220V
(U)	**Legal drinking age:**	18
(V)	**Systems of weights and measures:**	metric
(W)	**Legal age of incarceration**:	18
(X)	**Driving side of the road:**	right
(Y)	**Minimum expenditure expected of foreign visitors?** $	no
(Z)	**Name of currency**:	lira (Turkish)
(Za)	**Some places 0ff-limits to foreign visitors:**	n/a
(Zb)	**Some places, structures and items prohibited from being photographed:**	prior permit is required for museum, archaeological, historical sites

GREAT BRITAIN (U.K.)	Is customary Is allowed Is permissible Is used. Is OK	Is not customary Is frowned upon	Is disallowed Is forbidden Is a crime	(See last page for comments on items referenced here)
Smoking in public	✓			
Eating in public	✓			
Not flushing public toilet		✓		
Spitting in public		✓		
Feeding animals & birds in public	✓			
Whistling in public	✓			
Drinking alcohol in public			✓	
Kissing in public	✓			
Breast feeding in public	✓			
Drunkenness (in public)			✓	
Cursing in public			✓	
Religious preaching in public	✓			
Begging (panhandling) in public		✓		
Giving money to beggars/panhandlers	✓			
Giving food/drink to beggars/panhandlers	✓			
Brushing teeth in public (other than in restrooms)		✓		
Strolling with pets in major public roads/streets	✓			
Chewing gum in public	✓			
Chewing gum in government offices	✓			
Combing hair in public (other than in toilets/restrooms)	✓			
Undressing/dressing in public	✓			1
Wearing of dark glasses indoors in public places	✓			
Public display of wealth	✓			
Praying openly in public in non-designated areas	✓			
Walking bare feet in public	✓			
Chewing tobacco in public				n/a
Trimming one's finger or toe nails in public		✓		
Laughing aloud in public	✓			
Mingling of the sexes in public	✓			
Mixed bathing in public swimming pools	✓			
Distributing religious pamphlets (literature) in public/side streets	✓			

UNITED KINGDOM (U.K.)

	Is customary Is allowed Is permissible Is used. Is OK	Is not customary Is frowned upon	Is disallowed Is forbidden Is a crime	(See last page for comments on items referenced here)
Dancing on side street	✓			
Nude bathing	✓			
Littering			✓	
Binge Drinking		✓		
hitchhiking	✓			
Jaywalking		✓		
Drunk driving			✓	
Speeding			✓	
Skating on side streets (side-walk)	✓			
Graffiti painting			✓	
Pilfering			✓	
Prostitution			✓	
Haggling in the market place		✓		
Consumption of alcoholic beverages in bars and restaurants	✓			
Gambling	✓			
Possession of pornographic materials	✓			
Possession of the Christian Bible	✓			
Possession of the Moslem Koran	✓			
Possession of bullet-proof vest	✓			
Possession of toy gun	✓			2
Possession of fire crackers and fireworks	✓			
Possession of prescription drugs (without doctor's note)		✓		3
Possession of regulated drugs (narcotics)			✓	4
Possession of firearms (by foreigners)			✓	
Possession of pocket knife in public	✓			
Using walkie talkies	✓			5
Using of "boom boxes"(loud sounding stereo system)		✓		
Using "walkman" (very small radio/cassettes with ear plugs) in public places	✓			
Using "walkman" (very small radio/cassettes with ear plugs) while driving or riding	✓			

UNITED KINGDOM (U.K.)

	Is customary Is allowed Is permissible Is used Is OK	Is not customary Is frowned upon	Is disallowed Is forbidden Is a crime	(See last page for comments on items referenced here)
Use of cellular phone	✓			
Use of binoculars/periscopes other than in sports arena	✓			
Taking photographs of people (without their permission)	✓			
Taking photographs at airports, train and bus stations	✓			6
Taking photographs of airports	✓			7
Taking photographs of churches and synagogues	✓			
Taking photographs of religious statues	✓			
Taking photographs of public buildings	✓			
Taking photographs of bridges	✓			
Tipping (gratuity)	✓			
Tipping (when service is rendered)	✓			
Tipping (when service is not rendered)		✓		
Tipping waiters/waitresses at restaurants and hotels	✓			
Tipping taxi/cab drivers	✓			
Tipping baggage handlers, porters, door persons	✓			
Tipping of hair dressers/barbers	✓			
Overtipping	✓			
Undertipping	✓			
Spilling cigarette butt (ash) on side streets/on the floor		✓		
Men wearing lipstick		✓		
Wearing visible tattoo marks	✓			
Men painting/coloring their finger or toe nails		✓		
Cross dressing (men dressed like women & vice versa)		✓		
Walking in public without a shirt (i.e. with the upper half of the body naked)		✓		
Men wearing braided hair	✓			
Men wearing earrings	✓			
Men wearing dreadlock hair style	✓			
Homosexuality	✓			8
Lesbianism	✓			9

UNITED KINGDOM (U.K.)

	Is customary Is allowed Is permissible Is used Is OK	Is not customary Is frowned upon	Is disallowed Is forbidden Is a crime	(See last page for comments on items referenced here)
Females covering their hair (wearing headgear) in public	✓			
Females exposing their full face in public	✓			
Females driving automobiles	✓			
Females riding motorcycles	✓			
Females riding bicycles	✓			
Females smoking in public	✓			
Women wearing bras (braziers) in public			✓	
Use of lipstick by women	✓			
A woman extending her hands first when introduced	✓			
Female bashing		✓		
Females wearing trousers	✓			
Females wearing minis (short dresses)	✓			
Females wearing bikinis	✓			10
Females wearing shorts	✓			
Persons of opposite sex holding hands in public	✓			
Persons of same sex holding hands in public	✓			
Handshake between opposite sex	✓			
Hugging in public by same sex	✓			
Hugging in public by opposite sex	✓			
Men and women walking side by side in public	✓			
Man walking ahead (in public), with the woman following	✓			
Woman walking ahead (in public), with the man following	✓			
Men opening doors for women	✓			
Sitting with legs crossed in the presence of elders	✓			
Talking to an elderly person with one's hat/cap on	✓			
Talking to an elderly person with hands positioned on both sides of one's waist	✓			
Blowing one's nose in public	✓			
Blowing one's nose in the presence of others	✓			
Addressing people by their title	✓			

UNITED KINGDOM (U.K.)

	Is customary Is allowed Is permissible Is used. Is OK	Is not customary Is frowned upon	Is disallowed Is forbidden Is a crime	(See last page for comments on items referenced here)
Addressing people by their family name/surname/last name/given name	✓			
Addressing people by their first name/ given name	✓			
Women going through doors first	✓			
Men helping women with their coats	✓			
Men extending their hands to women first during greetings	✓			
Taking off one's hat when entering a private home	✓			
Removing one's shoes when entering a private home		✓		
Invited guests bringing food at social gatherings	✓			
Guests bringing drinks at social gatherings	✓			
Shaking hands when leaving a small group	✓			
Shaking hands with everyone present, upon arrival at a social gathering	✓			
Eating with the right hand	✓			
Eating with the left hand	✓			
Eating with both hands	✓			11
Presenting a gift or passing on an object with the left hand	✓			
Asking a man about his wife	✓			
Asking a woman about her husband	✓			
Making prior appointments before a meeting or visit				
Addressing an audience with one or both hands in the pocket	✓			
Carrying on conversation during meals	✓			
Females sitting with legs crossed	✓			
People discussing their wealth				12
Asking someone his or her age, or how old the person is	✓			
Complementing someone on his/her physical looks	✓			
Complementing someone on his/her attire	✓			
Use of both hands in handshake	✓			
In greeting, a handshake accompanied by a slight bow		✓		

UNITED KINGDOM (U.K.)

	Is customary Is allowed Is permissible Is used. Is OK	Is not customary Is frowned upon	Is disallowed Is forbidden Is a crime	(See last page for comments on items referenced here)
Salutations such as "Good morning", "Good afternoon", "Good evening"	✓			
The completion of a business deal with a handshake	✓			
Starting a negotiation session with a handshake	✓			
A gift for the host/hostess	✓			
Giving a business gift	✓			
A gift of money (use of money as gift)	✓			
Use of flowers as a gift	✓			
Use of business cards	✓			
Accepting/presenting gifts with both hands	✓			
Burning of the country's flag	✓			
Mutilation of the national currency	✓			
Casual wearing of clothings made with colors & marks of the national flag	✓			
Wearing of look-alike military (camouflage) fatigues (attire)	✓			
Sitting on the floor (on floor mats)	✓			13
Discussion of religion	✓			
Discussion of politics	✓			
Discussion of sex	✓			
Patting/slapping someone on the buttocks		✓		
Patting/slapping someone on the back				
Touching or patting someone's head/hair				
Casual touching of any part of someone's body	✓			
Drinking directly out of a bottle/can	✓			
Placing one's leg(s) on the table or chair	✓			

DO'S AND DON'TS AROUND THE WORLD: A COUNTRY GUIDE TO CULTURAL AND SOCIAL TABOOS AND ETIQUETTE

UNITED KINGDOM (U.K.)

	Is customary Is allowed Is permissible Is used. Is OK	Is not customary Is frowned upon	Is disallowed Is forbidden Is a crime	(See last page for comments on items referenced here)
Showing the sole of one's foot (feet)	✓			
People standing very close when talking	✓			
Maintaining steady eye contact (direct gaze) when talking to someone	✓			14
Kissing or exchange of kisses on the cheek	✓			
Counting money (change) in someone's palm	✓			n/a
Finger pointing in public (in a daring manner)	✓			
Seeking attention by winking the eyes	✓			
Tapping the head to indicate someone is crazy	✓			
Twirling the head to indicate someone is crazy	✓			
Whistling as a way of requesting something/seeking attention	✓			
Using "thumbs-up" sign to mean OK	✓			
Forming a circle with the thumb and index finger (forefinger) to mean OK	✓			
Using the fingers to make a "V" sign for victory	✓			
Beckoning to someone with the index finger (forefinger)	✓			
The left to right waving of the hand with open palms facing outward to indicate "Good bye"	✓			
The use of a nod to show acknowledgement	✓			
Stopping/beckoning a taxi using a stretched hand with the thumb pointing upward	✓			
Using the thumb finger pointed to a direction, to request a ride or a hike	✓			
Raising one's hand/waving with an open fist to summon a taxi	✓			
Tapping one's foot/feet on the floor in a public gathering	✓			
Wiggling one's leg(s) when in a sitting position	✓			
Use of the hand (by motorists and cyclists) to signal direction of traffic	✓			

UNITED KINGDOM (U.K.)

		(See last page for comments on items referenced here)
Foreign tourists are welcome in the country.	yes	
The use of seat belt is mandatory.	yes	
International driving license is accepted.	yes	15
U.S. driver's license is accepted.	yes	
It is considered impolite to yawn in public.	no	
Death penalty for drug trafficking is the law.	no	
Life imprisonment for drug trafficking is the law.	no	
Guilty until proven innocent in court is the law.	no	
Innocent until proven guilty in court is the law.	yes	
Pedestrians always have right of way.	no	16
Exit visas are required of visitors.	no	
Crash helmet is mandatory for motor cyclist.	yes	
Hanging is used as a form of legal punishment.	no	
Decapitation of a limb is used as a form of punishment.	no	
Caning is used as a form of legal punishment.	no	
Electric shock is used as a form of legal punishment.	no	
One is expected to stand up during the playing of the national anthem.	yes	
Crash helmet is mandatory for bicyclists.	no	
Guests are expected to eat every thing on their plates.	no	
Table manners are very informal.	yes	
One is expected to cover one's mouth when laughing.	no	
A vertical nod of the head means YES (OK).	yes	
A horizontal shaking of the head means NO (Not OK).	yes	
Prostitution is allowed only in designated areas.	no	
One is expected to take off one's hat during playing of national anthem.	yes	
Separate seating arrangements (between sexes) are maintained at movies.	no	
Separate seating arrangements (between sexes) are maintained at churches.	no	
Uninvited visitors or guests may not be welcome, even among acquaintances.	yes	
Pets (e.g. cats, dog) are allowed in some hotels and restaurants.	yes	
Couples invited for a meal may be separated during meals according to their sex.	no	
Punctuality is the order of business.	yes	
Automobiles are driven with headlights always turned on.	no	
Motorcycles are driven with headlights always turned on.	no	
Visitors with expired visa face mandatory jail time.	no	
Visitors without exit visa face jail time.	no	
Visitors without entry visa face mandatory (automatic) jail time.	no	

ADDITIONAL COUNTRY INFORMATION

(A)	**The types of gifts to avoid:**	white liliesn/a
(B)	**Appropriate gifts for a foreigner to give:**	chocolates, candy, liquor, flowers
(C)	**Best time to present gifts (at the beginning or at the end of a visit?):**	beginning, on arrival
(D)	**Best time to present gifts (on initial or later visits?):**	either
(E)	**Best place to present gifts (in private or in public?):**	n/a
(F)	**Number(s) with certain connotations and/or myths attached to them:**	n/a
(G)	**Basic shape(s) with negative connotations:**	n/a
(H)	**Basic color(s) with negative connotations:**	swastika
(I)	**Traditional greeting methods include:**	n/a
(J)	**Safe topics for discussion include:**	weather, fashion, travel, art, family, religion, domestic politics, food, sports,international politics, social conditions, money and personal wealth, sex
(K)	**Best time for conversations (before, during, after meals?):**	n/a
(L)	**Forms of legal punishment:**	jailing and fines deportation
(M)	**Approximately length of time one could be detained by law and order authorities before being charged in court:**	depends on the case
(N)	**January 15, 1999, for example, will normally be written as:**	15/1/99
(O)	**Emergency code number**:	999
(P)	**Ambulance code Number**:	999
(Q)	**Police code number:**	999
(R)	**Telephone (country) code:**	44
(S)	**Telex (country) code:**	851
(T)	**Electricity requirements**:	220v
(U)	**Legal drinking age:**	18
(V)	**Systems of weights and measures:**	metric
(W)	**Legal age of incarceration**:	18 for adults (detention centers for younger age)
(X)	**Driving side of the road:**	left
(Y)	**Minimum expenditure expected of foreign visitors? $**	none
(Z)	**Name of currency**:	sterling - pounds and pence
(Za)	**Some places 0ff-limits to foreign visitors:**	n/a
(Zb)	**Some places, structures and items prohibited from being photographed:**	n/a

ENDNOTES

Item Number: COMMENTS/EXPLANATIONS

n/a: Not applicable/Not available/No response

(1) At beach

(2) For children

(3) Depends on drug

(4) Depends on drug

(5) Need license

(6) Need permit in some places

(7) Need permit in some places

(8) Age limit 18

(9) Age limit 16

(10) At the beach

(11) With knife and fork

(12) Not disallowed

(13) If you wish to

(14) &/or not necessarily

(15) Not required by U.S. license holders

(16) Except at traffic lights

Final comments:

With points of "LAW" please check with the British Embassy. It is illegal to bring an animal into the U.K. - 6 months quarantine is required. Certain plants, foods and furs are also prohibited.

Appendix A

INTERNATIONAL GUIDE TO TIPPING*

	HOTELS	TAXIS	OTHERS
ANDORRA	10-20%	10%	YES
ANGUILLA	D	D	YES
ANTIGUA & BARBUDA	10%	D	YES
ARGENTINA	10-22%	10%	YES
ARMENIA	YES	OD	OD
AUSTRALIA	10%	D	YES
AUSTRIA	10-15%	10%	YES
AZERBAIJAN	YES	OD	OD
BAHAMAS	15%	15%	YES
BANGLADESH	5-10%	5-10%	YES
BARBADOS	10%	10%	YES
BELARUS	YES	OD	OD
BELGIUM	15%	D	YES
BELIZE	D 10%	D	YES
BENIN	D	D	D
BOLIVIA	10-23%	D	YES
BRAZIL	D	YES	
BURMA	10%	10%	YES
CAMEROON	10%	D	YES
CANADA	15-20%	15-20%	YES
CAYMAN IS	NC 10-15%	NC	YES
CHILE	10%	NC	YES
CHINA, PEOPLES REP.	F	F	F
CHINA, TAIWAN	D 10%	D 10%	YES
COLUMBIA	10%	NC	YES
COSTA RICA	10%	NC	YES
COTE D'IVOIRE	5-10%	5-10%	YES
CYPRUS	10%	NT	YES
CZECHOSLOVAKIA	OD 5-10%	5-10%	YES
DENMARK	15%	upto 15%	YES
DOMINICA	10%	D	YES
DOMINICAN REP.	10%		
ECUADOR	10%	NC	YES
EGYPT	10-12%	10%	YES
ETHIOPIA	5-10%	NC	YES
FIJI	D	D	YES
FINLAND	14-15%	NT	YES
FRANCE	upto 25%	15%	YES
FRENCH GUIANA	12 1/2%	NC	YES
GERMANY	10%	5%	YES
GHANA	YES	YES	YES
GIBRALTAR	10-12%	10%	YES
GREECE	10-15%	10%	YES
GRENADA	D	D	YES
GUADELOUPE	10-15%	YES	
GUATEMALA	10%	10%	YES

GUINEA	D	D	YES
GUYANA	10%	10%	YES
HAITI	NC 10%	D	YES
HONDURAS	10%	10%	YES
HONG KONG	10-15%	10%	YES
HUNGARY	OD 10-15%	YES	YES
ICELAND	NC	NC	NC
INDIA	10%	NC	YES
INDONESIA	NC 10%	NC 10%	YES
IRELAND	10-15%	YES	YES
ISRAEL	10%	NC	YES
ITALY	12-15%	15%	YES
JAMAICA	15%	10-20%	YES
JAPAN	NC 10-20%	NC	YES
JORDAN	10%	10%	YES
KAZAKHSTAN	OD	OD	OD
KENYA	10-15%	10%	YES
KOREA, SOUTH	NC 10%	NC 10-15%	YES
KUWAIT	10%	D	YES
KYRGYZSTAN	OD	OD	OD
LATVIA	NT	10-20%	YES
LIBERIA	10-15%	NC	YES
LIECHTENSTEIN	10-15%		
LITHUANIA	NC	NC	NC
LUXEMBOURG	NC 10-20%	15-20%	YES
MALAYSIA	NC 10%	NC 10%	YES
MALTA	10%	10%	YES
MARTINIQUE	10-15%	D	YES
MEXICO	7-15%	D	YES
MOLDOVA	OD	OD	OD
MONTSERRAT	10%	10%	YES
MOROCCO	10-15%	10-15%	YES
NEPAL		YES	
NETHERLANDS	15%	10-15%	YES
NEW CALEDONIA		F	F
NEW ZEALAND	NC 10%	NC	
NICARAGUA	10%	NC	YES
NIGERIA	10%	D	YES
NORWAY	15%	D	YES
PAKISTAN	5-10%	D	YES
PANAMA	10-15%	NC	YES
PAPUA NEW GUINEA	NC	NC	NC
PARAGUAY	10%	5-12%	YES
PERU	5-10%	NC	YES
PHILIPPINES	10%	D 10%	YES
POLAND	10%	10%	YES
PORTUGAL	10-15%	15%	YES
ROMANIA	NC	NC	
RUSSIA	10-15%	10-15%	YES
SAUDI ARABIA	10-15%	NC	YES
SENEGAL	10%	D	YES
SEYCHELLES	10%	D	YES
SINGAPORE	OD	10%	OD
SOUTH AFRICA	10%	10%	YES
SPAIN	5-10%	10-15%	YES
SRI LANKA	10%	D	YES

ST. KITTS	D	D	YES
ST. LUCIA	10%	10%	YES
ST. VINCENT	10-15%	10-15%	YES
ST. MAARTEN	10%	10%	YES
SURINAME	10%	NC	YES
SWEDEN	12-15%	10-15%	YES
SWITZERLAND	12-15%	12-15%	YES
TAJIKISTAN	OD	OD	OD
TANZANIA	5%	(OD) D	YES
THAILAND	D 10%	NC	YES
TOGO	OD	OD	
TRINIDAD & TOBAGO	10%	10-15%	YES
TUNISIA	10%	10%	YES
TURKEY	10-15%	D	YES
TURKMENISTAN	OD	OD	OD
UKRAINE	OD	OD	OD
UNITED KINGDOM	12-15%	10-15%	YES
UNITED STATES OF AMERICA	15%-20%	15%	YES
URUGUAY	10%	10%	YES
UZBEKISTAN	OD	OD	OD
VENEZUELA	10%	NC	YES
YUGOSLAVIA	10%	10%	YES
ZAIRE	10%	D	YES
ZAMBIA	10%	OD	YES

xxx YES, persons who perform other services such as porters, luggage handlers, door persons, etc. may be tipped or may expect to be tipped. Tipping and amount of tip is at your discretion.

D = Tipping is expected. Amount of tip is at your discretion.

OF = Tipping is Officially Discouraged although privately welcome.

NC = Tipping is not customary, nevertheless welcome.

NT = Not usually tipped

F = Tipping is prohibited

APPENDIX B

INTERNATIONAL ELECTRICITY REQUIREMENTS

COUNTRIES:	(Volts/AC)
AFGHANISTAN	20/50 AC
ALGERIA	110-115/50, 220/50 AC*
ANDORRA	125/50 AC
ANGUILLA	220
ANTIGUA	110/60 AC
ARGENTINA	220/60 AC
ARMENIA	220/50
AUSTRALIA	240 AC
AUSTRIA	220/50
AZERBAIJAN	220/50
BAHAMAS	120/60 AC
BAHRAIN	220/50 AC
BANGLADESH	220 AC
BARBADOS	110/50 AC
BELGIUM	220/50 AC
BELIZE	110/220/60 AC
BENIN	220/50
BERMUDA	110/60 AC
BHUTAN	110-220/50 AC*
BOTSWANA	220
BRAZIL+	110/60; 220/60, 127/60 AC*
BRITISH VIRGIN IS	115-210/60 AC
BULGARIA	220/50 AC
BURKINA FASO	220/50
BURMA	220/50 AC
BURUNDI	220/50
BYELARUS	220/50
CAMEROON	110-220
CANADA	110/60 AC
CAYMAN ISLANDS	110/60 AC
CENTRAL AF. REP.	220
CHAD	220
CHILE+	220/50 AC
CHINA	110/50
CHINA, TAIWAN	110/60 AC
COLOMBIA	150/60 AC, 110/60**
COMOROS	220/50
CONGO, REP.	220/50
COSTA RICA	110/60 AC
COTE D'IVOIRE	220/50 AC
CUBA	110/60
CYPRUS++	240/50 AC
CZECH REP.	220/50 AC
DENMARK	220/50
DOMINICA	220-240/50 AC
DOMINICAN REP.	110/60 AC
ECUADOR	110/60 AC
EGYPT	220/50, 110-120/50*
EL SALVADOR	110/60
ESTONIA	220/50
EQUAT. GUINEA	220/50
ETHIOPIA	220/60 AC
FIJI	240/50 AC
FINLAND	220/60 AC
FRANCE	220/50
FRENCH GUIANA	220 & 110/50 AC
GABON	220/240/50
GEORGIA	220/50
GERMANY	220/50 AC
GHANA	220-240/50 AC
GIBRALTAR	240-250/50 AC
GREECE+	220/50 AC
GRENADA	220-240/50 AC
GUADELOUPE	220/50 AC
GUAM	120/60 AC
GUATEMALA	110/60 AC
GUINEA	220/50
GUYANA	110-120/60 AC
HAITI	110/60 AC
HONDURAS	110 or 220/60 AC*
HONG KONG++	200-220/60 AC
HUNGARY	220/50 AC
ICELAND	220/50 AC
INDIA+	220/50 AC
INDONESIA	220/50 AC
IRAN	220/50
IRAQ	220 DC
IRELAND	220/50 AC
ISRAEL	220/50 AC
ITALY	220/50, 110-127/50 AC*
JAMAICA	110/50 AC
JAPAN	110/50, 100/60 AC*
JORDAN	220/50 AC
KAZAKHSTAN	220/50
KENYA	220/50 AC
KOREA, SOUTH	110/60 AC
KUWAIT	240/50 AC
KYRGYZSTAN	220/50

LATVIA	220/50
LEBANON	110-220/50
LESOTHO	220 AC
LIBERIA	120/60 AC
LIBYA	220/50
LIECHTENSTEIN	220/50 AC
LITHUANIA	220/50
LUXEMBOURG	220/110
MADAGASCAR	220/50
MALAWI	220
MALAYSIA	220/50 AC
MALI	220
MALTA	240/50 AC
MARTINIQUE	220/50 AC
MAURITANIA	220/50
MAURITIUS	220/230
MEXICO	110/60 AC
MICRONESIA	110/60 AC
MOLDOVA	220/50
MONTSERRAT	230/60 AC
MOROCCO	110-120/50 AC
MOZAMBIQUE	220/50
NAMIBIA	220/240/60
NEPAL	220/50 AC
NETHERLANDS ANT.	110-130/50, 120/60AC*
NETHERLANDS	220/50 AC
NEW CALEDONIA	220/50 AC
NICARAGUA	110/60 AC
NIGER	220-240/50
NIGERIA++	220/50 AC
NORWAY	220/50 AC
OMAN	220/240/50
PAKISTAN	220/240/50 AC
PANAMA	110/60 AC
PAPUA NEW GUINEA	240 AC
PARAGUAY+	220/50 AC
PERU	220/60 AC
PHILIPPINES	220/60 AC
POLAND	220/50 AC
PORTUGAL	210-220/50 AC
PUERTO RICO	110-115/60 AC
QATAR	220/50
REP. OF DJIBOUTI	220/50
CAPE VERDE	220/50
ROMANIA	220/50
RUSSIA	220/50
RWANDA	220/50
SAUDI ARABIA	110 & 120/60 AC
SENEGAL	110 & 220/50 AC
SEYCHELLES	240/50 AC
SIERRA LEONE	220/50
SINGAPORE++	230-250 AC
SAO TOME & PRIN.	220/50
SOMALIA	220/50
SOUTH AFRICA	220-230/50 AC
SPAIN	110-220/50 AC
SRI LANKA	230-240/50 AC
ST. KITTS	230/60 AC
ST. LUCIA	220/50 AC
ST. MARTIN	220/60 AC
ST. VINCENT	220-230/50 AC
SUDAN	240 AC
SURINAME	110-115/60 AC
SWAZILAND	240/50
SWEDEN+	220/50 AC
SWITZERLAND	220/50 AC
TAJIKISTAN	220/50
TANZANIA	240/50/60 AC
THAILAND	220/50 AC
TOGO	220/50 AC
TONGA	220 AC
TRINIDAD & TOB.	110/60 AC
TUNISIA	110-115/50, 220/50 AC*
TURKEY	220/50
TURKMENISTAN	220/50
TURKS & CAICOS	110/60
U.S.A	110-115/60 AC
UKRAINE	220/50
UNITED ARAB EM.	240/415 AC
UNITED KINGDOM	220/50 AC
URUGUAY	220/50 AC
UZBEKISTAN	220/50
VENEZUELA	110/60 AC
YEMEN, ARAB REP.	220/50 AC
YEMEN, P.D.R	220/240/50
YUGOSLAVIA	220/50 AC
ZAIRE	220/50
ZAMBIA	220/50 AC
ZIMBABWE++	220/240/50

----

* Electricity requirements vary in some parts of the country.

\+ Some parts of the country still use DC.

++ In some or most parts of the country, you may need three square pin plugs.

APPENDIX C

INTERNATIONAL TELEPHONE DIALING CODES

COUNTRY/City Codes

Algeria 213
City code not required.

American Samoa 684
City code not required.

Andorra 33
Use 628 for all cities.

Anguilla 809
Dial 1 + 809 + Local Number.

Antigua 809
Dial 1 + 809 + Local Number.

Argentina 54
Bahia Blanca 91. Buenos Aires 1, Cordoba 51, Corrientes 783, La Plata 21, Mar Del Plata 23, Mendoza 61, Merlo 220, Posadas 752, Resistencia 772, Rio Cuarto 586, Rosario 41, San Juan 64, San Rafael 627, Santa Fe 42, Tandil 293

Aruba 297
Use 8 for all cities.

Ascension Island 247
City code not required.

Australia 61
Adelaide 8, Ballarat 53, Brisbane 7, Canberra 62, Darwin 89, Geelong 52, Gold Coast 75, Hobart 02, Launceston 03, Melbourne 3, Newcastle 49, Perth 9, Sydne 2, Toowoomba 76, Townsville 77, Wollongong 42

Austria 43
Bludenz 5552, Graz 316, Innsbruck 5222, Kitzbuhel 5356, Klagenfut 4222, Krems An Der Donau 2732, Linz Donau 732, Neunkirchen Niederosterreich 2635, Salzburg 662, St. Polten 2742, Vienna 1, Villach 4242, Wels 7242, Wiener Neustadt 2622

Bahamas 809
Dial 1 + 809 + Local Number.

Bahrain 973
City code not required.

Bangladesh 880
Barisal 431, Bogra 51, Chittagong 31, Comilla 81, Dhaka 2, Khulna 41, Maulabi Bazar 861, Mymensingh 91, Rajshaki 721, Sylhet 821

Barbados 809

Dial 1 + 809 + Local Number.

Belgium 32
Antwerp 3, Bruges 50, Brussels 2, Charleroi 71, Courtrai 56, Ghent 91, Hasselt 11, La Louviere 64, Leuven 16, Libramont 61, Liege 41, Malines 15, Mons 65, Namur 81, Ostend 59, Verviers 87

Belize 501
Belize City (City code not required), Belmopan 08, Benque Viejo Del Carmen 093, Corozal Town 04, Dangviga 05, Independence 06, Orange Walk 03, Punta Gorda 07, San Ignacio 092

Benin 229
City code not required.

Bermuda 809
Dial 1 + 809 + Local Number.

Bolivia 591
Cochabamba 42, Cotoga 388, Guayafamerin 47, La Belgica 923, La Paz 2, Mineros 984, Montero 92, Oruro 52, Portachuelo 924, Saavedra 924, Santa Cruz 33, Trinidad 46, Warnes 923

Botswana 267
Francistown 21, Gaborone 31, Jwaneng 38, Kanye 34, Lobatse 33, Mahalapye 41, Maun 26, Mochudi 37, Molepoloe 32,

Orapa 27, Palapye 42, Ramotswana 39, Selibe (Phikwe) 8, Serowe 43

Brazil 55
Belem 91, Belo Horizonte 31, Brasilia 61, Curitiba 41, Fortaleza 85, Goiania 62, Niteroi 21, Pelotas 532, Porto Alegre 512, Recife 81, Rio de Janeiro 21, Salvador 71, Santo Andre 11, Santos 132, Sao Paulo 11, Vitoria 27

British Virgin Islands 809
Dial 1 + 809 + Local Number in the following cities: Anegada, Camanoe Island, Guana Island, Josh Vah Dyke, Little Thatch, Marina Cay, Mosquito Island, North Sound, Peter Island, Salt Island, Tortola, Virgin Gorda.

Brunei 673
Bandar Seri Begawan 2, Kuala Belait 3, Mumong 3, Tutong 4

Bulgaria 359
Kardjali 361, Pazardjik 34, Plovdiv 32, Sofia 2, Varna 52

Burkina Faso 226
Bobo Dioulasso 9, Fada N'Gorma 7, Koudougou 4, Ouagadougou 3

Burma 95
Akyab 43, Bassein 42, Magwe 63, Mandalay 2, Meikila 64, Moulmein 32, Pegu 52, Prom 53, Rangoon 1

Cameroon 237
City code not required.

Canada NPA's

Dial 1 + Area Code + Local Number.

Cape Verde Islands 238

City code not required.

Caymen Islands 809
Dial 1 + 809 + Local Number.

Chile 56
Chiquayante 41, Concepcion 41, Penco 41, Recreo 31, San Bernardo 2, Santiago 2, Talcahuano 41, Valparaiso 32, Vina del Mar 32

China 86
Beijing (Peking) 1, Fuzhou 591, Ghuangzhou (Canton) 20, Shanghai 21

Colombia 57
Armenia 60, Barranquilla 5, Bogota 1, Bucaramanga 73, Cali 3, Cartagena 59, Cartago 66, Cucuta 70, Giradot 832, Ibague 82, Manizales 69, Merdellin 42, Neiva 80, Palmira 31, Pereira 61, Santa Marta 56

Costa Rica 506
City code not required.

Cyprus 357
Kythrea 2313, Lapithos 8218, Lamaca 41, Lefkonico 3313, Limassol 51, Moni 5615, Morphou 71, Nicosia 2, Paphos 61, Platres 54, Polis 63, Rizokarpaso 3613, Yialousa 3513. The following cities are handled by the Turkish Telephone Network.
Use country code 90 for Turkey: Famagusta 536, Kyrenia 581, and Lefka 57817.

Czechoslovakia 42
Banska Bystrica 88, Bratislava 7, Brno 5, Ceske Budejovice 38, Decin 412, Havirov 6994, Hradec Kralove 49, Kablonec Nad Nisou 428, Karvina 6993, Kosice 95, Most 35, Ostrava 69, Pizen 19, Prague (Praha) 2, Usti Nad Labem 47, Zilina 89

Denmark 45
City code not required.

Djibouti 253
City code not required.

Dominica 809
Dial 1 + 809 + Local Number.

Dominican Republic 809
Dial 1 + 809 + Local Number.

Ecuador 593
Ambato 2, Cayambe 2, Cuenca 7, Esmeraldas 2, Guayaquil 4, Ibarra 2; Loja 4, Machachi 2, Machala 4, Manta 4, Portoviejo 4, Quevedo 4, Quito 2, Salinas 4, Santa Domingo 2, Tulcan 2

Egypt 20
Alexandria 3, Answan 97, Asyut 88, Benha 13, Cairo 2, Damanhour 45, El Mahallah (El Kubra) 43, El Mansoura 50, Luxor 95, Port Said 66,

Shebin El Kom 48, Sohag 93, Tanta 40

El Salvador 503
City code not required.

Estonia 7
Tallinn 0142

Ethiopia 251
Addis Ababa 1, Akaki 1, Asmara 4, Assab 3, Awassa 6, Debre Zeit 1, Dessie 3, Dire Dawa 5, Harrar 5, Jimma 7, Makale 4, Massawa 4, Nazareth 2, Shashemene 6

Faeroe Islands 298
City code not required.

Fiji Islands 679
City code not required.

Finland 358
Epoo-Ebbo 15, Helsinki 0, Joensuu 73, Jyvaskyla 41, Kuopio 71, Lahti 18, Lappeenranta 53, Oulu 81, Port 39, Tammefors-Tampere 31, Turku 21, Uleaborg 81, Vaasa 61, Vanda-Vantaa 0

France 33
Aix-en-Provence 42, Bordeaux 56, Cannes 93, Chauvigny 49, Cherbourge 33, Grenoble 76, Le Havre 35, Lourdes 62, Lyon 7, Marseille 91, Nancy 8, Nice 93, Paris 1, Rouen 35, Toulouse 61, Tours 47

French Antilles 596
City code not required.

French Guiana 594
City code not required.

French Polynesia 689
City code not required.

Gabon Republic 241
City code not required.

Gambia 220
City code not required.

Georgia 7
Sukhumi 88122, Tblisi 8832

Germany East 7
Berlin 2, Cottbus 59, Dresden 51, Erfurt 61, Frankfurt 30, Gera 70, Halle/Saale 46, Karl-Marx-Stadt 71, Leipzig 41, Magdeburg 91, Neubrandenburg 90, Postdam 33, Rostock 81, Schwerin (Meckl) 84, Suhl 66, Zittau 522

Germany West 49
Bad Homburg 6172, Berlin 30, Bonn 228, Bremen 421, Cologne (Koln) 221, Dusseldorf 211, Essen 201, Frankfurt 69, Hamburg 40, Heidellberg 6221, Koblenz 261, Mannheim 621, Munich 89, Numberg 911, Stuttgart 711, Wiesbaden 6121

Ghana 233
City code not required.

Gibraltar 350
City code not required.

Greece 30
Argos 751, Athens (Athinai) 1, Corinth 741, Iraklion (Kristis) 81, Kavala 51, Larissa 41, Patrai 61, Piraeus Pireefs 1, Rodos 241, Salonica (Thessaloniki) 31, Sparti 731, Thessaloniki 31, Tripolis 71, Volos 421, Zagora 426

Greenland 299
Goatham 2, Sondre Stromfjord 11, Thule 50

Grenada 809
Dial 1 + 809 + Local Number.

Guadeloupe 590
City code not required.

Guam 671
City code not required.

Guantanemo Bay 5399
City code not required.

Guatemala 502
Guatemala City 2. All other cities 9.

Guinea 224
City code not required.

Guyana 592
Anna Regina 71, Bartica 5, Beteryerwaging 20, Cove & John 29, Georgetown 2, Ituni 41, Linden 4, Mabaruma 77, Mahaica 28, Mahalcony 21, New Amsterdam 3, New Hope 66, Rosignol 30, Timehri 61, Vreed-En-Hoop 64, Whim 37

Haiti 509

Cap-Haitien 3, Cayes 5, Gonalve 2, Port au Prince 1

Honduras 504
City code not required.

Hong Kong 852
Castle Peak 0, Cheung Chau 5, Fan Ling 0, Hong Kong 5, Kowloon 3, Kwai Chung 0, Lamma 5, Lantau 5, Ma Wan 5, Peng Chau 5, Sek Kong 0, Sha Tin 0, Tai Po 0, Ting Kau 0, Tsun Wan 0

Hungary 36
Abasar 37, Balatonaliga 84, Budapest 1, Dorgicse 80, Fertoboz 99, Gyongyos 37, Kaposvar 82, Kazincbarcika 48, Komlo 72, Miskolc 46, Nagykaniza 93, Szekesfehervar 22, Szolnok 56, Varpalota 80, Veszprem 80, Zalaegerzeg 92

Iceland 354
Akureyi 6, Hafnafijorour 1, Husavik 6, Keflavik Naval Base 2, Rein 6, Reykjavik 1, Reyorarjorour 7, Sandgerol 2, Selfoss 9. Siglufijorour 6, Stokkseyri 9, Suoavik 4, Talknafijorour 4, Varma 1, Vik 9

India 91
Ahmedabad 272, Amritsar 183, Bangalore 812, Baroda 265, Bhopal 755, Bombay 22 Calcutta 33, Chandigarh 172, Hyderabad 842, Jaipur 141, Jullundur 181, Kanpur 512, Madras 44, New Dehli 11, Poona 212, Surat 261

Indonesia 62
Bandung 22, Cirebon 231, Denpasar (Bali) 361, Jakarta 21, Madiun 351, Malang 341, Medan 61, Padang 751, Palembang 711, Sekurang 778, Semarang 24, Solo 271, Surabaya 31, Tanjungkarang 721, Yogykarta 274

Iran 98
Abadan 631, Ahwaz 61, Arak 2621, Esfahan 31, Ghazvin 281, Ghome 251, Hamadan 261, Karadj 2221, Kerman 341, Mashad 51, Rasht 231, Rezaiyeh 441, Shiraz 71, Tabriz 41, Tehran 21

Iraq 964
Baghdad 1, Basiah 40, Diwanyia 36, Karbala 32, Kirkuk 50, Mosul 60, Nasryia 42

Ireland 353
Arklow 402, Cork 21, Dingle 66, Donegal 73, Drogheda 41, Dublin 1, Dundalk 42, Ennis 65, Galway 91, Kildare 45, Killamey 64, Sligo 71, Tipperary 62, Tralee 66, Tullamore 506, Waterford 51, Wexford 53

Israel 972
Afula 65, Ako 4, Ashkelon 51, Bat Iam 3, Beer Sheva 57, Dimona 57, Hadera 63, Haifa 4, Holon 3, Jerusalem 2, Nazareth 65, Netania 53, Rehovot 8, Tel Aviv 3, Tiberias 67, Tsefat 67

Italy 39
Bari 80, Bologna 51, Brindisi 831, Capri 81, Como 31, Florence 55, Genoa 10, Milan 2, Naples 81, Padova 49, Palermo 91, Pisa 50, Rome 6, Torino 11, Trieste 40, Venice 41, Verona 45

Ivory Coast 225
City code not required.

Jamaica 809
Dial 1 + 809 + Local Number.

Japan 81
Chiba 472, Fuchu (Tokyo) 423, Hiroshima 82, Kawasaki (Kanagawa) 44, Kobe 78, Kyoto 75, Nagasaki 958, Nagoya 52, Nahat (Okinawa) 988, Osaka 6, Sapporo 11, Sasebo 956, Tachikawa (Tokyo) 425, Tokyo 3, Yokohama 45, Yokosuka (Kanagawa) 468

Jordan 962
Amman 6, Aqaba 3, Irbid 2, Jerash 4, Karak 3, Maam 3, Mafruq 4, Ramtha 2, Sueeleh 6, Sult 5, Zerqa 9

Kazakhstan 7
Alma-Ata 3272, Chimkent 3252, Guryev 31222

Kenya 254
Anmer 154, Bamburi 11, Embakasi 2, Girgiri 2, Kabete 2, Karen 2882, Kiambu 154, Kikuyu 283, Kisumu 35, Langata 2, Mombasa 11, Nairobi 2, Nakuru 37, Shanzu 11, Thika 151, Uthiru 2

Kiribati 686
City code not required.

Korea 82
Chung Ju 431, Chuncheon 361, Icheon 336, Incheon 32, Kwangju (Gwangju) 62,

Masan 551, Osan 339, Osan Military (333+414), Pohang 562, Pusan (Busan) 51, Seoul 2, Suwon (Suweon) 331, Taegu (Daegu) 53, Ulsan 552, Wonju (Weonju) 371

Kuwait **965**
City code not required.

Kyrgyzstan 7
Osh 33222, Pishpek 3312

Latvia **7**
Riga 0132

Lebanon **961**
Beirut 1, Juniyah 9, Tripoli 6, Zahlah 8

Lesotho **266**
City code not required.

Liberia **231**

City code not required.

Libya **218**
Agelat 282, Benghazi 61, Benina 63, Derma 81, Misuratha 51, Sabratha 24, Sebha 71, Taigura 26, Tripoli 21, Tripoli International Airport 22, Zawai 23, Zuara 25

Liechtenstein **41**

Use 75 for all cities.

Lithuania **7**
Vilnius 0122

Luxembourg **352**
City code not required.

Macao **853**
City code not required.

Malawi **265**
Domasi 531, Likuni 766, Luchenza 477, Makwasa 474, Mulanje 465, Namadzi 534, Njuli 664, Thondwe 533, Thornwood 486, Thyolo 467, Zomba 50, City code not required for other cities.

Malaysia **60**
Alor Star 4, Baranang 3, Broga 3, Cheras 3, Dengil 3, Ipoh 5, Johor Bahru 7, Kajang 3, Kepala Batas 4, Kuala Lampur 3, Machang 97, Maran 95, Port Dickson 6, Semenyih 3, Seremban 6, Sungei Besi 3, Sungei Renggam 3

Maldives **960**
City code not required.

Mali **223**
City code not required.

Malta **356**
City code not required.

Marshall Islands **692**
Ebeye 871, Majuro 9

Mauritius **230**
City code not required.

Mayotte Islands **269**
City code not required.

Mexico **52**
Acapulco 748, Cancun 988, Celaya 461, Chihuahua 14, Ciudad Juarez 16, Conzumel 987, Culiacan 671, Ensenda 667, Guadalajara 36, Hermosillo 621, La Paz 682, Mazatlan 678, Merida 99, Mexicali 65, Mexico City 5, Monterrey 83, Puebla 22, Puerto Vallarta 322, Rasarito 661, San Luis Potosi 481, Tampico 121, Tecate 665, Tijuana 66, Torreon 17, Veracruz 29

Micronesia **691**
Kosrae 851, Ponape 9, Truk 8319, Yap 841

Moldova **7**
Kishinev 0422

Monaco **33**
Use 93 for all cities.

Mongolian People's Rep. **976**
Ulan Bator 1

Montserrat **809**
Dial 1 + 809 + Local Number.

Morocco **212**
Agardir 8, Beni-Mellal 48, Berrechid 33, Casablanca (City code not required). El Jadida 34, Fes 6, Kenitra 16, Marrakech 4, Meknes 5, Mohammedia 32, Nador 60, Oujda 68, Rabat 7, Tanger (Tangiers) 9, Tetouan 96
Mustique **809**

Dial 1 + 809 + Local Number.

Namibia 264
Gobabis 681, Grootfontein 673, Industria 61, Keetmanshoop 631, Luderitz 6331, Mariental 661, Okahandja 622, Olympia 61, Otjiwarongo 651, Pioneerspark 61, Swakopmund 641, Tsumeb 671, Windhoek 61, Windhoek Airport 626

Nauru Island 674
City code not required.

Nepal 977
City code not required.

Netherlands 31
Amsterdam 20, Arnhem 85, Eindhoven 40, Groningen 50, Haarlem 23, Heemstede 23, Hillegersberg 10, Hoensbraoek 45, Hoogkerk 50, Hoogvliet 10, Loosduinen 70, Nijmegen 80, Oud Zuilen 30, Rotterdam 10, The Hague 70, Utrecht 30

Netherlands Antilles 599
Bonaire 7, Curacao 9, Saba 4, Eustatius 3, St. Maarten 5

Nevis 809
Dial 1 + 809 + Local Number.

New Caledonia 687
City code not required.

New Zeland 64
Auckland 9, Christchurch 3, Dunedin 24, Hamilton 71, Hastings 70, Invercargill 21, Napier 70, Nelson 54, New Plymouth 67, Palmerston North 63, Rotorua 73, Tauranga 75, Timaru 56, Wanganui 64, Wellington 4, Whangarei 89

Nicaragua 505
Boaco 54, Chinandega 341, Diriamba 42, Esteli 71, Granada 55, Jinotepe 41, Leon 311, Managua 2, Masatepe 44, Masaya 52, Nandaime 45, Rivas 461, San Juan Del Sur 466, San Marcos 43, Tipitapa 53

Niger Republic 227
City code not required.

Nigeria 234
Lagos 1 (Only city direct dial)
Niue 683

Norfolk Island 672

Norway 47
Arendal 41, Bergen 5, Drammen 3, Fredrikstad 32, Haugesund 47, Kongsvinger 66, Kristiansund N. 73, Larvik 34, Moss 32, Narvik 82, Oslo 2, Sarpsborg 31, Skien 35, Stavanger 4, Svalbard 80, Tonsberg 33, Trondheim 7

Oman 968
City code not required.

Pakistan 92
Abbotabad 5921, Bahawalpur 621, Faisalabad 411, Gujtanwala 431, Hyderabad 221, Islamabad 51, Karachi 21, Lahore 42, Multan 61, Okara 442, Peshawar 521, Quetta 81, Sahiwal 441, Sargodha 451, Sialkot 432, Sukkur 71

Palm Island 809
Dial 1 + 809 + Local Number.

Panama 507
City code not required.

Papau New Guinea 675
City code not required.

Paragua 595
Asuncion 21, Ayolas 72, Capiata 28, Concepcion 31, Coronel Bogado 74, Coronel Oviedo 521, Encarnacion 71, Hermandarias 63, Ita 24, Pedro J. Caballero 36, Pilar 86, San Antonio 27, San Ignacio 82, Stroessner: Ciudad Pte. 61, Villarica 541, Villeta 25

Peru 51
Arequipa 54, Ayacucho 6491, Callao 14, Chiclayo 74, Chimbote 44, Cuzco 84, Huancavelica 6495, Huancayo 64, Ica 34, Iquitos 94, Lima 14, Piura 74, Tacna 54, Trujillo 44

Phillippines 63
Angeles 55, Bacolod 34, Baguio City 442, Cebu City 32, Clark Field (military) 52, Dagupan 48, Davao 35, Lloilo City 33, Lucena 42, Manila 2, San Fernando: La Union 46, San Fernando: Pampanga 45, San Pablo 43, Subic Bay Military Base 89, Subic Bay Residential Housing 89, Tarlac City 47

Poland **48**
Bialystok 85, Bydgoszcz 52, Crakow (Krakow) 12, Gdansk 58, Gdynia 58, Katowice 32, Lodz 42, Lubin 81, Olsztyn 89, Poznan 48, Radom 48, Sopot 58, Torun 56, Warsaw 22

Portugal **351**
Alamada 1, Angra Do Heroismo 95, Barreiro 1, Beja 84, Braga 53, Caldas Da Rainha 62, Coimbra 39, Estoril 1, Evora 66, Faro 89, Horta 92, Lajes AFB 95, Lisbon 1, Madalena 92, Madeira Islands 91, Montijo 1, Ponta Del Gada 96, Porto 2, Santa Cruz (Flores) 92, Santarem 43, Setubal 65, Velas 95, Vila Do Porto 96, Viseu 32

Qatar **974**
City code not required.

Reunion Island **262**
City code not required.

Romania **40**
Arad 66, Bacau 31, Brasov 21, Bucharest 0, Cluj-Napoca 51, Constanta 16, Crajova 41, Galati 34, Lasi 81, Oradea 91, Pitesti 76, Ploiesti 71, Satu-Mare 97, Sibiu 24, Timisoara 61, Tirgu Mures 54

Russia **7**
Magadan 41300, Moscow 095, St. Petersburg 812

Rwanda **250**
City code not required.

St. Kitts **809**
Dial 1 + 809 + Local Number.

St. Lucia **809**
Dial 1 + 809 + Local Number.

St. Pierre & Miquelon **508**
City code not required.

St. Vincent **809**
Dial 1 + 809 + Local Number.

Saipan **670**
Capitol Hill 322, Rota Island 532, Susupe City 234, Tinian Island 433

San Marino **39**
Use 541 for all cities.

Saudi Arabia **966**
Abha 7, Abqaiq 3, Al Khobar 3, Al Markazi 2, Al Ulaya 1, Damman 3, Dhahran (Aramco) 3, Jeddah 2, Khamis Mushait 7, Makkah (Mecca) 2, Medina 4, Najran 7, Qatif 3, Riyadh 1, Taif 2, Yenbu 4

Senegal **221**
City code not required.

Seychelles Islands **248**
City code not required.

Sierra Leone **232**
Freetown 22, Juba 24, Lungi 25, Wellington 23

Singapore **65**
City code not required.

Solomon Island **677**
City code not required.

South Africa **27**
Bloemfontein 51, Cape Town 21, De Aar 571, Durban 31, East London 431, Gordons Bay 24, Johannesburg 11, La Lucia 31, Pietermaritzburg 331, Port Elizabeth 41, Pretoria 12, Sasolburg 16, Somerset West 24, Uitenhage 422, Welkom 171

Spain **34**
Barcelona 3, Bibao 4, Cadiz 56, Ceuta 56, Granada 58, Igualada 3, Las Palmas de Gran Canaria 28, Leon 87, Madrid 1, Malaga 52, Melilla 52, Palma De Mallorca 71, Pamplona 48, Santa Cruz de Tenerife 22, Santander 42, Seville 54, Torremolinos 52, Valencia 6

Sri Lanka **94**
Ambalangoda 97, Colombo Central 1, Galle 9, Havelock Town 1, Kandy 8, Katugastota 8, Kotte 1, Maradana 1, Matara 41, Negomgo 31, Panadura 46, Trincomalee 26

Suriname **597**
City code not required.

Swaziland **268**
City code not required.

Sweden **46**
Alingsas 322, Boras 33, Eskilstuna 16,

Gamleby 493, Goteborg 31, Helsinborg 42, Karlstad 54, Linkoping 13, Lund 46, Malmo 40, Norrkoping 11, Stockholm 8, Sundsvall 60, Trelleborg 410, Uppsala 18, Vasteras 21

Switzerland 41
Baden 56, Basel 61, Berne 31, Davos 83, Fribourg 37, Geneva 22, Interlaken 36, Lausanne 21, Lucerne 41, Lugano 91, Montreux 21, Neuchatel 38, St. Gallen 71, St. Moritz 82, Winterthur 52, Zurich 1

Taiwan 886
Changhua 47, Chunan 36, Chunghsing-Hsintsun 49, Chungli 34, Fengyuan 4, Hsiaying 6, Hualien 38, Kaohsiung 7, Keelung 2, Lotung 39, Pingtung 8, Taichung 4, Tainan 6, Taipei 2, Taitung 89, Taoyuan 33

Tajikistan 7
Dushanbe 3772

Tanzania 255
Dar Es Salaam 51, Dodoma 61, Mwanza 68, Tanga 53

Thailand 66
Bangkok 2, Burirum 44, Chanthaburi 39, Chien Mai 53, Cheingrai 54, Kamphaengphet 55, Lampang 54, Nakhon Sawan 56, Nong Khai 42, Pattani 73, Pattaya 38, Ratchaburi 32, Saraburi 36, Tak 55, Ubon Ratchathani 45

Togo 228
City code not required.

Tonga Islands 676
City code not required.

Trinidad & Tabago 809
Dial 1 + 809 + Local Number.

Tunisia 216
Agareb 4, Beja 8, Bizerte 2, Carthage 1, Chebba 4, Gabes 5, Gafsa 6, Haffouz 7, Hamman-Souse 3, Kairouan 7, Kef 8, Khenis 3, Medenine 5, Tabarka 8, Tozeur 6, Tunis 1

Turkey 90
Adana 711, Ankara 41, Antalya 311, Bursa 241, Eskisehir 221, Gazianter 851, Istanbul 1, Izmir 51, Izmit 211, Kayseri 351, Konya 331, Malatya 821, Mersin 741, Samsun 361

Turka & Caicos 809
Dial 1 + 809 + Local Number.

Turkmenistan 7
Ashkkhabad 3632, Chardzhou 37822

Tuvalu 688

Ukraine 7
Kharkiv 0572, Kyiv 044, Lviv 0322

Uganda 256
Entebbe 42, Jinja 43, Kampala 41, Kyambogo 41

Union Island 809
Dial 1 + 809 + Local Number.

United Arab Emirates 971
Abu Dhabi 2, Ajman 6, Al Ain 3, Aweer 58, Dhayd 6, Dibba 70, Dubai 4, Falaj-al-Moalla 6, Fujairah 70, Jebel Ali 84, Jebel Dhana 52, Khawanij 58, Ras-al-Khaimah 77, Sharjan 6, Tarif 53, Umm-al-Quwain 6

United Kingdom 44
Belfast 232, Birmingham 21, Bournemouth 202, Cardiff 222, Durham 385, Edinburgh 31, Glasgow 41, Gloucester 452, Ipswich 473, Liverpool 51, London (Inner) 71, London (Outer) 81, Manchester 61, Nottingham 602, Prestwick 292, Sheffield 742, Southampton 703

Uruguay 598
Atlantida 372, Colonia 522, Florida 352, La Paz 322, Las Piedras 322,
Los Toscas 372, Maldonado 42, Mercedes 532, Minas 442, Montevideo 2, Parque De Plata 372, Paysandu 722, Punta Del Este 42, Salinas 372, San Jose 342, San Jose De Carrasco 382

Uzbekistan 7
Karish 37522, Samarkand 3662, Tashkent 3712

Vanuatu, Rep. of 678

Vatican City 39
Use 6 for all cities.

Venezuela 58
Barcelona 81, Barquisimeto 51, Cabimas 64, Caracas 2, Ciudad Bolivar 85, Coro 68, Cumana 93, Los Teques 32, Maiquetia 31, Maracaibo 61, Maracay 43, Maturin 91, Merida 74, Puerto Cabello 42, San Cristobal 76, Valencia 41

Vietnam 84
Hanoi 4, Ho Chi Minh City 8

Wallis & Futuna Islands 681

Western Samoa 685
City code not required.

Yeman (North) 967
Al Marawyah 3, Al Qaidah 4, Amran 2, Bayt Al Faquih 3, Dhamar 2, Hodeidah 3, Ibb 4, Mabar 2, Rada 2, Rawda 2, Sanaa 2, Taiz 4, Yarim 4, Zabid 3

Yugoslavia 38
Belgrade (Beograd) 11, Dubrovnik 50, Leskovac 16, Ljubjana 61, Maribor 62, Mostar 88, Novi Sad 21, Pirot 10, Rijeka 51, Sarajevo 71, Skopje 91, Split 58, Titograd 81, Titovo-Uzice 31, Zagreb 41

Zaire 243
Kinshasa 12, Lubumbashi 222

Zambia 260
Chingola 2, Kitwe 2, Luanshya 2, Lusaka 1, Ndola 26

Zimbabwe 263
Bulawayo 9, Harare 0, Mutare 20

APPENDIX D

COUNTRIES: BANKING, BUSINESS AND SHOPPING HOURS

AFGHANISTAN
Business/Shopping Hours: 8:AM - 6:AM (Sun-Thur) Businesses are closed Thursday and Friday afternoons

ALGERIA
Banking Hours: 9:AM - 4:PM (Sun-Thur) Business Hours: 8:AM - 12:Noon, 1:PM - 5:PM (Sat-Wed) Businesses are closed Thursday and Friday

AMERICAN SAMOA
Banking Hours: 9:AM - 2:PM (Mon-Thur) 9:AM - 5:PM (Fri)

ANDORRA
Banking Hours: 9:AM - 1:PM; 3:PM - 7:PM; Business Hours: 9:AM - 1:PM; 3:PM - 7:PM, Shopping Hours: 10:AM - 1:PM; 3:PM - 8:PM

ANGUILLA
Banking Hours: 8:AM - 12:00 Noon (Mon-Fri); 3:PM (Fri), Business Hours: 8:AM - 4:PM, Shopping Hours: 8:AM - 5:PM (Mon-Sat)

ANTIGUA AND BARBUDA
Banking Hours: 8:AM - 1:PM (Mon,Tue,Wed,Thur) 8:AM - 1:PM & 3:PM - 5:PM (Fri), Business Hours: 8:AM - 12:Noon & 1:PM - 4:PM (Mon-Fri), Shopping Hours: 8:AM - 12:Noon & 1:PM - 5:PM (Mon-Sat)

ARMENIA
Banking Hours: 9:AM - 6:PM, Business Hours: 9:AM - 6:PM, Shopping Hours: 8:AM - 9:PM

ARGENTINA
Banking Hours: 10:AM - 4:PM, (Mon-Fri), Business Hours: 9:AM - 6:PM (Mon-Fri), Shopping Hours: 9:AM - 8:PM (Mon-Sat)

AUSTRALIA
Banking Hours: 10:AM - 3:PM, (Mon-Thur); 10:AM - 5:PM (Fri)
Banks are closed on Saturdays
Business/Shopping Hours: 9:AM - 5:30PM (Mon-Thur); 8:30AM - 12:Noon (Sat)

AUSTRIA
Banking Hours: 8:AM - 12:30 PM, 1:30 - 3:30, PM (Mon, Tue, Wed, Fri); 1:30 - 5:30PM(Thur), Business Hours: 8:30 AM - 4:30 PM, Shopping Hours: 8:AM - 6:PM (Mon - Fri); 8:AM -12:Noon (Sat)

AZERBAIJAN
Banking Hours: 9:AM - 6:PM
Business Hours: 9:AM - 6:PM
Shopping Hours: 8:AM - 9:PM

BAHAMAS
Banking Hours: 9:30AM - 3:PM (Mon-Thur); 9:30AM - 5:PM (Fri)

BAHRAIN
Banking Hours: 7:30AM - 12:Noon (Sat-Wed); 7:30AM - 11:AM Thur)

BARBADOS
Banking Hours: 8:AM - 3:PM (Mon-Thur); 8:AM - 1:PM & 3:PM - 5:PM (Fri), Business Hours: 8:30AM - 4:PM (Mon-Fri), Shopping Hours: 8:AM - 4:PM (Mon-Fri); 8:AM - 12:Noon (Sat)

BANGLADESH
Banking Hours: 9:30AM - 1:30PM, (Mon-Thur); 9:AM - 11:AM (Fri-Sat)Business/Shopping Hours: 9:AM - 9:PM (Mon-Fri); 9:AM - 2:PM (Sat)

BELARUS
Banking Hours: 9:AM - 6:PM
Business Hours: 9:AM - 6:PM
Shopping Hours: 9:AM - 9:PM

BELGIUM
Banking Hours: 9:AM - 3:PM (Mon-Fri), Business Hours: 9:AM - 12:Noon & 2:PM - 5:30PM, Shopping Hours: 9:AM - 6:PM (Mon-Sat)

BELIZE
Banking Hours: 8:AM - 1:PM (Mon-

Fri); 3:PM - 6:PM (Fri) ;Business Hours: 8:AM - 12:Noon; 1:PM - 5:PM (Mon-Fri); Shopping Hours: 8:AM - 4:PM (Mon-Sat)

BENIN

Banking Hours: 8:AM - 11:AM; 3:PM - 4:PM (Mon-Fri); Business Hours: 8:AM - 12:30PM; 3:PM - 6:30PM (Mon-Fri); Shopping Hours: 9:AM - 1:PM, 4:PM - 7:PM (Mon-Sun)

BERMUDA

Business/Shopping: 9:AM - 5:PM (Mon-Sat)

BOLIVIA

Banking Hours: 9:AM - 12:Noon & 2:PM - 4:PM (Mon-Fri); Business Houre: 9:AM - 12:Noon & 2:30PM 6:PM (Mon-Fri); Shopping Hours: 9:AM - 6:PM; 9:AM - 12:Noon (Sat)

BOSNIA HERZEGOVINA

Banking Hours: 7:AM - Noon or &:AM - 7:PM; Business Hours: 8:AM - 3:30 PM; Shopping Hours: 8:AM - 8:PM (Mon-Fri)

BOTSWANA

Banking Hours: 8:15 - 12:45PM (Mon-Fri), 8:15AM - 10:45 AM (Sat); Shopping Hours: 8:AM - 6:PM (Mon-Sat)

BRITISH VIRGIN ISLANDS

Banking Hours: 9:AM - 2:PM (Mon-Fri); Business Hours: 8:30AM - 2:00PM & 4:PM - 5:PM (Mon-Fri); Shopping Hours: 8:AM - 5:PM (Mon-Sat)

BRAZIL

Banking Hours 10:AM - 4:30PM (Mon-Fri); Shopping Hours: 9:AM - 6:30PM (Mon-Fri) & 9:AM - 1:PM (Sat)

BURKINA FASO

Business Hours: 7:AM - 12:Noon, 3:PM - 5:PM (Mon-Fri); Shopping Hours: 7:AM - 12:Noon, 2:PM - 7:PM (Mon-Sat)

BURMA

Banking Hours: 10:AM - 2:PM (Mon-Fri); 10:AM - 12:Noon (Sat); Bussiness/Shopping Hours: 9:30Am - 4:PM (Mon-Sat)

BURUNDI

Business Hours: 8:AM - 12:Noon (Mon-Fri); Shopping Hours: 8:AM - 6:PM (Mon-Sat)

CAMEROON

Banking Hours: French Speaking Part: 8:AM - 11:AM, 2:30PM - 4:PM (Mon-Fri)English Speaking Part: 8:AM - 2:PM (Mon-Fri); Business Hours: French Speaking Part: 7:30AM - 12: Noon, 2:30PM - 6:PM (Mon-Fri); English Speaking Part: 7:30AM - 2:30PM - (Mon-Fri), 7:30AM - 1:PM; Shopping Hours: 8:AM - 12:30PM, 4:PM - 7:PM (Mon-Sat)

REPUBLIC OF CAPE VERDE

Banking Hours: 8:AM - 12: Noon (Mon-Fri); Business Hours: 8:AM - 12: Noon (Mon-Fri)

CAYMAN ISLANDS

Banking Hours: 9:AM - 2:30PM (Mon-Thur) & 9:AM -PM, :30PM - 4:30PM (Fri); Business Hours: 8:30AM - 5:PM; Shopping Hours: 8:30AM - 5:PM

CENTRAL AFRICAN REPUBLIC

Banking Hours: 8:AM - 11:30AM (Mon-Fri); Shopping Hours: 7:30AM - 9:PM (Mon-Sun)

CHAD

Banking Hours: 7:AM - 11:AM (Mon-Thur, Sat), 7:AM - 10:AM (Fri); Business Hours: 7:AM - 2:PM (Mon-Thur, Sat), 7:AM -12: Noon (Fri);Shopping Hours: 8:AM - 1:PM, 4:PM - 6:PM (Mon-Sat)

CHILE

Banking Hours: 9:AM - 1:PM & 2:30PM - 6:PM (Mon-Fri); 9:AM - 2:PM (Sat); Shopping Hours: 9:AM - 1:PM & 2:30PM - 6:PM (Mon-Fri)

CHINA, PEOPLES REPUBLIC

Banking Hours: varies (Mon-Sat)

CHINA, TAIWAN

Banking Hours: 9:AM - 3:30PM (Mon-Fri); 9:AM - 12:Noon (Sat)

COLUMBIA

Banking Hours: 9:AM - 3:PM (Mon-Thur); 9:AM - 3:30 (Fri); Business Hours: 8:30AM - 5:PM (Mon-Fri); Shopping Hours: 10:AM -- 7:PM (Mon-Sat)

COMOROS ISLAND

Banking Hours: 9:AM - 12:30PM, 3:PM - 5:PM (Mon-Fri), 9:AM - 12:30PM (Sat); Shopping Hours: 8:AM - 8:PM (Mon-Sat)

CONGO, PEOPLE'S REPUBLIC

Banking Hours: 7:AM - 2:PM (Mon-Fri); Shopping Hours: 7:AM - 7:PM (Mon-Sat)

COSTA RICA

Banking Hours: 9:AM - 3:PM (Mon-Fri); Shopping Hours: 8:30AM - 11:30AM & 2:PM - 6:PM (Mon-Fri) 8:30AM - 11:30AM (Sat)

COTE D'IVOIRE

Banking Hours: 8:AM - 11:30AM, 2:30PM - 4:PM (Mon-Fri); Business Hours: 8:AM - 12:Noon, 2:30PM - 5:30PM (Mon-Fri); Shopping Hours: 8:30AM - 12:Noon, 2:30PM - 7:PM (Mon-Sat)

CUBA

Banking Hours: 9:AM - 3:PM (Mon-Fri); Business Hours: 8:30AM - 12:30PM & 1:30PM - 5:30PM (Mon - Fri); Shopping Hours: 9:AM - 5:PM (Mon-Fri); 9:AM - 12:Noon (Sat)

CYPRUS

Banking Hours: 8:30AM - 12: Noon (Mon-Sat); Business Hours: 8:AM - 1:PM, 2:30PM - 6:PM (Mon-Fri) 8:AM -i:PM (Sat); Shopping Hours: 8:AM - 1:PM; 4:PM - 7:PM (Mon-Fri) Closed Wednesday and Saturday afternoons.

CZECH REPUBLIC

Banking Hours: 8:AM - 4:PM (Mon-Fri); Business Hours: 8:30AM - 5:PM; Shopping Hours: 9:AM - 6:PM (Mon-Fri), 9:AM - 1:PM (Sat)

DENMARK

Banking Hours: 9:30AM - 4:PM (Mon,Tue,Wed, & Fri), 9:30AM - 6:PM (Thur); Business Hours: 8:AM - 4:PM (Mon-Fri); Shopping Hours: 9/10:AM - 5:30/7:PM (Mon-Thur) 9/10:AM - 7/8:PM (Fri) 9/10:AM - 1/2:PM (Sat)

REPUBLIC OF DJIBOUTI

Banking Hours: 7:15AM - 11:45AM (Sun-Thur); Shopping Hours: 7:30AM - 12:Noon, 3:30PM - 7:30PM (Sat-Thur)

DOMINICA

Banking Hours: 8:AM - 1:PM (Mon-Fri); 3:PM - 5:PM (Fri); Business Hours: 8:AM - 1:PM & 2:PM - 4:PM (Mon-Fri); 8:AM - 1:PM (Sat); Shopping Hours: 8:AM - 1:PM & 2:PM - 4:PM (Mon-Fri); 8:AM- 1:PM (Sat)

DOMINICAN REPUBLIC

Banking Hours: 8:AM - 12:Noon (Mon-Fri); Business Hours: 9:AM - 6:PM (Mon-Fri) & 9:AM -12:Noon (Sat); Shopping Hours: 8:30AM - 12:Noon & 2:30PM - 6:PM (Mon-Fri); 8:30AM - 1:PM (Sat)

ECUADOR

Banking Hours: 9:AM - 1:30PM (Mon-Fri) Shopping Hours: 8:30AM - 12:30PM (Mon-Sat) & 3:30PM - 7:PM (Mon-Sat)

EGYPT

Banking Hours: 8:30AM - 1:PM (Mon-Thur, Sat), 10:AM - 12:Noon (Sat); Shopping Hours: 10:AM - 7:PM (Tue-Sat), 10:AM - 8:PM (Mon - Thur)

EL SALVADOR

Banking Hours: 8:AM - 12:Noon & 2:PM - 4:PM (Mon-Fri); Shopping Hours: 8:AM - 12:Noon & 2:30PM - 6:PM (Mon-Sat)

EQUATORIAL GUINEA

Banking Hours: 8:AM - 3:PM (Mon-Fri), 8:AM - 1:PM(Sat); Business Hours; 8:AM - 3:PM (Mon-Fri), 8:AM - 1:PM (Sat); Shopping Hours: 8:AM -3:PM, 5:PM - 7:PM (Mon-Sat)

ESTONIA

Banking Hours: 9:AM - 3:PM; Business Hours: 9:AM - 6PM; Shopping Hours: 9:am - 9:PM (Mon-Sat)

ETHIOPIA

Banking Hours: 9:AM - 5:PM (Mon-Fri); Business Hour: 8:AM - 12:Noon, 1:PM - 4:PM (Mon-Fri); Banks close for 3 hours for lunch

FIJI

Banking Hours: 10:AM - 3:PM (Mon-Thur); 10:AM - 4:PM (Fri) Business/Shopping Hours: 8:AM - 5:PM

FINLAND

Banking Hours: 9:15AM - 4:15PM (Mon-Fri); Business Hours: 8:30AM - 4:PM (Mon-Fri);Shopping Hours: 9:AM - 5/6:PM (Mon-Fri), 9:AM - 2/3:PM (Sat)

FRANCE

Banking Hours: 9:AM - 4:30PM (Mon-Fri); Business Hours: 9:AM - 12:Noon; 2:PM - 6:PM (Mon-Fri), 9:AM - 12:Noon (Sat); Shopping Hours: 9:AM - 6:30PM (Tue-Sat)

FRENCH GUIANA

Banking Hours: 7:15AM - 11:45AM (Mon,Tue,Thur, Fri); 7:AM - 12:Noon (Wed)

GABON

Banking Hours: 7:AM - 12:Noon (Mon-Fri); Business Hours: 8:AM - 12:Noon, 3:PM - 6:PM (Mon-Fri); Shopping Hours: 8:AM - 12:Noon, 4:PM - 7:PM (Mon-Sat)

GEORGIA

Shopping Hours: 9:AM - 7:PM

THE GAMBIA

Banking Hours: 8:AM - 1:PM (Mon-Fri); 8:AM - 11:AM (Sat); Business/Shopping Hours: 8:AM - 5:PM (Mon-Fri); 8:AM -12:Noon (Sat)

FEDERAL REPUBLIC OF GERMANY

Banking Hours: 8:30AM - 12:30PM; 1:45PM - 3:45PM (Mon-Fri), Thur- 5:45PM; Business Hours: 8:AM - 5:PM; Shopping Hours: 8:AM - 6:30PM (Mon-Fri), 8:AM - 2:PM (Sat)

GHANA

Banking Hours: 8:30AM - 2:PM (Mon-Fri); Business Hours: 8:30AM - 5:PM (Mon-Fri); Shopping Hours: 8:30AM - 5:PM (Mon-Sat)

GIBRALTAR

Banking Hours: 9:AM - 3:30PM (Mon-Fri), 4:30PM - 6:PM (Fri); Business Hours: 9:AM - 6:PM; Shopping Hours: 9:AM - 1:PM & 3:30PM - 7:PM (Mon-Fri), 9:-1:PM (Sat)

GREECE

Banking Hours: 8:AM - 2:PM (Mon-Fri); Business Hours: 8:30AM - 1:30PM, 4:PM - 7:30PM; Shopping Hours: 8:AM - 2:30PM (Mon, Wed, Sat), 8:AM - 1:30PM, 5:PM- 8:PM (Tue, Thur, Fri)

GRENADA

Banking Hours: 8:AM - 12:Noon (Mon-Fri) & 2:30 PM - 5:PM (Fri); Business Hours: 8:AM - 4:PM (Mon-Fri) 8:AM - 11:45 AM (Sat) Shopping Hours: 8:AM - 4:PM (Mon Fri); 8:AM - 11:45 AM (Sat)

GUADELOUPE

Banking Hours: 8:AM - 12:Noon & 2:PM - 4:PM; Shopping Hours: 9:AM - 1:PM & 3:PM - 6:PM (Mon-Fri); Sat mornings

GUATEMALA

Banking Hours: 9:AM - 3:PM (Mon-Fri); Shopping Hours: 9:AM - 7:PM (Mon-Sat)

GUINEA,REPUBLIC

Banking Hours: 7:30AM - 3:PM (Mon-Sat); Business Hours: 7:30 - 3:PM (Mon-Sat);Shopping Hours: 8:AM - 6:PM (Mon-Sun)

GUYANA

Banking Hours: 8:AM - 12:30PM; (Mon-Fri); Business Hours: 8:AM - 4:PM (Mon-Fri); Shopping Hours: 8:AM - 12:Noon; 2:PM - 4:PM

HAITI

Banking Hours: 9:AM - 1:PM (Mon-Fri); Business Hours: 8:AM - 5:PM (Mon-Fri); 8:AM - 12:Noon (Sat); Shopping Hours: 8:AM - 5:PM (Mon-Fri); 8:AM - 12:Noon (Sat)

HONDURAS

Banking Hours: 9:AM - 3:30PM (Mon-Fri); Shopping Hours: 8:AM - 6:30PM (Mon-Sat)

HONG KONG

Banking Hours: 10:AM - 3:PM (Mon-Fri); 9:AM - 12:Noon (Sat) Business/Shopping Hours: 9:AM - 5:PM; 9:AM - 1:Pm (Sat)

HUNGARY

Banking Hours: 8:30AM - 3:PM (Mon-Sat); Business Hours: 8:30AM - 5:PM; Shopping Hours: 10:AM - 6:PM (Mon-Fri); 10:AM - 2:PM (Sat)

ICELAND

Banking Hours: 9:15AM - 4:PM (Mon-Fri); Business Hours: 9:AM - 5:PM (Mon-Fri); Shopping Hours:

9:AM - 6:PM (Mon-Fri); 9:AM - 12:Noon (Sat)

INDIA

Banking Hours: 10:30AM - 2:30PM (Mon-Fri); 10:30AM - 12:30PM (Sat) Business/ShoppingHours:Government Offices: 10:AM - 1:PM; 2:PM - 5:PM (Mon-Sat); Non-Gov't Offices: 9:30AM - 1:PM; 2:PM - 5:PM (Mon-Sat)

INDONESIA

Banking Hours: 10:AM - 3:PM (Mon-Fri); 9:AM - 12:Noon (Sat)

IRAN

Banking Hours: 8:AM - 1:PM; 4:PM - 6:PM (Sat-Thur); Business/Shopping Hours:Gov't Office: 8:AM - 4:30PM (Sat-Wed) Non-Gov't. Offices: 8:AM - 4:30PM (Sat-Thur) Offices closed on Friday

IRELAND

Banking Hours: 10:AM - 12:30PM; 1:30PM - 3:PM (Mon-Fri); Business Hours: 9:AM - 1:PM, 2:PM - 5:PM;Shopping Hours: 9:AM - 5:30PM (Mon-Sat)

ISRAEL

Banking Hours: 8:30AM - 12:30PM; 4:PM - 5:30PM (Sun-Tue,Thur) 8:30AM -12:30PM (Wed); 8:30AM -12:Noon (Fri); Business Hours: Non-Gov't Office: 8:AM - 4:PM (Mon-Fri) Offices close early on Friday

ITALY

Banking Hours: 8:35AM - 1:35PM; 3:PM - 4:PM (Mon-Fri); Business Hours: 8:30AM - 12:30PM, 3:30PM-7:30PM; Shopping Hours: 9:AM - 1:PM, 3:30/4:PM - 7:30/8:PM

JAMAICA

Banking Hours: 9:AM - 2:PM (Mon - Thur); 9:AM - 12:Noon & 2:PM-5:PM (Fri); Business Hours: 8:AM - 4:PM; Shopping Hours: 8:30AM - 4:30PM

JAPAN

Banking Hours: 9:AM - 3:PM (Mon-Fri); 9:AM 12:Noon (Sat); Business/Shopping: 9:AM - 5:PM (Mon-Fri); 9:AM - 12:Noon (Sat)

JORDAN

Banking Hours: 8:AM - 12:30PM (Sat-Thur)
Business/Shopping Hours: 8:AM - 6:PM (Sat-Thur)

KENYA

Banking Hours: 9:AM - 2:PM (Mon - Fri); 9:AM - 11;AM (1st & last saturday of month); Business Hours: 8:30AM - 4:30PM (Mon -Fri), 8:30 - 12:Noon (Sat); Shopping Hours: 8:30AM - 12:30PM, 2:PM - 5:PM (Mon - Sat)

KOREA, SOUTH

Banking Hours: 9:30AM - 4:30PM (Mon-Fri); 9:30AM - 11:PM (Sat)
Business/Shopping Hours: 9:AM - 5:PM (Mon-Fri): 9:AM - 1:PM (Sat)

KUWAIT

Banking Hours: Mostly in the morning; Business/Shopping Hours: Gov't Offices: 7:30AM - 1:30PM Non-Gov't Offices: 7:30AM - 2:30PM (Sat-Wed);7:AM - 1:PM; 5:PM - 8:PM

KYRGYZSTAN

Banking Hours: 9:AM - 6:PM
Business Hours: 9:AM - 6:PM
Shopping Hours: 8:AM - 9:PM

LATVIA

Banking Hours: 9:AM - 12:Noon
Business Hours: 9:AM - 6:PM
Shopping Hours: 8:Am - 10:PM

LEBANON

Banking Hours: 8:30AM - 12:30PM (Mon-Fri); 8:30AM - 12:Noon (Sat)

LESOTHO

Banking Hours: 8:30AM - 1:PM (Mon-Fri); 9:AM - 11:AM (Sat); Business Hours: 8:AM - 4:30PM (Mon-Fri); Shopping Hours: 8:AM - 4:30PM (Mon-Fri); 8:AM - 1:PM (Sat)

LIBERIA

Banking Hours: 9:AM - 5:PM (Mon-Sat); Business Hours: 9:AM - 6:PM (Mon-Sat)

LIBYA

Banking Hours: 8:AM - 4:PM (Sat-Thur); Business Hours: 8:AM - 4:PM (Sat-Thur)

LIECHTENSTEIN

Banking Hours: 8:30AM - 12:Noon, 1:30 - 4:30PM (Mon-Fri); Business

Hours: 8:AM - 12:Noon, 2:30PM - 6:PM ; Shopping Hours: 8:AM - 12:15PM, 2:PM - 6:30PM (Mon-Fri), 8:AM - 4:PM (Sat)

LITHUANIA

Banking Hours: 9:AM - 12:Noon; Business Hours: 9:AM - 1:PM, 2:PM - 6:PM (Mon-Sat)

LUXEMBOURG

Banking Hours: 9:AM - 12:Noon; 2:PM - 5:PM (Mon-Sat); Business Hours: 9:AM - 12:Noon, 2:PM - 5:30PM; Shopping Hours: 8:AM - 12:Noon, 2:PM - 6:PM (Mon-Sat)

MADAGASCAR

Banking Hours: 8:AM - 11:AM, 2:PM - 4:PM (Mon-Fri); Shopping Hours: 9:AM - 6:PM (Mon-Sat); Business Hours: 8:AM - 12:Noon, 2:PM - 6:PM (Mon-Fri)

MALAWI

Banking Hours: 8:AM - 1:PM (Mon-Fri); Business Hours: 7:30AM - 5:PM (Mon-Fri);Shopping Hours: 8:AM - 6:PM

MALAYSIA

Business/Shopping Hours: 8:30/9:AM - 1:PM, 2:30PM - 4:30PM (Mon-Fri); 9:AM - 1:PM (Sat) Gov't Offices: 9:AM - 4:30Pm (Mon-Fri); 9:AM -1:PM (Sat)

MALI

Banking Hours: 8:AM - 12:Noon, 2:PM - 4:PM (Mon-Fri); Business Hours: 7:30AM - 2:30PM (Mon-Sat), 7:30AM - 12:30PM (Fri); Shopping Hours: 9:AM - 8:PM (Mon-Sat)

MALTA

Banking Hours: 8:30AM - 12:30PM (Mon-Fri), 8:30AM - 11:30AM (Sat); Business Hours: 8:30AM - 5:30PM (Mon-Fri), 8:30AM - 1:PM (Sat); Shopping Hours: 9:AM - 1:PM, 4:PM - 7:PM (Mon-Fri), 9:AM - 1:PM, 4:PM - 8:PM (Sat)

MARTINIQUE

Banking Hours: 7:30AM - 4:PM (Mon-Fri); Shopping Hours: 8:30AM - 6:PM (Mon-Fri);
8:30AM - 1:PM (Sat)

MAURITANIA

Banking Hours: 8:AM - 3:PM (Sun-Thur); Business Hours: 8:AM - 3:PM (SunThur); Shopping Hours: 8:AM - 1:PM, 3:PM - 6:PM (Sun-Thur)

MAURITIUS

Banking Hours: 10:AM - 2:PM (Mon - Fri), 9:30AM - 11:30AM (Sat); Shopping Hours: (Varies) 9:AM - 5:PM (Mon-Fri), 9:AM -12:Noon (Sat, Sun)

MEXICO

Banking Hours: 9:AM - 1:30PM (Mon-Fri); Business Hours: 9:AM - 6:PM (Mon-Fri); Shopping Hours: 10:AM - 5:PM (Mon-Fri); 10:AM - 8:/9:PM

MICRONESIA

Banking Hours: 9:30Am - 2:30PM (Mon-Fri)

MONACO

Banking Hours: 9:AM - 12:Noon, 2:PM - 4:PM (Mon-Fri); Business Hours: 8:30AM - 6:PM; Shopping Hours: 9:AM - 12:Noon, 2:PM - 7:PM (Mon-Sat)

MONTSERRAT

Banking Hours: 8:AM - 1:PM (Mon-Thur); Business Hours: 8:AM - 4:PM; Shopping Hours: 8:AM - 4:PM

MOROCCO

Banking Hours: 8:30AM - 11:30AM, 3:PM - 5:30PM (Mon-Fri); Business Hours: 8:30AM - 12:Noon, 2:30PM - 6:30PM (Mon-Fri), 8:30AM - 12:Noon (Sat); Shopping Hours: 8:30AM - 12:Noon, 2:PM - 6:30PM (Mon-Sat)

MOZAMBIQUE

Banking Hours: 7:30 -12:Noon, 2:PM - 5:PM (Mon-Fri), 7:30AM - 12:Noon (Sat); Business Hours: 7:30AM - 12:Noon, 2:PM - 5:PM (Mon-Fri), 7:30AM - 12:Noon (Sat)

NAMIBIA

Banking Hours: 9:AM - 3:30PM (Mon-Fri), 8:30AM - 11:AM (Sat) Business Hours: 8:30AM - 5:PM (Mon-Fri); Shopping Hours: 8:30AM - 5:30PM (Mon-Fri)
9:AM - 1:PM (Sat)

NEPAL

Banking Hours: 10:AM - 3:PM (Sat-Thur);10:AM - 12:Noon (Sat)

NETHERLANDS

Banking Hours: 9:AM - 4/5:PM (Mon-Fri); Business Hours: 8:30 - 5:30PM; Shopping Hours: 8:30/9:AM - 5:30/6:PM (Mon-Fri)

NETHERLANDS ANTILLES

Banking Hours: 8:30AM - 11:AM; 2:PM - 4:PM (Mon-Fri); Business/Shopping Hours:8:AM - 12:Noon; 2:PM - 6:PM (Mon-Sat)

NEW CALEDONIA

Banking Hours: 7:AM - 10:30AM; 1:30PM - 3:30PM (Mon-Fri); 7:30 - 11:AM (Sat)

NEW ZEALAND

Banking Hours: 10:AM - 4:PM (Mon-Fri); Business/Shopping Hours: 9:AM - 5:PM (Mon-Fri)

NIGARAGUA

Banking Hours: 8:30AM - 12:Noon; 2:PM - 4:PM (Mon-Fri); 8:30AM - 11:30AM (Sat); Business/Shopping Hours: 8:AM - 5:30PM (Mon-Sat)

NIGER

Banking Hours: 7:30AM - 12:30PM, 3:30PM - 5:PM; Business Hours: 7:30AM - 12:30:PM, 3:30PM - 6:30PM; Shopping Hours: 7:30AM - 12:30PM, 3:30PM - 6:30PM

NIGERIA

Banking Hours: 8:AM - 3:PM (Mon), 8:AM - 1:30PM (Tues-Fri):; Business Hours: Gov't Offices: 7:30AM - 3:30PM (Mon-Fri) Private Firms: 8:AM - 5:PM (Mon-Fri)

NORWAY

Banking Hours: 8:15AM - 3:30PM (Mon, Tue, Wed, Fri); 8:15AM - 5:PM (Thur); Business Hours: 9:AM - 4:PM; Shopping Hours: 9:AM - 5:PM (Mon-Fri); 9:AM - 6/7:PM (Thur); 9:AM- 1/2:PM (Sat)

PAKISTAN

Banking Hours: 9:AM - 1:PM (Mon-Thur); 9:AM - 11:30AM (Sat) Business/Shopping Hours: 9:30AM - 1:PM (Mon-Thur); 9:AM -10:30AM (Sat)

PANAMA

Banking Hours: 8:30AM - 1:PM (Mon-Fri); Business Hours: 8:30AM - 12:30PM & 1:30PM - 4:PM (Mon-Fri)); Shopping Hours: 8:30AM - 6:PM (Mon-Sat)

PARAGUAY

Banking Hours: 7:AM - 12:Noon (Mon-Fri); Shopping Hours: 7:AM - 12:Noon & 3:PM - 7:PM

PERU

Banking Hours: 9:AM - 1:PM (Mon-Fri); Business Hours: 9:AM - 5:PM (Mon-Fri); Shopping Hours: 9:AM - 7:PM (Mon-Sat)

PHILIPPINES

Banking Hours: 9:AM - 6:PM (Mon-Fri); 9:AM 12:30 (Sat);

POLAND

Banking Hours: 8:AM - 1:PM; Business Hours: 8:30AM - 3:30PM; Shopping Hours: 9:AM - 8:PM

PORTUGAL

Banking Hours: 8:AM - 3:PM (Mon-Fri); Business Hours: 10:AM - 6:PM; Shopping Hours: 9:AM - 1:PM, 3:PM - 7:PM (Mon-Fri), 9:AM - 12:Noon (Some Shops)

PUERTO RICO

Banking Hours: 9:AM - 5:PM (Mon-Fri); Business Hours: 8:AM - 5:PM (Mon-Fri); Shopping Hours: 9:AM - 6:PM (Mon-Sat)

QATAR

Banking Hours: 7:30AM - 11:30AM (Sat-Thur)

REUNION ISLAND

Business/Shopping Hours: 8:AM - 12:Noon; 2:PM - 6:PM

ROMANIA

Banking Hours: 8:30 - 11:30AM; Business Hours: 8:AM - 4:PM (Mon-Fri), 8:AM - 12:30PM (Sat); Shopping Hours: 9:AM - 1:PM, 4:PM-6/8:PM

RUSSIA

Banking Hours: 9:AM - 6:PM; Business Hours: 9:AM - 6:PM; Shopping Hours: 9:AM - 9:PM (Mon-Sat)

RWANDA

Banking Hours: 8:AM - 11:AM, 2:PM - 5:PM (Mon-Fri), 8:AM - 1:PM (Sat); Business Hours: 7:AM - 12:Noon, 2:PM - 6:PM (Mon-Fri); Shopping Hours: 8:AM - 6:PM (Mon-Fri), 11:AM - 6:PM (Sat)

SRI LANKA

Banking Hours: 9:AM - 1:PM (Mon-Fri); 9:am - 11:AM (Sat)

ST. KITTS & NEVIS

Banking Hours: 8:AM - 1:PM (Mon-Fri); 8:AM - 1:PM; 3:PM -5:PM (Fri); Business Hours: 8:AM - 12:Noon, 1:PM - 4:30PM (Mon, Tues); 8:AM - 12:Noon; 1:PM - 4:PM (Wed Thur, Fri); Shopping Hours: 8:AM - 12:Noon, 1:PM - 4:PM Shops closed on Thursday afterNoons

ST. LUCIA

Banking Hours: 8:AM - 12:30PM (Mon-Thur); 8:AM - 12:Noon & 3:PM - 5:PM (Fri); Shopping Hours: 8:AM - 4:30PM (Mon-Fri); 8:AM - 1:PM (Sat)

SAN MARINO

Banking Hours: 8:30AM - 12:Noon, 2:30PM - 3:15PM; Business Hours: 8:AM - 12:Noon, 2:PM - 6:PM; Shopping Hours: 8:AM - 12:Noon 3:PM - 7:PM

ST. MAARTEN

Banking Hours: 8:30AM - 1:PM (Mon-Thur); 8:30AM - 1:PM & 4:PM - 5:PM (Fri); Business Hours: 8:AM -12:Noon & 2:PM - 6:PM; Shopping Hours: 8:AM - 12:Noon & 2:PM - 6:PM

ST. MARTIN

Banking Hours: 9:AM - 12:Noon & 2:PM - 3:PM (Mon-Fri); Shopping Hours: 9:AM - 12/12:30 & 2:PM - 6:PM (Mon-Sat)

SAO TOME AND PRINCIPE

Banking Hours: 7:30AM - 12:30PM, 2:30PM - 4:30PM (Mon-Fri); Businss Hours: 7:30AM - 12:30PM, 2:30PM - 4:30PM (Mon-Fri); Shopping Hours: 9:AM - 12:30PM, 2:30PM - 6:PM (Mon-Sat)

ST. VINCENT & THE GRENADINES

Banking Hours: 8:AM - 12/1:PM (Mon - Thur); 8:AM - 12:/1:PM & 2:/3:PM -5:PM (Fri) ;Business Hours: 8:AM - 12:Noon & 1:PM - 4:PM (Mon - Fri); 8:AM- 12:Noon (Sat)

SAUDI ARABIA

Banking Hours: 7/8:AM - 2:30PM (Sat-Thur); Business Hours: Gov't Offices: In Winter 8:AM -4:PM (Sat-Wed); In Summer 7:AM - 3:PM; During Ramadan 8:AM - 2:PM Others: 8:30AM- 1:30PM; 4:30AM - 8PM (Sat-Thur) closed Friday

SENEGAL

Banking Hours: 8:AM - 11:AM, 2:30PM - 4:30PM (Mon-Fri); Business Hours: 8:AM - 12:Noon , 3:PM - 6:PM (Mon-Fri), 8:AM - 12:Noon (Sat); Shopping Hours: 8:AM - 7:PM (Mon-Sat)

SEYCHELLES

Banking Hours: 8:30AM - 1:30PM (Mon-Sat); Business Hours: 8:AM - 12:Noon, 1:PM - 4:PM (Mon-Fri); Shopping Hours: 8:AM - 5:PM (Mon-Fri), 8:AM - 1:PM (Sat)

SIERRA LEONE

Banking Hours: 9:AM - 2:PM (Mon-Fri); Business Hours: 9:AM - 2:PM (Mon-Fri); Shopping Hours: 9:AM - 6:PM (Mon-Sat)

SINGAPORE

Banking Hours: 10:AM - 3:PM (Mon-Fri); 9:30AM - 11:30AM (Sat); Business Hours: Gov't: 9:AM - 4:30PM (Mon-Fri); 9:AM - 1:PM (Sat);Shopping Hours: 9:AM - 6:PM (Mon-Sat)

SOUTH AFRICA

Banking Hours: 9:AM - 3:PM (Mon,Tue,Thur,Fri); 9:AM - 1:PM (Wed); 9:AM -11:AM (Sat); Business/Shopping Hours: 8:30AM - 5:PM (Mon-Fri); 8:30AM - 12:Noon (Sat) Some stores

SPAIN

Banking Hours: 9:AM - 2:PM (Mon-Fri), 9:AM - 1: PM (Sat); Business Hours: 9:AM - 2:PM, 4:PM - 7:PM; Shopping Hours: 9:AM - 1:PM, 4:PM - 8:PM

SUDAN

Banking Hours: 8:30AM - 12:Noon (Sat-Thur); Business/Shopping Hours: 8:AM - 1:PM; 5:PM - 8:PM (Sat-Thur)

SURINAME

Banking Hours: 8:AM - 3:PM (Mon-Fri); Business Hours: 7:AM - 3:PM (Mon-Fri); Shopping Hours: 7:30AM - 4:PM (Mon-Fri)

SWEDEN

Banking Hours: 9:30AM - 3:PM

(Mon,Tue,Wed,Fri), 9:30AM -3:PM, 4:PM - 5:30PM (Thur); Business Hours: 8:AM - 5:PM; Shopping Hours: 9:30AM - 6:PM (Mon-Fri), 9:30AM - 1:PM (Sat), Noon - 4:PM (Sun)

SWITZERLAND

Banking Hours: 8:30AM - 4:30PM (Mon-Fri); Business Hours: 8:AM - 12:Noon; 2:PM - 6:PM; Shopping Hours: 8:AM - 12:15PM, 1:30PM - 6:30AM (Mon-Fri); 8:AM - 4:PM (Sat)

SYRIA

Banking Hours: 8:AM - 12:30PM (Sat-Thur)
Business Hours: 8:AM - 1:30PM; 4:30PM - 9:PM (Sat-Thur)

TANZANIA

Business/Shopping Hours: 8:AM - 5/6:PM (Mon-Sat)

TAJIKISTAN

Bankng Hours: 9:AM - 6:PM
Business Hours: 9:AM - 6:PM
Shopping Hours: 8:AM - 9:PM

THAILAND

Business/Shopping Hours: 8:30AM - 7/8:PM

TOGO

Banking Hours: 7:30AM - 11:30AM; 1:30 - 3:30PM (Mon-Fri); Business/Shopping Hours: 8:AM - 6:PM (Mon-Fri); Sat morning

TONGA

Banking Hours: 9:30AM - 4:30PM (Mon-Fri)

TRINIDAD AND TOBAGO

Banking Hours: 9:AM - 2:PM (Mon-Thur) & 9:AM - 12:Noon; 3:PM - 5:PM (Fri); Shopping Hours: 8:AM - 4:PM (Mon-Fri); 8:AM - 12:Noon (Sat)

TUNISIA

Banking Hours: 8:AM - 11:AM; 2:PM - 4:PM (Mon-Fri)

TURKEY

Banking Hours: 8:30AM - 12:Noon, 1:30 - 5:PM (Mon-Fri); Business Hours: 8:30AM - 12:30PM, 1:30PM - 5:30PM; Shopping Hours: 9:AM - 1:PM, 2:PM - 7:PM (Mon-Sat)

TURKMENISTAN

Banking Hours: 9:AM - 6:PM
Business Hours: 9:AM - 6:PM
Shopping Hours: 8:AM - 9:PM

TURKS AND CAICOS

Banking Hours: 8:30AM - 3:30PM
Business Hours: 8:30AM - 5:PM
Shopping Hours: 9:AM - 7:PM

UKRAINE

Banking Hours: 9:AM - 6:PM
Business Hours: 9:AM - 6:PM
Shopping Hours: 8:AM - 9:PM

UNITED KINGDOM

Banking Hours: (Varies) England & Wales: 9:AM - 3:PM (Mon-Fri) Scotland: 9:30 - 12:30PM, 1:30 - 3:30PM (Mon - Wed), 9:30AM - 12:30PM, 1:30 - 3:30PM, 3:30PM - 4:30PM-6PM (Thur) 9:30AM - 3:30PM (Fri), North Ireland: 10:AM - 3:30PM (Mon - Fri); Business Hours: 9:AM - 5:PM; Shopping Hours: 9:AM - 5:30PM

UNITED STATES OF AMERICA

Banking Hours: 9:AM - 5PM (Mon-Fr); 9:AM - Noon (Sat). Some locations have extended hours. Business Hours: 9:AM - 5PM (Mon-Fri); Shopping Hours: 9:AM -5PM (Mon-Fri); 9:AM-5PM (Sat); Noon-5PM (Sun) Some locations have extended hours.

URUGUAY

Banking Hours: 1:PM - 5:PM (Mon-Fri); Business Hours: 7:AM - 1:30PM (Mon-Fri) Summer & 12:30 - 7:PM (Mon-Fri) Winter; Shopping Hours: 10:AM - 7:PM (Mon-Sat)

UZBEKISTAN

Banking Hours: 9:AM - 6:PM
Business Hours: 9:AM - 6:PM
Shopping Hours: 8:AM - 9:PM

VENEZUELA

Banking Hours: 9:AM - 12:Noon & 3:PM - 5:PM (Mon-Fri); Business Hours: 8:AM - 12:Noon & 2:PM - 5:PM (Mon-Fri); Shopping Hours: 9:AM - 12:Noon &
2:PM - 5:PM (Mon-Sat)

VIETNAM

Banking Hours: 8:AM - 11:30AM; 2:PM - 4:PM (Mon-Fri); 8:AM - 11:AM (Sat)

WESTERN SAMOA

Banking Hours: 9:30AM - 3:PM

(Mon-Fri); 9:30AM - 11:30AM (Sat)

YUGOSLAVIA

Banking Hours: 7:AM - 12:Noon or 7:AM - 7:PM; Business Hours: 8:AM - 12:30PM; Shopping Hours: 8:AM - 12:Noon, 4:PM - 8:PM or 8:AM - 8:PM (Mon-Fri) 8:AM - 3:PM (Sat)

ZAIRE

Banking Hours: 8:AM - 11:30 (Mon-Fri); Business/Shopping Hours: 8:AM - 12:Noon; 3:PM - 6:PM (Mon- Sat)

ZAMBIA

Banking Hours: 8:AM - 1:PM (Mon-Fri); 8:AM -11:AM (Sat); Business/Shopping Hours: 8:AM - 5:PM (Mon-Fri); 8:AM - 3:PM (Sat)

ZIMBABWE

Banking Hours: 8:30AM - 2:PM (Mon,Tue, Thur, Fri); 8:30AM - 12:Noon (Wed); 8:30AM - 11:AM (Sat); Business/Shopping Hours: 8:AM - 5:PM

APPENDIX E

INTERNATIONAL EMERGENCY CODES

Country	Emergency #	Ambulance #	Police #
Algeria			17
Andorra		182-0020	21222
Andorra	11/15	20020	
Anguilla	999		
Antigua	999		20045/20125
Argentina			101
Austria		144	133
Bahamas		3222221	3224444
Barbados			112/60800
Belgium	900/901	906	101
Belize			2222
Bermuda			22222
Bolivia	118		110
Brazil	2321234		2436716
Columbia			12
Costa Rica	2158888		117
Cyprus	999		
Czech Republic	155		
Denmark	000		
Dominican Republic			6823000
Egypt			912644
Ethiopia			91
Fiji Islands	000		
Finland	000	002/003	
France	17	12/17	
French Guiana			18
Germany	110		
Gibraltar	199		
Great Britain	999		
Greece	100		171
Guyana	999		
Haiti	0		
Hong Kong	999		
Hungary	04		
Iceland			
(Reykavik)	11100	11166	
(elsewhere dial 02 for the operator who will then place the call)			
India		102	100
Ireland	999		
Israel			100
Italy		113	112
Jamaica		110	119
Japan		119	100

Jordan	19		
Kenya	999		
Liechtenstein		144	117
Luxembourg	012		
Malaysia	0		
Malta	99		
Maltese Island		196	191
Monaco		933-01945	17
Morocco			19
Nepal	11999		
Netherlands			
Amsterdam	559-9111	5555555	222222
(elsewhere dial 008 for the operator who will then place the call)			
New Zealand	111		
Norway		003	110011
Pakistan	222222		
Papua New Guinea			255555
Paraguay			49116
Peru	05		
Phillipines		599011	
Poland		999	997
Portugal	115		
San Marino	113		
Singapore	999		
Spain	091		
Sri Lanka			26941/21111
St. Vincent			71121
St. Kitts & Nevis	999		
St. Lucia	95		99
Suriname	99933		711111/77777
Sweden	90000		
Switzerland		144	117
Tanzania	999		
Thailand			2810372/2815051
Tunisia			243000
U.S. Virgin Is.		922	915
United States of America	411	411	411
Uruguay	401111		890
Venezuela			169/160
Yugoslavia	94		92

NOTES

OTHER BOOKS IN THE SERIES FROM WORLD TRAVEL INSTITUTE

[Edition, ISBN, Page Count, Price, Availability/publication date]

Book Specification: **6 x 9, Paperback**

AUTHOR: Gladson I. Nwanna (Ph.D)

Series Title: DO'S AND DON'TS AROUND THE WORLD: A COUNTRY GUIDE TO CULTURAL AND SOCIAL TABOOS AND ETIQUETTE

Edition:	ISBN#:	Pages:	Price:	Availability
EUROPE	**1-890605-00-X**	**332**	**$29.99**	**Jan. 98**
SOUTH AMERICA	**1-890605-03-4**	**245**	**$19.99**	**Jan. 98**
AFRICA	**1-890605-04-2**	**440**	**$34.99**	**May 98**
THE CARIBBEAN	**1-890605-02-6**	**220**	**$19.99**	**March 98**
ASIA	**1-890605-01-8**	**250**	**$24.99**	**March 98**
RUSSIA & THE INDEPENDENT STATES	**1-890605-06-9**	**160**	**$12.99**	**March 98**
USA, CANADA & AUSTRALIA	**1-890605-08-5**	**75**	**$12.99**	**March 98**
OCEANIA & JAPAN	**1-890605-07-7**	**185**	**$15.99**	**May 98**
THE MIDDLE EAST	**1-890605-05-0**	**145**	**$12.99**	**March 98**

INDIVIDUAL COUNTRY REPORTS ARE AVAILABLE!!!
at $7 per report per country.
Individual Country Reports can only be ordered directly from the publisher or through the internet at www.worldtravelinstitute.com

COUNTRY REPORTS

[Note: Individual Country reports are currently available at $7 per country, per report. Price includes postage]

AFRICA
ALGERIA
BENIN
BOTSWANA
BURKINA FASO
BURUNDI
CAMEROON
CAPE VERDE, REP. OF
CENTRAL AFR. REP.
CHAD
COMOROS
CONGO, PEOPLE'S REP.
COTE D'IVOIRE
DJIBOUTI, REP. OF
EGYPT
ERITREA
ETHIOPIA
GABON
GAMBIA, THE
GHANA
GUINEA
GUINEA BISSAU
KENYA
LESOTHO
LIBERIA
LIBYA
MADAGASCAR
MALAWI
MALI
MAURITIUS
MOROCCO
MOZAMBIQUE
NAMIBIA
NIGER
NIGERIA
RWANDA
SAO TOME & PRINCIPE
SENEGAL
SEYCHELLES
SIERRA LEONE
SOMALIA
SOUTH AFRICA
SUDAN
SWAZILAND
TANZANIA
TOGO
TUNISIA
UGANDA
ZAIRE
ZAMBIA
ZIMBABWE

ASIA
AFGHANISTAN
BANGLADESH
BHUTAN
BRUNEI-DARUSSALEM
CAMBODIA
CHINA, PEOPLE'S REP.
CHINA, TAIWAN
CYPRUS
HONG KONG
INDIA
INDONESIA
JAPAN
KOREA, SOUTH
KOREA, NORTH
LAOS
MACAO
MALAYSIA
MALDIVES
MONGOLIA
MYANMAR (BURMA)
NEPAL
PAKISTAN
PHILIPPINES
SINGAPORE
SRI LANKA
THAILAND

EUROPE
ALBANIA
ANDORRA
AUSTRIA
BELGIUM
CROATIA
CZECH REP.
BULGARIA
DENMARK
FINLAND
FRANCE
GREECE
GREENLAND
HUNGARY
ICELAND
IRELAND
ITALY
LIECHESTEIN
LUXEMBOURG
MACEDONIA
MALTA
MOLDOVA
MONACO
NETHERLANDS
NORWAY
POLAND
PORTUGAL
ROMANIA
SAN MARINO
SLOVAK REP.
SLOVENIA
SPAIN
SWEDEN
SWITZERLAND
TURKEY
UNITED KINGDOM
YUGOSLAVIA

OCEANIA & JAPAN
AMERICAN SAMOA
COOK ISLANDS
FAROE ISLAND
FIJI
FRENCH POLYNESIA (TAHITI)
JAPAN
JERSEY CHANNEL IS
KIRIBATI
MARSHALL ISLAND
MICRONESIA
NAURU
NIEU
NEW CALEDONIA
NEW ZEALAND
PAPUA NEW GUINEA
SAMOA
SOLOMON ISLAND
ST. HELENA IS.
TUVALU
VANUATU

THE CARIBBEAN
ARUBA
ANGUILLA
ANTIGUA & BARBUDA
BAHAMAS
BARBADOS
BERMUDA
BRITISH VIRGIN ISLANDS
CAYMAN IS
CURACAO
DOMINICA
DOMINICAN REP.
FRENCH GUIANA
GRENADA
GUADELOUPE
HAITI
JAMAICA
MONTSERRAT
NETHERLANDS ANTILLES
ST. KITTS & NEVIS
ST. LUCIA
ST. MARTIN
ST. PIERRE & MIQUELON
ST. VINCENT
TRINIDAD & TOBAGO
TURKS & CAICOS

MIDDLE EAST
BAHRAIN
IRAN
IRAQ
ISRAEL
JORDAN
KUWAIT
LEBANON
OMAN
QUATAR
SAUDI ARABIA
SYRIA
UNITED ARAB EMIRATES
YEMEN
YEMEN, P.D.R.

RUSSIA & THE INDEPENDENT STATES
ARMENIA
AZERBAIJAN
BYLERUS
ESTONIA
GEORGIA
KAZAKHSTAN
KYRGYZSTAN
LATVIA
LITHUANIA
RUSSIAN FEDERATION
TAJIKISTAN
TURKMENISTAN
UKRAINE
UZBEKISTAN

SOUTH AMERICA
ARGENTINA
BELIZE
BOLIVIA
BRAZIL
CHILE
COLOMBIA
COSTA RICA
CUBA
ECUADOR
EL SALVADOR
GUATEMALA
GUYANA
HONDURAS
MEXICO
NICARAGUA
PANAMA
PARAGUAY
PERU
PUERTO RICO
SURINAME
URUGUAY
VENEZUELA

USA, CANADA & AUSTRALIA
CANADA
AUSTRALIA
USA

*Please check our website www.worldtravelinstitute.com) for a complete and updated list of available Country Reports.

OTHER WTI BOOKS BY THE SAME AUTHOR

Americans Traveling Abroad: What You Should Know Before You Go (2nd Ed.) Bestseller! paperback, 658 pages, ISBN: 0-9623820-7-8, $39.99 [Available at major bookstores throughout the United States. It may also be ordered from Access Publishers Network at 1-800-345-0096 or directly from the publisher-World Travel Institute].

Practical Tips For Americans Traveling Abroad: Ignore Them At Your Own Risk, paperback, 265 pages, ISBN: 1-890605-09-3, $19.99. On-line version is also available for purchase ($19.99) at **www.worldtravelinstitute.com**

ABOUT THE AUTHOR

Dr. Gladson I. Nwanna (Ph.D) is a university professor, a former consultant to the World Bank, and a veteran traveler. He has over the past 17 years traveled to numerous countries of the world, logging thousands of miles in the process.

LIBRARY RECOMMENDATION FORM

(This form should be hand delivered to your local Head Librarian or Reference Librarian)

Sir/Madam:

I regularly use the following book(s) published by **World Travel Institute**:

(1)______________________ ISBN#:__________ Price $______

(2)______________________ ISBN#:__________ Price $______

(3)______________________ ISBN#:__________ Price $______

(4)______________________ ISBN#:__________ Price $______

(5)______________________ ISBN#:__________ Price $______

(6)______________________ ISBN#:__________ Price $______

(7)______________________ ISBN#:__________ Price $______

(8)______________________ ISBN#:__________ Price $______

Your records indicate that the library does not carry these valuable and comprehensive travel reference books. Could you please place an order them for our library?

Name of Recommender:______________________________

Address:______________________________

____

Phone:______________________________

LIBRARY RECOMMENDATION FORM

(This form should be hand delivered to your local Head Librarian or Reference Librarian)

Sir/Madam:

I regularly use the following book(s) published by **World Travel Institute**:

(1)______________________ ISBN#:__________ Price $______

(2)______________________ ISBN#:__________ Price $______

(3)______________________ ISBN#:__________ Price $______

(4)______________________ ISBN#:__________ Price $______

(5)______________________ ISBN#:__________ Price $______

(6)______________________ ISBN#:__________ Price $______

(7)______________________ ISBN#:__________ Price $______

(8)______________________ ISBN#:__________ Price $______

Your records indicate that the library does not carry these valuable and comprehensive travel reference books. Could you please place an order them for our library?

Name of Recommender:______________________________

Address:______________________________

____

Phone:______________________________

ORDERING INFORMATION

MAIL OR FAX YOUR ORDERS TO:

World Travel Institute
P.O. Box 326740-1A,
Baltimore, MD 21282-2674 U.S.A.
Fax: (410) 922-8115.
Make check or money order payable to **World Travel Institute (WTI)**. We also accept, international money orders; VISA & MASTERCARD.

Shipping/Postage Cost for books:
U.S. Residents add $4 U.S. dollars per book for postage.
Canadian Residents add $5 U.S. dollars per book for postage.
Mexican Residents add $7 U.S. dollars per book for postage.
Other Countries: add $15 U.S. dollars for airmail delivery; $7 for surface mail delivery.

Shipping/Postage Cost for Reports:
[Save on postage by ordering & downloading on-line version]
U.S. Residents reports are mailed free-of-charge.
Canadian Residents add $2 U.S. dollars for postage.
Mexican Residents add $2 U.S. dollars for postage.
Other Countries: add $5 U.S. dollars for airmail delivery; $3 dollars for surface mail delivery.

Books may also be ordered through Access Publishers at 1-800-345-0096 ([Bookcrafters at 1-800-507-2665 after 5pm]. (BOOKS ONLY!!!). Only book orders placed directly with publisher qualifies for the pre-publication discounts mentioned elsewhere in this document.

Remember, individual country reports are now available at $7 (U.S. dollars) per country. Reports can only be ordered through the publisher!!! or through the web at **www.worldtravelinstitute.com**

ORDER FORM

Telephone Orders: Call Access Publishers Network at 1-800-345-0096. (Bookmasters at 1-800-507-2665, after 5pm). Have Your Credit Card ready. Order any time, day or night, 7 days a week, 24 hours a day.

Fax Orders: 1-410-922-8115 (Send this form)

Postal Orders: World Travel Institute, P.O. Box 32674-1A, Baltimore, Maryland 21282-2674-8674 U.S.A.{tel: (410) 922-4903}. Make check payable to WTI.

☐ Please enter my order for the following books:

- **Do's and Don'ts**:

Europe	$29.99 + $____	postage:	Total $____
South America	$19.99 + $____	postage:	Total $____
Africa*	$34.99 + $____	postage:	Total $____
The Caribbean	$19.99 + $____	postage:	Total $____
Asia	$24.99 + $____	postage:	Total $____
Russia/The Independent States	$12.99 +$____	postage:	Total $____
USA, Canada & Australia	$12.99 + $____	postage:	Total $____
The Middle East*	$12.99 + $____	postage:	Total $____
Oceania & Japan*	$15.99 + $____	postage:	Total $____

(* *Please check availability/publication date*)

(Please refer to the section containing postage/shipping information for applicable postage rates.)

- **Americans Traveling Abroad..** $39.99 + $____ postage Total $____
- **Practical Tips for Americans..** $19.99 + $____ postage Total $____
- **Do's and Don'ts - COUNTRY REPORTS:**
  for the following countries at $7.each $____ + $____ postage Total $____

List Countries:____

____

Sales Tax: (Maryland Residents Only) Add 5% $______________________

Enclosed is my Total Payment of $______________ by

☐ Check ☐ Money Order ☐ Credit Card ☐ VISA ☐ MASTERCARD

Card Number:__________________ **Card Holder's Name:**__________________

Expiration Date:________________ **Card Holder's Signature:**________________

☐ This is a gift from:________________________

Ship to:________________________ **Firm Name:**________________________

Your Name:______________________ **Address:**__________________________

City:________________ **State:**__________ **Zip:**________ **Country**:______________

Inquiries: *All inquiries regarding your order or this book should be directed to our headquarters at the address and phone number shown above. The toll-free number is for orders only. No inquiries will be accepted at that number. Note! Country Reports are available through the publisher only. It cannot be ordered from Access Publisher or by calling the toll-free number shown above.*

COMMENT FORM

YOUR OPINION MEANS A LOT TO US
Please use this post card to tell us how you feel about any of our books. We are also interested in learning more about other cultural and social **do's and don'ts** of countries that you may want us to include in our data base and future editions, in particular, those we may not have included in any of our publications. Remember, we may quote you and/or use your comments, testimonials or suggestions in our promotions and future editions.

Title of Book:______________________________

Name:______________________________
Organization:____________________ **Position:**__________
Address:______________________________
City, State, Zip & Country:______________________________
____
( ) **Check here if we may quote you. Signature:**__________ **Date:**______
[Mail your comments to WTI, P.O. Box 32674 Baltimore, MD 21282-2674, USA.]

COMMENT FORM

YOUR OPINION MEANS A LOT TO US
Please use this post card to tell us how you feel about any of our books. We are also interested in learning more about other cultural and social **do's and don'ts** of countries that you may want us to include in our data base and future editions, in particular, those we may not have included in any of our publications. Remember, we may quote you and/or use your comments, testimonials or suggestions in our promotions and future editions.

Title of Book:______________________________

Name:______________________________
Organization:____________________ **Position:**__________
Address:______________________________
City, State, Zip & Country:______________________________
____
( ) **Check here if we may quote you. Signature:**__________ **Date:**______
[Mail your comments to WTI, P.O. Box 32674 Baltimore, MD 21282-2674, USA.]

NOTES

NOTES

NOTES

SELECT BOOKS AND REPORTS FROM WORLD TRAVEL INSTITUTE

□ Do's and Don'ts Around the World: A Country Guide to Cultural and Social Taboos and Etiquette - **EUROPE**

□ Do's and Don'ts Around the World: A Country Guide to Cultural and Social Taboos and Etiquette - **ASIA**

□ Do's and Don'ts Around the World: A Country Guide to Cultural and Social Taboos and Etiquette - **SOUTH AMERICA**

□ Do's and Don'ts Around the World: A Country Guide to Cultural and Social Taboos and Etiquette - **AFRICA**

□ Do's and Don'ts Around the World: A Country Guide to Cultural and Social Taboos and Etiquette - **THE CARIBBEAN**

□ Do's and Don'ts Around the World: A Country Guide to Cultural and Social Taboos and Etiquette - **THE MIDDLE EAST**

□ Do's and Don'ts Around the World: A Country Guide to Cultural and Social Taboos and Etiquette - **OCEANIA & JAPAN**

□ Do's and Don'ts Around the World: A Country Guide to Cultural and Social Taboos and Etiquette - **USA-CANADA-AUSTRALIA**

□ Do's and Don'ts Around the World: A Country Guide to Cultural and Social Taboos and Etiquette - **RUSSIA & THE INDEPENDENT STATES**

□ Do's and Don'ts Around the World... COUNTRY REPORTS (over 170 countries)

□ Practical Tips For Americans Traveling Abroad: Ignore Them At Your Own Risk

□ Americans Traveling Abroad: What You Should Know Before You Go.

See Pages 316-321 for Ordering Information